HEALTHY BREAD

in Five Minutes a Day

ALSO BY JEFF HERTZBERG, M.D., AND ZOË FRANÇOIS

Artisan Bread in Five Minutes a Day:
The Discovery That Revolutionizes Home Baking

HEALTHY BREAD
in Five Minutes a Day

100 New Recipes Featuring Whole Grains, Fruits,
Vegetables, and Gluten-Free Ingredients

JEFF HERTZBERG, M.D., and ZOË FRANÇOIS

Photography by MARK LUINENBURG

THOMAS DUNNE BOOKS
ST. MARTIN'S PRESS ❧ NEW YORK

THOMAS DUNNE BOOKS.
An imprint of St. Martin's Press.

HEALTHY ARTISAN BREAD IN FIVE MINUTES A DAY. Copyright © 2009 by Jeff Hertzberg and Zoë François. All rights reserved. Printed in the United States of America. For information, address St. Martin's Press, 175 Fifth Avenue, New York, N.Y. 10010.

www.thomasdunnebooks.com
www.stmartins.com

Design by Phil Mazzone
Photography copyright © 2009 by Mark Luinenburg

Library of Congress Cataloging-in-Publication Data

Healthy bread in five minutes a day : 100 new recipes featuring whole grains, fruits, vegetables, and gluten-free ingredients / Jeff Hertzberg and Zoë François ; photography by Mark Luinenburg.—1st ed.
       p.   cm.
Includes bibliographical references and index.
ISBN 978-0-312-54552-9
1. Gluten-free diet—Recipes. 2. Bread. I. François, Zoë. II. Title.
RM237.86.H47 2009
641.8'15—dc22

                                                              2009016846

10   9   8   7   6

To my grandparents Esther and Abe Weissman, who taught me that bread is better than cake.

—Jeff

To my mom for a lifetime of love, grace, generosity, and humor—the most important ingredients of all.

—Zoë

CONTENTS

ACKNOWLEDGMENTS

Sometimes, it's the second time that's a charm. So many things went more smoothly for us in our second book, and we're grateful to the friends and colleagues who have kept us on track and were so willing to help us. Our spouses, Laura Silver and Graham François, continued to put up with the crazy hours, interrupted dinners, houses coated with flour dust, and carbohydrates at every meal. We're not trained as writers, but Laura is, and she made sure our editors got manuscript versions that had already been vetted. And Graham created our incredible Web site, where we spend most of our time these days.

Friends once again generously agreed to test our recipes and provide all kinds of help when we needed it. Thanks to Christa Anders and Tom McLeod (who also lent us their gorgeous kitchen for a photo shoot), Betsy Carey, Marion and John Callahan, Allison Campbell, Alex Cohn, Barbara Fenzl (who invited us to teach our method at Les Gourmettes Cooking School), Shelly Fling, Leslie Held, Theresa and Jim Murray, Lorraine Neal (Zoë's mom), John Rosengren, Danny Sager and Brian McCarthy, Jen Sommerness and Debora Villa and Ralph Gualtieri. Neither of us are celiacs nor eat a gluten-free diet, so we are particularly grateful to Danny and Shauna James Ahern of the Gluten-Free Girl Web site, who advised us on the gluten-free chapter.

Rebekah Denn connected us with great new sources for artisan flours. Writers Beth Fouhy and Peggy Orenstein helped us navigate the murky waters of book publicity, and as always, we relied on the wisdom of our literary agent, Jane Dystel. At St. Martin's Press, thanks to Peter Wolverton for helping us with the process of creating a second book; thanks to our editor, Ruth Cavin, and of course to our managing editor, Amelie Littell. Amelie's dedication and thoroughness got us through the nitty-gritty of actually finishing. And of course, we wouldn't be writing any books if not for Ruth Cavin, who took a chance on us in the first place and let us tell our story. Judy Hunt helped us create a great index, perhaps the most important pages of the book. Lynne

Rossetto Kasper, Sally Swift, and Jennifer Russel of *The Splendid Table* radio program gave us our first national exposure.

Many more people gave of their time, their knowledge and their support to this book: Mike Anderson (for Web support), Brett Bannon and Jon Templeton at Bret's Table, Leslie Bazzett, Karl Benson and all of the wonderful folks at Cooks of Crocus Hill, Jay, Tracey, Gavin, and Megan Berkowitz, Sarah Berkowitz, Barb Davis, Fran Davis, Nan Fletcher (whose talents as a makeup artist made us feel like movie stars, if only for a moment), Anna and Ewart François, Jaden Hair, Judy and Larry Hicks, Raghavan Iyer, the staff at the Joie de Vivre Hotel Group in San Francisco, Mary Jo Katz and the kitchen staff from the Intercontinental Hotel in Buckhead, Klecko, Kathy Kosnoff and Lyonel Norris, Dusti Kugler, Kelly Lainsbury, Emily Luchetti and her pastry staff for lending their kitchen at Farallon, Alec Neal and Katherine Ball, Barbara and Kristin Neal, Carey Neal and Heather Pamula, Craig and Patricia Neal, Don Newcomb and Jim Price from ChicagoGourmets, Jimmy Alexander, John Peters and Mitchell Schmieding from Powerhouse restaurant, Ray from Mohawk Valley Trading Company, Cy Rohan, the staff at Quang, Suvir Saran and Charlie Burd, the Schmitt family, Sally Simmons and David Van De Sande, Jen Sommerness (for providing a second home to Zoë's boys in all the crunch times), and a special thanks to all the lovely people we met on our Web site (healthybreadinfive.com), who taught us so much, made our first book a success, and then paid us the compliment of asking for a second one. And the community on Twitter who inspire us daily.

Gratitude to Zoë's mentors and colleagues in the baking and culinary world from the past and present: Robin Asbell, Steven Brown, Jennifer Burkholder, Stephen Durfee, Michelle Gayer, Thomas Gumpel, Jacqueline Hopkins, Riad Nasr, Suvir Saran, and Andrew Zimmern.

Once again, some of the most fun and creative times were spent with our friend, photographer, and visual mentor Mark Luinenburg, who not only advised us about our own pictures for the Web site, but also produced the stylish and delicious photographs that appear in both of our books. Food and recipes are more than just a collection of information. Thanks to Mark for pictures that convey beauty, texture, and taste—a sensual feast.

Most of all we are thankful for the love and support of our families: Zoë's husband, Graham, and her two boys, Henri and Charlie, and Jeff's wife, Laura, and his girls, Rachel and Julia. They're our best taste testers and most honest critics.

It does not cost much. . . . It leaves you filled with peace, and the house filled with one of the world's sweetest smells . . . probably there is no chiropractic treatment, no Yoga exercise, no hour of meditation . . . that will leave you emptier of bad thoughts than this homely ceremony of making bread.

—M. F. K. FISHER IN *HOW TO COOK A WOLF*, 1942

THE SECRET

The "Secret" works with super-healthy ingredients, too: Mix enough dough for many loaves and store it in the refrigerator.

It's easy to have freshly baked whole grain and other healthy breads whenever you want them, with only five minutes a day of active effort. First, mix the ingredients into a container all at once, and let them sit for two hours. Now you are ready to shape and bake the bread, or you can refrigerate the dough and use it over the next five to fourteen days (depending on the recipe). You've prepared enough dough for many loaves. When you want fresh-baked, crusty whole grain or gluten-free bread, take a piece of the dough from the container and shape it into a loaf. Let it rise and then bake. Your house will smell like a bakery and your family and friends will love you for it.

1

INTRODUCTION
HEALTHY BREADS CAN BE MADE
IN FIVE MINUTES A DAY, TOO!

∽

We love food, and we love bread best of all. It was our bread obsession that brought us together for a cookbook in the first place. Our first book (*Artisan Bread in Five Minutes a Day: The Discovery That Revolutionizes Home Baking*) created an unlikely team: a doctor and a pastry chef. But it turned out to be a great combination. One review of our book called us "the Chemist and the Alchemist," though on any given day we reverse roles at will. Our partnership worked because amateurs found the result extraordinarily easy, yet aficionados found it utterly delicious. In writing that book, we wanted to discard everything that was intimidating and make the process fast enough to fit into people's busy lives. *Artisan Bread* replaced the time-consuming traditional yeast bread method with something quicker, without compromising quality. This technique calls for mixing large batches of dough in advance, storing them in the refrigerator, and then tearing off dough for loaves as needed over two weeks. Quite a lot of people tried it, and our book became part of a home-baked bread revolution.

Along the way, we started our blog at www.artisanbreadinfive.com, so that we could be in touch with readers who had questions or comments. It became a place to share new information that we'd learned. It's been great fun—people have even written poems to us about their bread. We've heard emotional stories about entire families making bread together: grandmas making pizza with their grandkids, and siblings baking long-distance (some even across oceans). Our blog space is a forum for feedback and requests, and the most common ones have been for breads with more whole grains, seeds, nuts, and even for gluten-free breads. The requests came from as far away as Europe, Asia, and Australia. It seems that the world is becoming a healthier place. People were asking for whole grain breads that they could bake themselves, but they still wanted the same five-minute method. So the idea for our second book came from our readers. *Healthy Bread in Five Minutes a Day* became our next logical step for making breads and even desserts part of a healthy diet.

We both eat *some* sugar, white flour, and butter. In other words, we're not health-food fanatics. But that's not to say we aren't health-conscious. We both exercise, and ultimately we watch what we eat. We wrote our first book with the goal of getting people back into their kitchens to bake really great bread, with recipes mostly inspired by the European tradition. That meant lots of white flour. We ate it in moderation while we tested the book, and believe it or not, despite the much-maligned reputation of carbohydrates, we didn't gain weight. We were both pleasantly surprised. Bread and desserts can be part of a healthy lifestyle, so long as you eat them in moderation.

Whether you are looking for more whole grains, whether you're vegan, gluten-free, watching your weight, trying to reduce your cholesterol, or just care about what goes into your body, *Healthy Bread in Five Minutes a Day* has recipes for you. We all want to be healthy, and now we can do it without sacrificing flavor or precious time. It's obvious why this would make sense for Jeff (the doctor). His background in health care and preventive medicine leads him to alternatives that are lower in calories, with healthier fats and higher fiber. Then, there's his passion for bread baking, which led to the discovery we wrote about in our first book, making artisan breads quickly and easily. Not everyone needs to make their brioche without butter, but if doing so means that someone who can't eat butter can enjoy fabulous brioche, then by all means let's do it, and do it right.

That's where Zoë (the pastry chef), comes into the picture. She grew up the daughter of hippies and cut her teeth on the ultra-healthy bread served at the Vermont commune where she was raised. In her twenties Zoë was a vegetarian; she didn't eat refined sugar and headed off to the Culinary Institute of America (CIA) to follow her passion, pastry. Her goal: bake without refined sugar, but create ethereal pastries that didn't weigh a ton and taste like sweetened tree bark. But while studying at the CIA, Zoë was tempted by the miracles of sugar, bleached flour, heavenly butter, and all of the other ingredients she had once shunned. She was being seduced away from the whole grains, fruit sweeteners, and carob that had been the staples of her counterculture childhood. Years later, Zoë would figure out a way to have it all: great-tasting but healthy pastries, desserts, and of course, breads.

So we both were drawn to write a new book that combines superfast bread with healthy ingredients. *Healthy Bread in Five Minutes a Day* is about taking the speedy methods of *Artisan Bread in Five Minutes a Day* and adapting them for breads made with less white flour (sometimes none), lower refined sugars, and healthier ingredients. We're not going to claim that eating these breads is the key to a longer life. But we can show bread eaters who want to use more nutritious ingredients how to get results as delicious and fast as those they achieved with our first book. So *Healthy Bread in Five Minutes a Day* will *not* be 250 pages of preaching and scolding about health and diet; neither of us has the patience for that.

We'll use the same wet, stored-dough method and we won't make anyone knead. But as you'll see, we're switching to healthier alternatives: whole grains, canola and olive oils, nuts, seeds, natural sweeteners, and in some cases, gluten-free ingredients. Where white flour (or butter) is required, we've tried to decrease the total amount that goes into the recipe. And we kept active daily preparation time to five minutes for the basic recipes. We assume that this newfound interest in health hasn't been accompanied by a newfound wealth of free time! A doctor and a pastry chef turn out to be a great match to create recipes that are not only good for you but that also taste fantastic. So now healthy eaters can have their bread (or pastry) and eat it, too!

As you read through the book, please visit our Web site (www.healthybreadinfive.com), where you'll find instructional text, photographs, videos, and a community of other five-minute-a-day bakers. Another easy way to keep in touch is to follow us on the social networking site "Twitter," at http://twitter.com/ArtisanBreadIn5.

Happy baking, and enjoy all the bread!

Why Eat Healthy Bread: A Wee Bit of Science

Being alive takes energy, and that energy comes from burning carbohydrate fuels with oxygen in our bodies (that's called *oxidation*). Even though oxidation is perfectly natural and healthy, it releases some nasty chemicals. So does exposure to sunlight, chemicals, pollutants, and radiation. All that oxidation and energy can create what biochemists call "superoxide radicals," which we've heard of as "free radicals," high-energy chemicals that can do damage to our cells. Free-radical damage has a role in a host of chronic diseases, including cancer, hardening of the arteries, heart disease, stroke, and arthritis. **The good news:** Our bodies get help in getting rid of free radicals from phytochemicals (beneficial plant chemicals) and vitamins in our food, both natural substances with powerful health benefits. They act as potent antioxidants, chemicals that absorb damaging energy from free radicals. Phytochemicals with antioxidant activity tend to be richly colored: green, yellow, blue, and red. Some of the most colorful fruits and vegetables have the largest stores of phytochemicals. As you work through chapter 7, Breads with Hidden Fruits and Vegetables, you'll feast your eyes on a stunning and colorful palette of breads. Substances like phytochemicals are the reason that the U.S. government recommends that you eat nine or more servings of fruits and vegetables per day. These breads will help you do it.

Vitamins are essential helpers for the body's normal chemical functions (metabolism), allowing the chemical reactions we depend upon to take place. Lack of vitamins cause some of the world's most devastating but curable deficiency diseases, which have pretty much disappeared in the industrialized world. But deficiency diseases are the tip of the iceberg—many vitamins don't just act as metabolic catalysts, they're also antioxidants. This is especially clear for vitamin E. There is strong evidence that normal levels of vitamin E prevent heart, blood, muscle, and eye problems. Vitamin E is found in wheat germ (from whole grain wheat), vegetable oils, seeds, and nuts. Vitamin C, another powerful antioxidant, works in concert with vitamin E. Throughout the book, we'll jump in with sidebars about the vitamins—vitamin A, the eight B vitamins (see Appendix, page 307), plus vitamins C, D, E, and K (please do not ask us why there is no vitamin F, G, H, or I!). Most nutritionists agree that vitamin requirements are best met through a diet rich in fruits and vegetables, rather than by taking vitamin supplements. That's not to say supplements aren't ever helpful; they certainly can be when daily requirements aren't being met through food intake. But the vitamins

∽

EAT YOUR CRUSTS! There's evidence that the browning process that occurs when you bake bread creates additional antioxidants. So bread crust is healthy in addition to being delicious.

that occur naturally in food are better because they're more easily absorbed through digestion than supplements are, probably resulting in higher levels of vitamins and antioxidants in our bloodstream and tissues. This book will help you put more of those natural vitamins and antioxidants into your family's diet.

There are a lot of wild nutrition claims out there, and we've steered clear of them in this book—we do not believe that there is a magic bullet to promote health or cure disease with particular food sources or supplements. But there are some scientifically based statements that will probably stand the test of time:

1. Whole grain flour is better for you than white flour. Because whole grains include the germ and the bran, in addition to the starch-rich but fiber- and vitamin-poor endosperm (see chapter 2, Ingredients, page 7), whole grain flours bring a boatload of healthy substances into your diet, including phytochemicals (beneficial plant chemicals), vitamins, and fiber. Those are pretty much absent from white flour. Iron, niacin, folic acid, riboflavin, and thiamine are added back in enriched commercial white flour, but no other nutrients—so whole wheat delivers more complete nutrition than white flour even when it's been enriched. But there's more—because bran and germ in whole grains dilute the effect of pure starch in the endosperm, the absorption and conversion of starches into simple sugars is slowed, so blood glucose (the simplest sugar) rises more slowly after consumption of whole grains than it does after eating refined white flour products. Complex, high-bran carbohydrates are said to have a lower "glycemic index," a measure of how fast your blood sugar rises after eating a particular food. The evidence for better handling of blood sugar convinced the American Diabetes Association (ADA) and the U.S. Department of Agriculture to make two recommendations in their current guidelines:

- **Consume a high-fiber diet,** with at least 14 grams of dietary fiber per 1,000 calories consumed. For most people, that's going to mean 28 to 40 grams a day (depending on body size at normal weight).
- **Make sure that at least half of your grain intake is *whole* grain.** The recipes in this book will help you meet that goal.

2. Monounsaturated and polyunsaturated oils are better for you than saturated fats (like butter and hydrogenated oil). See our ingredients list for a more complete discussion (page 18). Switching to these oils or other heart-healthy fat sources can benefit those with high blood cholesterol.

3. Low-salt breads will benefit people with hypertension, heart failure, and kidney failure. This applies to all our breads—they all can be made salt-free, though the flavor will of course be different.

4. Nuts and seeds contain heart-healthy oils. Though they're concentrated calorie sources, nuts and seeds are rich in vitamins, minerals, and heart-healthy fats (monounsaturated and omega-3 polyunsaturated fats).

5. Fruits and vegetables are the best sources for phytochemicals and vitamins. We have a whole chapter of breads enriched by fruits or vegetables, which are fiber-rich and loaded with vitamins and antioxidants. We'll discuss the unique benefits of the particular fruit or vegetable in sidebars next to the recipes.

And finally, a word of advice: Please don't obsess about food. This is supposed to be fun. If you can put some healthy ingredients into your bread and you like the flavor, do it. Otherwise, eat something else.*

Making Your Own Great Bread Saves You Money

When the economy goes into a tizzy (and even when it doesn't) you have to wonder why anyone is willing to pay $6.00 for a loaf of bread in specialty bakeries. If you buy your bread in a supermarket, you'll still pay $3.00 a loaf. Making your own bread, on the other hand, is very, very economical. Even when whole wheat flour is 70 cents a pound (right at this moment in some of the stores near us), an entire batch of whole wheat bread uses a little more than two pounds of flour, costing about $1.40. It's a few pennies more for yeast and salt, and you get four 1-pound loaves that cost about 40 cents each.

An added benefit: The world's most heavenly source of home heating this winter will be your oven, cranking out the aroma of freshly baked bread.

*But we really, really like bread.

2

INGREDIENTS

Our first book concentrated on ingredients from the traditional European baker's cupboard. We've updated our discussion to include whole grains, vital wheat gluten, and even ingredients for gluten-free breads. Perhaps the most crucial new ingredient to get familiar with is vital wheat gluten. It's essential for achieving a light loaf when using lots of whole grains, never kneading, and still storing the dough in the refrigerator.

Flours, Grains, and Wheat Extracts

Whole grains of wheat are seeds that have three main parts:

- The brown or reddish-brown fibrous outer *bran* layer that protects the seed's contents. It contains no gluten and is slightly bitter in taste. Bran is a naturally occurring fiber that absorbs water in the intestine and promotes normal digestive function.
- The brown-colored *germ*, which is the future baby wheat plant. It's highly nutritious but contains no gluten. The oil in wheat germ is particularly rich in vitamins A, D, E, and K.
- The white *endosperm*, containing starch and protein, nourishes the new plant when it sprouts. In wheat, the protein is mostly gluten.

Let's first consider vital wheat gluten (sometimes called vital wheat gluten flour).

Vital wheat gluten: In order to mix up dough that's really high in whole grains, *but can still be successfully stored*, you need to boost the dough's gluten level or the bread won't rise nicely and will be too dense, especially as a batch ages. We boost gluten by using a powdered extract of wheat called *vital wheat gluten*. We find that stored whole grain dough really needs this ingredient, about one to two teaspoons per cup of flour or dry grain ingredient. Why? In whole grain wheat flours, the nutritious bran and germ are ground into the flour and take the place of some of the gluten-rich endosperm (the white part of the wheat kernel). So, whole wheat flour has significantly less gluten than white flour, and this will mean less rising power and a less "open" airy crumb (interior of the bread). Gluten is strengthened when the proteins align themselves into strands after water is added. Resilient, stretchy, gas-trapping gluten (with lined-up strands) can be formed in two ways:

- **The dough can be kneaded:** Not the way we like to spend our time. OR . . .
- **By using lots of water:** The gluten strands become mobile enough to *align themselves.*

Creating a wet environment is the basis for all no-knead methods. Gluten alignment creates a protein network that traps gas bubbles and creates an airy crumb in the interior of bread. Without gluten or something like it (in gluten-free breads), loaves won't rise; untrapped gas produced by yeast just bubbles out of the mixture. What's worse is that whole wheat's bran particles have sharp edges that cut and disrupt developing gluten strands. So breads made with whole wheat flour really need some help.

Storing the dough creates another challenge. In our five-minute approach, the initial rise traps enough gas to allow the dough to be used successfully for up to two weeks (depending on the recipe). With whole grain dough, we use vital wheat gluten to bolster the protein network and trap more gas. Otherwise, stored whole grain dough can yield a dense result.

Two supermarket brands of vital wheat gluten are generally available in the United States: Bob's Red Mill and Hodgson Mill. King Arthur Flour also has one available online or through mail order. Vital wheat gluten is easy to incorporate into recipes but can form very firm lumps in dough if not handled properly. To prevent that, **always whisk vital wheat gluten with the dry ingredients *before* adding liquids.** Product labeling varies by brand in terms of how much to use in recipes. We experimented to find a dose of vital wheat gluten that gave us a nice rise and an open crumb, but didn't result in a "rubbery" feel that comes when you've used too much. The less white flour in a recipe, the more you need, and if there are seeds, nuts, fruit, or vegetables that weigh down the crumb, that also raises the requirement for vital wheat gluten. Bob's Red Mill and Hodgson Mill can be used interchangeably, but if you use something else, you may need to experiment to find a level that gives you the result you like.

Refrigerate vital wheat gluten in an airtight container after opening the package.

Whole wheat flour: Whole wheat flour contains both the germ and bran of wheat; both of which are healthful and tasty. The germ is rich in vitamins; the bran promotes healthy digestive function because it's loaded with dietary fiber. Together they add a slightly bitter, nutty flavor to bread that most people enjoy. In general, you can use any kind of whole wheat flour that's available to you. Stone-ground whole wheat flour will be a bit coarser and more rustic; the result will be denser. The same is true for the whole wheat available at most natural food co-ops. Coarser whole wheat has larger, more jagged particles of bran, which cut gluten strands as they develop. That leads to a denser loaf than you get with more finely ground supermarket whole wheat products.

HOW MUCH DIETARY FIBER DO YOU NEED?
According to the U.S. Department of Agriculture and the American Diabetic Association, adults need 14 grams of fiber for every 1,000 calories they consume in an ideal-calorie diet each day. For a 2,000-calorie diet (appropriate for most women), that means about 28 grams of fiber a day. For a 2,500-calorie diet (appropriate for most men), that means 35 grams a day). 100% whole wheat bread contains a little less than 2 grams of fiber per slice if you cut a thin 1-ounce slice, and 3 to 4 grams if you cut a 2-ounce slice. White bread contains a quarter of that.

Whole wheat flour labels generally don't specify whether the flour is for bread (high protein) as opposed to all-purpose (lower in protein). All whole wheat flours are high in fiber; there are 15 grams per cup in most brands. **Storing whole wheat flour:** Oils in whole wheat flour can go rancid if stored for long periods at room temperature. So if you don't use it often, store it in an airtight container in the freezer.

White whole wheat: King Arthur Flour released the first "white" whole wheat flour, and it's terrific. White whole wheat flour is made from wheat varieties that have very pale-colored, mild-tasting bran layers, but it packs the same nutrition as regular whole wheat. It measures like regular whole wheat and can be substituted for traditional whole wheat in any of our recipes. We use it in recipes when we don't want the assertive taste of whole wheat to come through other, more delicate flavors. Don't expect it to taste like white flour and don't try to substitute it 1:1 for all-purpose. It absorbs water like regular whole wheat, so if you substitute 1:1 for all-purpose, you'll get a dry, tight dough that won't store well at all. King Arthur, Bob's Red Mill, Hodgson Mill, and Trader Joe's now all carry terrific white whole wheat flour products.

Unbleached white all-purpose flour: Many of our whole-grain breads use some white flour, because it creates a more open crumb structure and a lighter result.

Unbleached all-purpose white flour has a protein content of about 10 percent (mostly gluten). Our recipes were tested with all-purpose flours in the range of 10 to 11.7 percent.

Don't use bleached flour. We prefer unbleached flours for their natural creamy color, not to mention our preference for avoiding unnecessary chemicals. Even more important, bleaching removes some of the protein, and that throws off our recipes because protein absorbs water. *If you use bleached flour, your dough will be too wet and you'll need to decrease the water by about a quarter cup (or increase the flour).* Cake or pastry flours are too low in protein (around 8 percent) to make successful bread.

White bread flour: This flour has about 12 percent protein (mostly gluten). You can boost the gluten content of your breads by substituting white bread flour for white all-purpose. You need to slightly increase the water if you make this substitution in our recipes (about a quarter cup). We've found that substituting bread flour for all-purpose does not make vital wheat gluten unnecessary; you just need less (and you'll need to experiment). Since one of our goals is to simplify the process, our recipes that include white flour call for unbleached all-purpose.

Graham flour: This flour was created by Sylvester Graham in the nineteenth century as an alternative to white flour. Graham was convinced that bran was the cure-all. The flour differs from whole wheat only in the way that it is processed. Graham flour is made by separating the bran and germ from the wheat berry, grinding them separately, and then reintroducing that flour to the ground endosperm (white flour). The bran is not ground as fine and therefore this flour creates a slightly different texture than regular whole wheat flour. The difference is subtle enough that you can substitute one for the other in our recipes. A Bob's Red Mill product is now readily available in supermarkets.

Rye flour: Even though there is a wide range of rye flour available in the United States, most rye flour that's easily available is very high in rye bran; it really could be labeled as whole grain flour. Exceptions are "light" and "medium" rye, which are lower in bran than the alternatives. Since they're hard to find and we wanted a healthier result, we tested our recipes with high-bran products such as Bob's Red Mill and Hodgson Mill. See the Appendix, page 308, for protein and fiber content in nationally available rye flours.

Oats: Oat products add a wonderful hearty flavor and contribute to a toothsome texture, but they don't have much gluten. So, like rye flour, oats need to be paired with wheat flour to produce a loaf that rises. We've also used vital wheat gluten for the same reason. Rolled oat varieties sold as "old-fashioned" (they are not pre-cooked) are best—the milling process actually rolls the whole kernel flat. Steel-cut oats are coarser ground and will yield a coarser result—the kernel is not flattened but rather broken into fragments. Steel-cut oats are often sold as "Scottish" or "Irish" oats. With about 16 grams of fiber per cup, rolled oats have more fiber than whole wheat flour.

Bulgur: Bulgur is made of wheat kernels that are boiled, dried, husked, and cracked. It is sometimes called "Middle Eastern pasta," because it is so versatile, takes on many flavors, and cooks quickly. It is even higher in fiber than oats (26 grams per cup).

Barley: Barley is one of the oldest grains; it has been found worn as necklaces by mummies in Egyptian tombs. Now mostly associated with beer making, the grain has a pleasant taste and is particularly high in fiber (20 grams per cup). Barley is low in gluten, so it needs to be mixed with wheat and vital wheat gluten.

Wheat germ: Wheat germ has a wonderful flavor and is very high in omega-3 fatty acids, one of the healthiest fats of all, not to mention vitamins A, D, E, and K. We add wheat germ to some recipes to boost flavor and nutrition.

Spelt flour: A variety of wheat that is very high in protein, but slightly lower in gluten. It has a delicious flavor and creates a terrific moist crumb in baked bread. We've never found a variety that wasn't whole grain; a refined product isn't sold in the United States and that's fine with us! Many people use spelt because it is lower in gluten than wheat flour. If you are trying to reduce gluten in your diet, then omit the vital wheat gluten from the recipes. Just be aware that it will produce a much denser loaf.

Emmer flour: Emmer is one of the truly ancient grains, having been under human cultivation even longer than spelt, to which it's related. Like spelt, it's related to wheat and contains gluten. Confusing the picture is that both grains are sometimes called *farro*, especially when left in whole-kernel form and served as a side dish. But emmer is higher in protein than spelt, and some of our diabetic readers are using it in the hope that it might be slower to raise blood sugar than other wheat relatives (the jury is still out on that one). The germ and bran make up a larger portion of the emmer grain than they do in spelt, and while this is a very nutritious package, it can create a dense bread if used in high proportion in recipes. Like spelt, only whole grain versions are available in the United States.

Organic flours: Many of our readers told us that they bake their own bread so that they can eat organic bread and not go broke doing it—store-bought organic bread is expensive! Unfortunately, store-bought organic bread is often not very good, either. If you use organic products, by all means use them (we often do). There are now a number of organic flour brands available in the supermarket, but the best selection remains at your local organic food co-op.

GLUTEN-FREE GRAINS *(double-check with your doctor before consuming any new grain if you are allergic or intolerant of wheat gluten)*

Buckwheat: Buckwheat is actually a cousin to the rhubarb plant, and is not a grain at all, but its seeds behave and taste like a grain when ground into flour. The unground kernels are called groats. It is high in antioxidants and protein.

Cornmeal and corn masa: Look for whole grain varieties and avoid cornmeal products labeled as "degerminated"; this process strips away the germ, which contains most of the nutrients (though degerminated cornmeal has a longer shelf life). Yellow cornmeal is higher in vitamin A than the white variety. In Latin American cultures, corn is treated with alkali to create *masa* (also known as *masa harina*); this releases niacin, an essential B vitamin. Untreated corn is a poor source of niacin because it remains bound to indigestible parts of the kernel.

Cornstarch: Cornstarch is often found in gluten-free recipes. It has very little nutritional value, but helps to create a nice smooth texture and acts as a binder in the dough.

Mesquite flour: Mesquite is a woody plant native to northern Mexico and the southwestern United States. Many people have had southwestern specialties grilled over the plant's fragrant branches, but less well known are the edible pod and seed, which can be ground into a high-protein and nutritious flour. It makes a fabulous and unusual bread or *focaccia* (see pages 171 and 220). It has a naturally sweet flavor that is well complemented by agave syrup.

Millet: This is a tiny ancient grain that is very high in protein and vitamin B. The unground grain has a very mild flavor that becomes nutty when toasted.

Quinoa (*keen-wah*): Quinoa is a relative of Swiss chard and beets. It has a lovely flavor, cooks quickly, and has lots of high-quality protein, which means it contains all the essential amino acids. It is also high in calcium, iron, and B vitamins.

Rice and rice flours: Brown rice is rice with its external bran left in place. It's high in nutrients but gluten-free. Flour made from brown rice is much higher in fiber than white rice flour but has half the fiber content per cup compared with whole wheat. White rice flour has very little nutritional value or fiber, but is used in many gluten-free recipes for its nice texture and its neutral flavor, which goes with just about anything.

Sorghum: Sorghum is a very popular cooking grain related to sugarcane. It is used around the world but has just recently found its way into American kitchens.

Soy flour: This flour is milled from soy beans, which are very high in protein. They are also one of the few foods that contain all of the essential amino acids. Soy flour is an excellent way to get protein in breads that are gluten-free.

Tapioca: Tapioca is made from a root that's known by many names: cassava, manioc, or yucca. It is extracted and ground into a flour that is high in starch, calcium, and vitamin C, but low in protein. It is most often associated with its thickening properties, but it is now frequently used in gluten-free baking. It is sold as both tapioca starch and flour, but they are exactly the same.

Teff: A very popular grain in Ethiopia, teff has been virtually unheard of in the rest of the world until recently. It is a type of millet that is very small but packed with iron and calcium. It is a wonderful sweet grain that is gluten-free and therefore gaining in popularity.

Wild rice: Although technically an aquatic grass like plain rice, wild rice from North America distinguishes itself from its Asian counterpart by its distinct flavor and texture. It's long been prized by traditional Native American cultures, and more recently its nutritional profile and flavor has attracted interests from health-conscious gourmets.

Xanthan gum: This powdered additive is used in gluten-free breads to replace the stretchiness and chew that breads would otherwise get from gluten in wheat. It is a naturally derived gum that creates gas-trapping structure in dough that mimics the action of gluten in regular wheat breads.

Water

Throughout the book, we specify luke-warm water. This means water that feels just a little warm to the touch; if you measured it with a thermometer it would be no higher than 100°F (38°C). We never use a thermometer and we've never had a yeast failure due to excessive tempera-ture. If you use cold water from the tap, it will work but the initial rise will take much longer (the bread will be just as good).

About water sources: We find that the fla-vors of wheat and yeast overwhelm the contribution of water to bread's flavor, so we use ordinary tap water run through a home water filter, but that's only because it's what we drink at home. Assuming your own tap water tastes good enough to drink, use it filtered or unfiltered; we can't tell the difference in finished bread.

Yeast

Some readers of our first book preferred a lower yeast level in their breads, and it's really a matter of taste. Less yeast will work for nearly all of our recipes, but be aware that the initial rise will be slower, and the resting/rising time will also be increased. We've had good results using as little as

∞

YEAST LOVE TO KEEP COOL: Jefferson University yeast biochemist Hannah Silver, Ph.D., loves great bread, and bakes her own with our method. We asked her where the great flavor comes from, especially with dough that has aged a few days: "Yeast extracts are sometimes used as a flavor enhancer in commercial food, and they introduce a savory, complex flavor, sometimes called *umami*, the so-called fifth basic taste recognized by the human tongue (in addition to sweet, salty, bitter, and sour). The flavor you get with stored dough comes from chemicals produced by yeast as they use sugars and starches to make carbon dioxide gas (which forms bubbles to leaven the bread) and alcohol (which boils off in baking)."

We asked Dr. Silver why the yeast stays active enough for leavening even after two weeks. "It's the refrigeration. In the lab, we store ours at 176 degrees below zero, and yeast pretty much go to sleep. But if you

(continued)

(continued)

leave them out on the counter with a starch or sugar source, they get over-active and stinky. You'd never get away with two-week dough storage without refrigeration—the yeast would soon use up all the nutrients and become inactive."

Someone once asked us why, in five thousand years of bread baking, had no one come up with our approach. Well, it's really just one hundred years—that's how long refrigeration has been around.

〜

MODERN YEAST almost never fails if used before its expiration date, so you do not need to wait until the yeast "proofs" (bubbles), nor do you need to add sugar. Skip it. It wastes five precious minutes when you could be fishing around for compliments from your family about the fresh bread you've baked.

one-quarter of the specified level of yeast (rising time will be much longer).

Use whatever yeast is readily available; with our approach you won't be able to tell the difference between the various national brands of yeast, nor between instant, regular, granulated, or cake yeast (though you will have to double the quantity if you use cake yeast). The long storage time of our doughs acts as an equalizer between all of these. *One strong recommendation: Buy in bulk or in commercially available jars, rather than in envelopes. The envelopes are much more expensive, ounce for ounce.* Between the two of us, we've had only one yeast failure in many years of baking, and it was with an outdated envelope. Excellent results can be had with bulk-purchased yeast. Just be sure it's fresh. ***The real key to avoiding yeast failures is to use water that is no warmer than lukewarm (about 100°F). Even cold water will work, though rising will take much longer. Hot water kills yeast.*** After several days of high-moisture storage, yeasted dough begins to take on a flavor and aroma that approximates the flavor of the natural sourdough starters used in many artisan breads. Sours and starters like *biga* (Italian), *levain* (French), and *poolish* (referred to in Eastern European, French, and Italian recipes) all require significant time and attention, so our books don't ask you to make them.

Salt: Adjust It to Your Taste

In traditional bread recipes, salt is used not only for flavor, but also to help tighten and strengthen the gluten. Because our dough is slack in the first place, and is stored for so long, we don't detect differences in dough strength between high- and low-salt versions of our breads. In our recipes, salt makes its appearance mostly for flavor, so adjust it to suit your palate. So, how much? We love the taste of salt, but for this health-oriented book, we decided to turn down the salt, compared with our first book. If you're missing the salt, feel free to increase it to taste. If health reasons require it, you can decrease it and the recipes will still work well. Cutting the salt in half can be a good option for people who want to restrict sodium in their diet. In fact, you can bring the salt all the way down to zero, if you like.

Salt-free breads for people with health problems: In Italy, the Tuscans have had a long tradition of salt-free bread, apparently arising during a time of high taxation on salt from papal authorities. Many older baking books include recipes for salt-free Tuscan bread. It's particularly nice for dipping into soups and in other situations where it's not eaten alone. Obviously, the flavor will be very different. You'll get a sense of how salt brings out the subtle flavors of wheat, but at the same time, you'll develop an appreciation for the grain's pure essence. Be aware that salt-free yeast dough might behave badly at high altitude (see page 46).

All of our recipes were tested with a noniodized coarse Morton brand kosher salt, measuring the salt by volume rather than weight. If you're using something finer or coarser, you need to change the amount, because finer salt packs denser on the spoon. You'll get the same saltiness from these tablespoon amounts:

> **Table salt (finer):** 2/3 tablespoon
> **Morton Kosher Salt (coarse):** 1 tablespoon
> **Diamond Kosher Salt (coarsest):** 1 1/3 tablespoons

SALT SUBSTITUTE

Salt substitutes are made from potassium chloride, which, like table salt (sodium chloride), is a naturally occurring mineral that's required by all living things. Unlike sodium chloride, potassium salt does not tend to raise blood pressure and promote fluid retention, so it's sometimes recommended for people with high blood pressure and others on a sodium-restricted diet. In fact, potassium may help control blood pressure in some people. When added to bread dough, it does replace some of the salt flavor that you lose when you omit sodium salt from our recipes. It can be substituted volume for volume with kosher salt in our recipes. *Consult your doctor before using salt substitute because some medications and medical conditions, including kidney disease, can cause retention of potassium and dangerous buildup of potassium in the bloodstream.*

Oils and Solid Fats

Butter: Butter is delicious, but because it's high in saturated fat, it increases "bad" cholesterol (LDL). In this book, we use it sparingly, and give you zero saturated and zero trans fat options. But if truth be told, life's too short to use anything other than a little butter as a spread on fresh bread. If you need some justification, butter is high in vitamins A and E, both essential nutrients. If you're going to eat butter once in a while, spread some European-style artisan salted butter on the freshest and most delicious bread you make. Just use it in moderation, as a treat.

    Ghee is butter that has been clarified and slightly toasted. It is a staple in Indian kitchens because of its wonderful flavor. Since the heat-sensitive milk solids are toasted and then strained off, *ghee* can be heated to a much higher temperature than regular butter. *Ghee* can be found in many Asian markets, but we prefer to make our own. The following recipe will yield ¾ pound (about 1⅔ cups). Melt 1 pound of unsalted butter in a medium saucepan over low heat. When it is completely melted, bring it up to a boil and cook until it is frothy. Reduce the heat low and cook gently until the milk solids have settled on the bottom of the pot and are golden brown. Strain the ghee through a fine-mesh sieve. Allow it to cool completely, cover, and refrigerate. The *ghee* will last in the refrigerator for a month.

Butter substitutes: Butter substitute spreads are made by blending unsaturated oils with by-products of butter in patented manufacturing processes. They're designed to deliver buttery flavor with little or no saturated and trans fat. Based on today's understanding of nutrition and health, many of the products are successful in doing that. Despite being unsaturated, they're solid at room temperature and perform well in brioche. But we recommend them with some reservations. They are manufactured products, like margarine or vegetable shortening, and they do not exist in nature. Health authorities have been burned before by endorsing, for example, hard stick margarine as being more heart-healthy than butter, only to find out, years later, that trans fats in hard margarine were countering much of the benefit from margarine's decreased saturated fat content. Plus, some of these products were designed for people with cholesterol problems, and it's possible that there are side effects for those whose cholesterol is normal in the first place. Research is accumulating all the time, so be aware that today's "safe" butter substitute may not be seen that way forever. If these appeal to you, you can substitute them for butter, margarine, or oil in our recipes. See the table of fats and oils in the Appendix, page 309.

Canola oil: Canola oil is virtually flavorless, so we use it when we don't want olive oil's distinctive flavor to come through. It's high in monounsaturated fat and polyunsaturated fat, and has a high smoking point so it's suited for deep-frying (see Indian Spiced Whole Grain Doughnuts, page 287) Canola has more super-healthy omega-3 fat than olive oil, but less monounsaturated fat.

Margarine: Old-style hard stick margarine is made with unhealthy hydrogenated oils, and it has trans fat, the worst kind of all. Don't use it! Margarine manufacturers are touting their newer soft "tub" margarines: look for a zero trans fat, zero hydrogenated oil brand, and this should be as healthy as using vegetable oil. It's a little hard to find salt-free versions, so decrease the salt a bit if you end up using a salted brand.

Olive oil: In our opinion, olive oil has one of the most delightful flavors in Western cooking: There is nothing like it (except maybe olives). It's a cornerstone of the so-called Mediterranean diet, based on olive oil as a major fat source, abundant vegetables and grains, limited meat, and a bit of red wine (see sidebar, page 137). It's also central to the flavors in many of our Mediterranean-inspired pizzas, flatbreads, and breadsticks. Olive oil has more monounsaturated fat than canola but much less omega-3 polyunsaturated fat. Don't use olive oil for deep-frying—its smoking point is too low for that.

Saturated fats: These are found mostly in animal products. They include unhealthy trans fats, are solid at room temperature, and are the unhealthiest fats of all. They tend to raise "bad" cholesterol (LDL) and lower "good" cholesterol (HDL). See the Appendix (page 309) for more about saturated versus unsaturated fats in various ingredients. Butter substitutes and some margarines are an exception to the liquid/solid rule. They're solid at room temperature, but they're generally made with processed unsaturated and monounsaturated oils, plus butter flavorings that have been processed to get rid of some of the saturated fat. Check product labeling if your doctor has recommended that you avoid saturated fat.

One other area of confusion is product labeling that promotes a product as being cholesterol-free. Only animals produce cholesterol, so *all* vegetable oils are cholesterol-free. Beware of ads that promote cholesterol-free vegetable products in general. Preformed cholesterol in food is much less important to our blood cholesterol than the types of fats we eat (saturated, trans, polyunsaturated, and monounsaturated), and whether our weight is under control. Butter is the only fat we use that has pre-formed cholesterol in it. We use it sparingly, and so should you. See our table in the Appendix (page 309) for more information on fats, oils, and spreads that you might use in our breads.

THERE ARE TWO KINDS OF UNSATURATED FAT

Monounsaturated fat: Olive oil is particularly high in monounsaturated fat.

Polyunsaturated fat: Canola oil is high in polyunsaturated fat, and in particular, omega-3 polyunsaturated fat, which appears to have the most potent effect on improving cholesterol profile. It's also quite high in monounsaturated fat, but not quite so high as olive oil.

Unsaturated fats: Unsaturated fats like neutral-flavored canola oil and flavorful olive oil are among the healthiest options for enriching breads. They raise "good" cholesterol (HDL) and lower "bad" cholesterol (LDL). While safflower, peanut, corn, and blended oils are also heart-healthy, they tend to have stronger flavors. Canola works nicely as a neutral-flavored oil in our breads. And when you don't need a neutral-flavored oil, nothing tastes like olive oil; we'd probably drink it if someone came up with an appropriate cocktail!

Between olive oil and canola, there's scant and conflicting health evidence to strongly favor one over the other. Healthwise, they're both terrific, so we use whichever fits a recipe's flavor best. All cooking oils contain 14 grams of fat per tablespoon (120 calories), so if you're trying to lose weight, oil choice won't have a major effect. Canola and olive oil promote heart health because they're high in unsaturated fats (usually liquid at room temperature); unsaturated fats are considered to be the healthiest. Neither canola nor olive oil contains any "trans" fat, which is considered to be the unhealthiest fat of all.

Seeds and Nuts

We boost the nutrition of many of our breads by topping them with a mixture of healthy seeds, usually including sesame, flaxseed, caraway, raw sunflower, poppy, and anise. They'll stick to the bread best if you first paint the surface of the loaf with water before sprinkling them on the loaf.

Anise seeds: Anise seeds have the flavor of licorice. Like other seeds, they occasionally turn rancid, so taste a few if your jar is older than a year. Freeze them if you are storing them longer than 3 months.

Caraway seeds: These are so central to the flavor of many rye breads that a lot of people think that caraway is actually the flavor of the rye grain. It's not, but for us, something does seem to be missing in unseeded rye bread. The only problem you can run into with caraway seeds (or any other) is that the oil inside the seed can go rancid if they are very old. Taste a few if your jar is older than a year. Otherwise use whatever brand or bulk source you like. Freeze them if you are storing them longer than 3 months.

Flaxseeds: These little brown beauties are slightly larger than a sesame seed and pack lots of omega-3 fatty acids, lignans (which may have anti-cancer properties), manganese, fiber, protein, and other nutrients our bodies need. They seem to protect against everything from heart disease, cancer, diabetes, and high blood pressure to even hot flashes. We use them whole to top loaves, but the nutrients are more readily absorbed by the body when they are ground into a powder, so that's how they're used in the dough mixtures. Buy ground flaxseed in small amounts—because of its high oil content it tends to become rancid more quickly than other flours. If your flaxseed breads have an unpleasant fishy taste, you know you used rancid flax. You can also buy whole seeds and grind them in a spice or coffee grinder.

Two other points: the Flax Council of Canada (Canada is the world's largest producer of flax) says:

1. Ground flaxseed can be stored for 30 days in a cool place in an airtight, opaque container, while whole seeds can be kept at room temperature for up to a year. Freeze them if you are storing them longer than 3 months.

2. Despite older references that suggest high heat can break down flax's nutrients, more recent studies have shown that it can be heated to high temperatures without damage.

Nuts: Store nuts in the freezer so that the oils will not go rancid. Buy them either natural or blanched.

Poppy seeds: Poppy seeds are used in Western, Middle Eastern, and Asian cuisines. They, like other seeds, occasionally turn rancid. Taste a few if your jar is older than a year. Freeze them if you are storing them longer than 3 months.

Pumpkin seeds (*pepitas*): Buy the dark green prehusked seeds, which are the most nutritious part of the pumpkin. They are rich in minerals, protein, and monounsaturated fat. You can't eat the husk, so don't try to use seeds straight out of a pie pumpkin! Freeze them if you are storing them longer than 3 months.

Sesame seeds: Not only do they have a wonderful nutty flavor, but these tiny seeds are full of nutrients. They are a good source of calcium, iron, vitamin B_1, zinc, and fiber. Black sesame seeds have a stronger flavor than white ones. Try both and see what you think. Freeze them if you are storing them longer than 3 months.

Sunflower seeds: These seeds are a great source of vitamins E and B_1, along with a host of minerals. You can use roasted or raw sunflower seeds in a dough, but if you're using them on a top crust, use the raw seeds or they will burn at temperatures higher than 375°F. Freeze them if you are storing them longer than 3 months.

Other Flavorings

Caramel coloring: Caramel color powder is actually a natural ingredient made by overheating sugar until it almost burns. It's crucial for pumpernickel breads (pages 115, 118), in which it provides more than just color—it imparts a bitterness that really complements the wheat and rye flavors in pumpernickel bread. The easiest way to use it is to buy the powder from a baking specialty store or from King Arthur Flour (see Sources for Bread-Baking Products, page 311), but if you can't easily get it, you can make your own. What you make will be a liquid that is added to recipes; you should decrease liquid ingredients in the recipe to account for the extra you are adding in the form of caramel. Put 3 tablespoons sugar and 1 tablespoon water into a small saucepan. Melt the sugar over a low flame, then increase the heat to medium-high, cover, and bring it to a boil for 2 minutes. Add a pinch of cream of tartar and continue to boil it, uncovered, until the mixture becomes very dark. Be careful that it does not burn. Remove it from the heat and allow it to cool partially. Very carefully, add ¼ cup of boiling water to the pan (it may sputter and water may jump out of the pan, so wear gloves and keep your face away from it). Dissolve the caramelized sugar and cool it to room temperature. Use about ¼ cup of this mixture in place of commercial caramel color powder in our Bavarian-Style Whole Grain Pumpernickel Bread recipe (page 115); decrease the water in the recipe by ¼ cup to account for the difference between liquid caramel and powdered caramel color.

Chocolate: Some of our enriched breads call for chocolate, either cocoa powder, bar chocolate, or chunks. You will notice an improvement in flavor and recipe performance if you use the highest quality chocolate available. For bittersweet bar chocolate, Valrhona is our favorite, but Callebaut, Scharffen Berger, Lindt, Perugina, Ghirardelli, and other premium brands also work quite well. Our favorite unsweetened cocoa powder is Valrhona, but Droste's, Ghirardelli, and other premium brands also give good results. In our recipes, it doesn't matter if the cocoa powder is Dutch-processed (alkali-treated) or not: The question of Dutch-process is only important for baked goods risen with baking soda or baking powder. Yeast doesn't seem to care. If premium chocolates are unavailable, try the recipes with your favorite supermarket brands. The premium stuff is not an absolute requirement by any means.

Natural Sweeteners

These sweeteners have trace amounts of plant nutrients (refined white sugar has none). But they still spike blood sugar levels and contain lots of calories. For diabetics or anyone on a weight-loss program, these should be used in moderation. Like salt, sugars help to hold moisture in the bread and keep bread from getting stale—salt and sugar are hygroscopic (water-attracting).

Agave syrup: Agave syrup (sometimes labeled "agave nectar") tastes the tiniest bit like tequila, and no wonder. The agave plant is the source of the fermentable juice that makes the world's best tequila, and agave syrup is the concentrated sweetener made from that juice. It provides a smooth and distinct flavor in Mesquite Bread (page 171), and is available from natural food co-ops and by Web or mail order from Native Seeds/SEARCH (see Sources for Bread-Baking Products, page 311). You can substitute it for honey or maple syrup if you prefer the flavor in recipes calling for those natural sweeteners.

Barley malt: Made from sprouted barley, it is very dark, sweet with malt sugar, and quite thick. It adds a beery, yeasty flavor to bread. Barley malt is the main ingredient in beer, and malt sugar is one of the best sugars for feeding yeast.

Brown sugar and raw sugar: Like white sugar, these less refined sugars are made from sugarcane or sugar beets, but they retain trace amounts of the nutrition found in molasses. They impart a caramel flavor as well. Raw sugars are most commonly found as demerara, muscovado, and turbinado and have a larger grain than regular brown sugar.

Honey: This is the sweetener we call for most frequently in the book, produced by busy bees the world over from naturally occurring sugars in the nectar of flowers that they visit. Honey's flavor is determined by the type of plant nectar the honeybee collects. Some honeys have very intense flavor, such as buckwheat honey, while others are quite mild, like clover honey. We've had nice results with all kinds of honey, so experiment with different types and see which you prefer.

Maple syrup: The most commonly found maple syrup is Grade A, which is lightest in color and mildest in flavor. Many consider it the more desirable grade, but we actually prefer to use Grade B, which is made later in the production season and has a darker color, stronger flavor, and more of the minerals magnesium and zinc. It is great for baking because the flavor stands up to the other ingredients, but either Grade A or B will work nicely.

Molasses: Molasses is an unrefined sweetener derived from sugarcane. Blackstrap molasses is the product of three boilings of the sugarcane, and so it concentrates the nutrients. Its iron, magnesium, calcium, copper, potassium, and vitamin B_6 content makes it one of the most nutrient-rich sweeteners, more so than molasses that isn't labeled as blackstrap. It is used in the recipes to add color and a deep, rich flavor. Unsulphured molasses has the best flavor.

Dairy Products

Cheese: We add a number of different cheeses to our doughs. They are not only a great source of flavor, but also add protein and calcium to the bread. Many cheeses are high in saturated fat, so eat them in moderation.

Milk: The addition of milk to bread dough adds not only a slight sweetness, but also protein. And lactose (milk sugar) helps to keep the loaf fresher longer. Too much milk in dough, however, can have an adverse effect on the rising power of your loaf. With our whole grain breads we can't afford to lose any rise! In *CookWise*, food scientist Shirley O. Corriher suggests scalding the milk first, which helps to eliminate the problem. We don't call for it in the recipes, but if your dough is dense it is worth a try.

Yogurt: Plain yogurt, either whole milk, lowfat, or nonfat, contains lactic acid, which helps to promote strong gluten development. It also acts as a preservative to prevent baked bread from going stale so quickly. It adds a lovely tangy flavor to the bread and is a great source of protein, calcium, and zinc.

Miscellaneous Ingredients

Beer: The addition of beer to the dough adds yeasty flavors that we often don't taste using our method until the dough has stored for at least twenty-four hours. By using a little beer you can achieve the complex flavors much faster. You can use any beer except strongly flavored stouts and porters in these recipes.

Wine: Red wine might have some health benefits (see sidebar, page 137), so we tossed some into our Red Wine and Cheese Bread (page 137). Use any wine you'd enjoy drinking; it doesn't have to be top-shelf.

3

EQUIPMENT

~

W e've learned a thing or two since we wrote our first book and have discovered a few additional pieces of equipment that make bread baking even easier.

EQUIPMENT FOR BAKING WITH STEAM (You Only Need One)

Broiler tray to hold boiling water for steam: This is our first choice for creating the steam environment needed for breads to achieve a crispy crust. Highly enriched breads (eg., challah, brioche, etc.) don't benefit from baking with steam, because fat in dough softens the crust anyway. Pour hot tap water (or drop a handful of ice cubes) into the preheated broiler tray just before closing the oven door. **Two important warnings about glass: 1. Do not use a glass pan to catch water for steam, or it will shatter! 2. Some of our readers have reported cracked oven window glass after spilling water on its hot surface. If you want extra assurance that this won't happen to you, cover the window with a towel before throwing water into the pan; remove before closing the oven door.**

Some oven doors (and most professional ones) don't make a great seal for holding in steam. *If your oven allows steam to dissipate and you're not getting a beautiful crust, try one of these three alternatives to the broiler tray method:*

Food-grade water sprayer: Mist the bread three times with water from the sprayer during the first two minutes of baking.

Metal bowl or aluminum-foil roasting pan for covering loaves in the oven: By trapping steam next to a loaf as it bakes on the hot stone, you can create the humid environment that produces a crisp crust without using a broiler tray or a sprayer. The bowl or dish needs to be heat-tolerant and tall enough so that the rising loaf won't touch it when it rises, but not so large that it hangs beyond the edge of the stone, or it won't trap the steam. This is a great technique for outdoor grills, which don't trap steam even when the lid is down.

Bake inside a *cloche* or a covered cast-iron pot: The *cloche* is a time-honored way to bake—the covered unglazed clay baking vessel traps steam inside, so the crackling crust forms without the need for a broiler tray or sprayer. If you use a *cloche*, follow its directions carefully, as these can be finicky until they're well seasoned. The Sassafras La Cloche product comes with directions that recommend against preheating before use, but we get better results with a preheated Cloche. We don't soak clay pots in water before use as sometimes advocated. Covered cast-iron pots also work well for much the same reason and are a little less finicky to use, but like the Cloche, they should be preheated for 20 minutes before dropping in the rested dough. Handle hot baking implements carefully to avoid burning yourself. Most enameled cast-iron vessels won't need to be greased, but experiment with yours and grease it lightly after preheating the first time you try it. Rest the loaf on a pizza peel prepared with either cornmeal or parchment paper. Slash the dough and carefully slide the loaf, parchment and all, if you're using it, into the preheated pot.

   To bake bread dough in either of these vessels, preheat the *cloche* or cast-iron pot 50°F hotter than the recipe calls for. After the 20-minute preheat, reduce the oven to the specified temperature and add the rested dough. Some cast-iron pots will need a heat-resistant replacement knob. Finish baking, uncovered, for the last third of the baking time.

OTHER EQUIPMENT

Oven thermometer: This item isn't optional; you need to know the actual oven temperature to get predictable bread-baking results. A hot oven drives excess water out of wet dough, but if it's too high you'll burn the crust before fully baking the crumb (the bread's interior). Home ovens are often off by up to 75 degrees. With an inexpensive oven thermometer, you can be certain to get results as good as ours. Without the thermometer, your bread-baking experiments are going to require an annoying element of trial and error.

Baking stone: For best results, you'll want a high-quality, half-inch-thick baking stone (thinner ones are more likely to crack). Look for a large rectangular one, preferably with a lifetime replacement guarantee against cracking. Baking your loaves right on a stone helps create a thin, crisp crust by doing two things:

1. The stone absorbs excess moisture from your wet dough, allowing the crust to become crisp.

2. The weight and density of the stone makes for great heat retention, evenness of heating, and heat transfer to the loaves, even in ovens that deliver uneven heat. You can bake wet dough on a cookie sheet or other nonporous surface, but the crust won't be as good.

A bucket, large plastic storage container, or a glass, stainless steel, or crockery container with a lid: You can mix and store the dough in the same vessel—this will save you from washing one more item (it all figures into the five minutes a day). Look for a food-grade container that holds about five quarts, to allow for the initial rise. Round containers are a little easier to mix in than square ones, in which flour gets caught in the corners. Great options are available on our Web site, or from Tupperware, King Arthur Flour's Web site, and kitchen supply specialty stores, as well as discount chains like Costco and Target. Some food storage buckets include a tiny vent for microwave steaming, which works nicely to let gases escape early in the fermentation process. Another vented option is a beer fermentation bucket, which is sold at beer-making (home-brew) stores. You can usually close the vent (or seal the lid) after the first two days because gas production has really slowed by then. Plastic buckets are generally not airtight even when fully closed, but be careful with glass or crockery containers—you don't want a truly airtight screw-top to be completely sealed at any time in the batch's life. They can shatter from gas pressure. If you don't have a vented container, just leave the lid open a crack for the first few days of storage.

And of course, you can always use a mixing bowl covered with plastic wrap.

Pizza peel: This is a flat board with a long handle used to slide bread or pizza onto a hot stone (in Britain, it's known as a pizza paddle, pie paddle, or a pizza blade). You can't use anything made of plastic to transfer bread into the oven—it would melt upon contact with the very hot baking stone. Cover the peel with cornmeal or parchment before putting wet dough loaves on it or they will stick to the peel and possibly to the stone. If you don't have a pizza peel, a flat cookie sheet with no sides will do, but it will be more difficult to handle. Another alternative is a handled wood cutting board.

Cookie sheets and silicone mats: You might opt to bake your first bread on a greased cookie sheet that you already own. Similar results are obtained with the new non-stick, flexible silicone baking mats, which don't need to be greased and are used on top of a cookie sheet or dropped onto a hot stone (cleanup is a breeze). Be sure to get a silicone mat rated to at least 450°F (230°C), which is the baking temperature for most of our non-enriched doughs. The silicone mats are reusable thousands of times; or, you can line your cookie sheet with single-use parchment paper, which also provides a nice nonstick surface and easy cleanup (see below). All these nonporous options give respectable results, but don't expect the crust to be quite as good as bread baked directly on the stone, because moisture can't transfer away from the bottom crust. For improved results, remove the bread from the cookie sheet or silicone mat and bake directly on the oven rack for the last third of baking. One advantage of the silicone mat is that it eliminates the need to grease a cookie sheet.

Parchment paper: Parchment paper is a great alternative to cornmeal for preventing loaves from sticking to the pizza peel as they're slid into the oven. The paper goes with the loaf onto the preheated stone. Most kitchen parchment products have a silicone coating that blocks moisture transfer to the stone, so you should peel the paper off the loaf for the last third of baking. Otherwise you won't get a crispy bottom crust. One other advantage of parchment, even for cookie-sheet bakers, is that it eliminates the need to grease the cookie sheet.

Baguette pan (metal or silicone): Both the metal and the silicone perforated baguette pans work wonderfully—they allow moisture to vent through the bottom crust and can replace the baking stone. They are a great way to bake several beautifully shaped baguettes at once, without crowding. They also prevent sideways spreading, which sometimes gives baguettes an odd shape when using longer-aged or wetter dough.

Banneton/brotform: Wicker rising baskets (French = *banneton*, German = *brotform*) have long been favored by artisan bakers for the beautiful flour patterns they impart to the loaves, but we also found they are a great way to keep our very soft doughs from spreading sideways while the loaves are rising. Smaller ones are the easiest to work with, preferably designed for one or one and a half pounds of dough (see Bavarian-Style Whole Grain Pumpernickel Bread, page 115).

Loaf pans and mini loaf pans: Like cookie sheets and silicone mats, loaf pans work well but don't promote the development of a crisp and beautifully colored crust—wherever the pan touches the bread, it's going to be pale compared to your free-form loaves. One word of caution about loaf pans: With our wet doughs, you must use a pan with a nonstick coating, and even then, we find that a light greasing is still needed. Traditional loaf pans will stick no matter how much you grease them. We prefer the smaller loaf pans, because it's easier to get high-moisture dough to bake all the way through in these. Ideally, pans intended for one pound of dough are the best bet, though we specify more dough since we like them filled generously (we find that so-called "one-pound" loaf pans take more like two pounds when three-quarters full). Dimensions of 8½ by 4½ inches (length/width) work best, but those numbers are approximate.

For smaller sandwich breads, it's fun to use the mini loaf pans. They're sometimes labeled as "number-1" loaf pans, measure about 6 by 3 inches (length/width), and hold about three-quarters of a pound of dough. They bake faster than larger loaf pans, so check for doneness sooner than the recipe calls for when using them.

Brioche pans: Traditionally, brioche is baked either in a fluted brioche mold or in a loaf pan. The fluted mold is easy to find either online or in any baking supply store. They are available in several sizes, with or without a nonstick coating; flexible silicone brioche molds are also available.

Bread knife: A serrated bread knife is very helpful, because it does a great job of cutting through fresh bread without tearing or compressing, and also because it's the best implement we've found for slashing high-moisture loaves just before baking the bread. Razor blades and French *lames*, usually referenced in traditional artisan baking methods, catch and stick in very wet dough—not so for serrated bread knives.

Serrated steak knife: This is Jeff's tool of choice for cutting a portion of dough out of a bucket. The free ones from the gas station work beautifully.

Kitchen shears/scissors: These are handy for cutting pita bread or even pizza. Zoë prefers them to a serrated knife for cutting dough out of the storage bucket. You want shears with long blades for best results cutting the *epi* (page 71).

Cooling rack: These are fashioned of wire or other thin metal and are usually intended for cake. They are very helpful in preventing the soggy bottom crust that can result when you cool bread on a plate or other nonporous surface.

Dough scraper: The dough scraper (also called a bench scraper) makes it much easier to work with wet dough. Without one, there'll be the temptation to use too much flour to prevent dough from sticking to the work surface. Keep our doughs wet by dusting lightly and scraping them off the work surface when they stick, rather than by working in flour. *Once you start making pizza and other rolled-out flatbreads, you really* *need to have one of these, because rolling them thin leads to sticking.* The scraper is also the easiest way to scrape excess cornmeal or flour off a hot baking stone.

Measuring cups: We have only one word of advice, and that is to avoid 2-cup measuring cups, because they overestimate the flour quantity when using the scoop-and-sweep method (see page 55) that we describe in our recipes, due to excessive packing-down into the cup.

Measuring spoons: Seek out a set that includes a half-tablespoon measure in addition to the usual suspects. Many of our recipes call for 1½ tablespoons of certain ingredients. If you can't find a half-tablespoon measure, you can approximate a half tablespoon by using a rounded teaspoon, or, to be more exact, measure out 1½ teaspoons.

Pastry brush: These look like small paintbrushes, and are used to paint egg wash or water onto the surface of loaves just before baking. We both prefer the bristle ones over the silicone, but that's a matter of taste.

Scale: We specify loaf size in pounds, but weighing is by no means necessary. We give both a weight and a visual cue for loaf size. A pound of dough is about the size of a grapefruit. But there's an even better use for the new digital scales, which are getting cheaper all the time—you may prefer weighing ingredients, rather than using measuring cups. Chapter 4, Tips and Techniques, has tables of weight and volume equivalents (including metric units) on pages 36–38, and you can use them to convert any recipe in this book.

Microplane zester: Microplane zesters or micro zesters are used for removing the zest from citrus fruit without getting the bitter pith. In Chocolate Tangerine Bars (page 304), we use the coarse holes on an ordinary box grater to get a more assertive tangerine flavor.

Whisk: Whisks, either wire or plastic, are the best way to mix vital wheat gluten into the other dry ingredients (before adding liquids), a crucial step for the doughs in this book. Whisking distributes the vital wheat gluten and keeps it from clumping into lumps when the liquids are added.

Food processors and mixers: As mentioned in all the recipes, you can use a 14-cup food processor (with dough attachment) or a heavy-duty stand mixer (with paddle) rather than a spoon to mix the dough.

Immersion blenders: These are great for breaking up a lump of old dough, known in French as *pâte fermentée* (páht fair-mon-táy). *Pâte fermentée* can be used to jump-start the sourdough process in stored dough (see page 39). These blenders are also nice for breaking up pieces of whole tomatoes for pizza toppings. Be sure that the immersion blender is fully submerged in the liquid mixture before turning it on, otherwise you'll be spattered with ingredients.

Safety note: Remember that immersion blenders don't have a protective safety interlock, so it's possible to touch the sharp spinning blades while the unit is on. Be careful, and don't let children use an immersion blender.

Convection ovens: They produce a terrific browned crispy crust and speed the baking by circulating hot air around bread in the oven. This has the effect of transferring heat more quickly. Baking tends to be completed about 15 percent faster. You need to turn the oven temperature down by 25°F if you choose the convection mode in your oven, and in some ovens, it will be beneficial to turn the loaf around at the halfway point, so that each side is exposed directly to the fan. Ignore oven instructions that claim you can skip the preheat—that won't give a happy result, especially if you're using a baking stone. As always, use an oven thermometer to check temperature; air circulation in convection ovens can "fool" thermostats in some ovens.

These instructions apply only to range-based convection ovens, not microwaves with convection modes, which we have not tested.

4

TIPS AND TECHNIQUES

෦ඛ

This chapter will help you perfect your whole grain breads made from stored high-moisture dough. In the discussion that follows, we provide tips and techniques to achieve breads with professional-quality crust (exterior) and crumb (interior).

Measuring Ingredients by Weight

Many readers of our first book asked us for weight equivalents, especially readers outside the United States, who commonly bake this way. We have to admit, this is the quickest way to mix up a batch of dough. Below are some useful U.S. and metric equivalents so that you can convert recipes in the book to a weighed version (the Master Recipe's already converted, see page 54). Be aware that this table reflects minor rounding errors that won't affect your recipes. **All cup measurements were performed using the scoop-and-sweep method described in chapter 5, page 55):**

INGREDIENT	VOLUME (U.S.)	WEIGHT (U.S. OUNCES)	WEIGHT (GRAMS)
Unbleached all-purpose flour	1 cup	5	140
Whole wheat flour (traditional or white)	1 cup	$4\frac{1}{2}$	130
Rye flour, whole grain	1 cup	$4\frac{1}{4}$	120
Emmer flour	1 cup	$4\frac{1}{4}$	120
Spelt flour	1 cup	$4\frac{1}{2}$	130
Barley flour	1 cup	$4\frac{1}{4}$	120
Wheat bran	1 cup	3	85
Vital wheat gluten	1 tablespoon	0.33	10
	$\frac{1}{4}$ cup	$1\frac{3}{8}$	35
Cooked brown rice	1 cup	$6\frac{1}{2}$	185
Cooked wild rice	1 cup	$5\frac{1}{8}$	145
Yeast, granulated	1 tablespoon	0.37	10
Salt, kosher (Morton brand)	1 tablespoon	0.55	15
Cocoa powder	$\frac{1}{2}$ cup	2	55
Vegetable oil (canola, olive, etc.)	$\frac{1}{2}$ cup	$3\frac{3}{4}$	110
Butter, 1 stick	$\frac{1}{2}$ cup (8 tablespoons)	4	115
Water	1 cup	8	225

(continued)

INGREDIENT	VOLUME (U.S.)	WEIGHT (U.S. OUNCES)	WEIGHT (GRAMS)
Honey	½ cup	6	170
Raisins	½ cup	3	85

Conversion Tables for Common Measures

Volumes

U.S. SPOON AND CUP MEASURES	U.S. LIQUID VOLUME	METRIC VOLUME
1 teaspoon	⅙ ounce	5 ml
1 tablespoon	½ ounce	15 ml
¼ cup	2 ounces	60 ml
½ cup	4 ounces	120 ml
1 cup	8 ounces	240 ml
2 cups	16 ounces	475 ml
4 cups	32 ounces	950 ml

U.S. and Metric Weight Conversion

U.S. WEIGHT (OUNCES)	U.S. WEIGHT (POUNDS)	METRIC WEIGHT
1 ounce	1/16 pound	28 grams
2 ounces	1/8 pound	56 grams

(continued)

U.S. and Metric Weight Conversion (*continued*)

U.S. WEIGHT (OUNCES)	U.S. WEIGHT (POUNDS)	METRIC WEIGHT
4 ounces	¼ pound	112 grams
8 ounces	½ pound	225 grams
16 ounces	1 pound	450 grams

Oven Temperature: Fahrenheit to Celsius conversion

DEGREES FAHRENHEIT	DEGREES CELSIUS
350	180
375	190
400	200
425	220
450	230
475	240
500	250
550	288

WEIGHING SMALL-QUANTITY INGREDIENTS

Our recipes only require a fraction of an ounce of some ingredients (like salt and yeast). Since many scales for home use are accurate only to within the nearest eighth of an ounce (3 or 4 grams), measuring small amounts this way introduces inaccuracy, but that becomes less important with measuring larger quantities for the doubled recipes.

Storing Dough to Develop Flavor

All of our recipes are based on dough that can be stored for up to 14 days in the refrigerator. That makes our method incredibly convenient, but there's another benefit to storing the dough. Sourdough flavor progressively develops over the lifespan of the batch. That means that your first loaves won't be the same as your last ones. Some of our readers have taken to mixing staggered batches, so that they're never baking with brand-new dough.

How much to make: In order to have artisan fresh-baked bread in only 5 minutes a day, you'll want to make enough dough to last a week or more. Your initial time investment (mixing the dough) is the most significant one, though it generally takes no more than 15 minutes. By mixing larger batches, you can spread that investment over more days of bread making. So we really recommend mixing enough dough to last 7 to 10 days. For larger households, that might mean doubling or even tripling the recipes. If you make larger batches, be sure you're using a larger container as well.

Dough Moisture Content: How Wet Is Wet Enough?

Our recipes were carefully tested, and we arrived at the ratio of wet to dry ingredients with an eye toward creating a relatively slack and wet dough. But flours can vary in their protein content, the degree to which they're compacted into their containers, and in the amount of water they've absorbed from the environment. All of this means that our recipes' specified dry ingredients may produce slightly variable results depending on humidity, compaction, and the flour brand you're using.

If you find that your doughs are too stiff (especially if they don't show much rising capacity after a few days in the refrigerator), decrease the flour by ¼ cup at a time in subsequent batches (or increase the water by the same amount). And if they're too loose and wet, and don't hold a shape well for free-form loaves, increase the flour (or decrease the water) in subsequent batches again by ¼ cup at a time. If you don't want to wait till your next batch to correct a problem with moisture content, you can work extra flour into a too-wet batch (give it some time to ferment after doing this), but it's difficult to work additional water into a too-dry batch unless you use a stand mixer with a paddle attachment.

You'll find that overly wet dough still works well as flatbreads or in loaf pans. The same is true for long-saved dough (more than 10 days or so).

Vary moisture content in our recipes based on your taste. To summarize:

If you modify a recipe, using . . .

. . . MORE LIQUID (GIVING YOU WETTER DOUGH), YOU'LL GET . . .	. . . LESS LIQUID (GIVING YOU DRIER DOUGH), YOU'LL GET . . .
Larger air holes and a desirable "custard" crumb (see below)	Smaller air holes, with dense crumb
Dough can become gummy if overly wet and will have a "wet sponge" crumb	Crumb will be drier
May be difficult for free-form loaf to hold shape, may spread sideways; will do very well as flatbread or in loaf pans	Free-form loaves will hold shape well and remain high and domed
Requires less resting time before baking	Requires more resting time before baking

"Custard" Crumb

Perfectly baked high-moisture dough can produce a delightful "custard" crumb (interior). When mixed with water and then baked, wheat flour's protein, mostly gluten, traps the water and creates a chewy and moist texture. A shiny surface is seen in the larger air holes; that's the "custard" effect. As you adjust flour amounts for your favorite recipes, you'll find that this is an effect you can manipulate. Too much flour, and you will lose the custard crumb character. Too little, and the dough will be difficult to shape and the breads gummy. If your batch is too wet, you can work in more flour at the shaping step, or in its storage container. If the batch is too dry, add more water, using wet hands at the shaping step. If you work flour or water into dough that's already risen, you need to allow the dough to rest longer before baking to develop hole structure again.

Resting and Baking Times Are Approximate

Our first book concentrated on bread recipes that were mostly based on white flour, which is high in gluten and is forgiving of short resting/rising times. We opted for the shortest possible rest time so that our method would fit into people's busy schedules. But when using whole grains, it's important to let the loaves sit for a longer rest, otherwise the bread may be too dense. So readers of our first book will notice that the resting times are longer in this book; remember that this is still passive time. Have a glass of red wine (see sidebar, page 137) while your whole wheat loaf is resting.

All of our resting and baking times are approximate. Since artisan loaves are formed by hand, their size can vary from loaf to loaf (though you can weigh out the dough if you like). There can be significant changes in resting and baking time requirements with changes in loaf size. Although large flat loaves will rise and bake rapidly, large high-domed loaves will require dramatically longer resting and baking times. So unless you're weighing out exact 1-pound loaves and forming the same shapes each time, your resting and baking times will vary and our listed time should be seen only as a starting point for 1-pound free-form loaves (or 2-pound loaf-pan loaves). Here are some basic guidelines for varying resting and baking times based on what you're baking. **Increase resting and/or baking time if any of the following apply:**

- The temperature of your kitchen is low: This only affects rising and resting times, not baking.
- Larger loaf: A 3-pound loaf will take nearly twice as long to bake, compared with a 1-pound loaf, though resting time won't change that much.
- You use more whole grain.

A good rule of thumb, if you want the loaves to develop maximum rise and air holes, is to wait until the dough no longer feels dense and cold.

Underbaking Problems

The crust is crispy when it comes out of the oven, but it softens as it comes to room temperature: This is most often a problem with very large breads, but it can happen with any loaf that's been slightly underbaked. Internal moisture, so high in wet dough, can soften the crust as it cools. You need to drive off that moisture with heat. As you gain experience, you will come to understand just how brown the loaf must be to prevent this problem for any given loaf size. We use brownness and crust firmness as our measure of doneness (there might be a few blackened bits on the loaf in non-egg-enriched breads). **If you have a crust that is initially crisp but softens as it cools, it can be returned to the oven until you have the desired result.**

The loaf has a soggy or gummy crumb (interior):

- Check your oven temperature with a thermometer.
- Make sure you are allowing the dough to rest for the full time period we've recommended (page 41).
- Your dough may benefit from being a little drier. Increase the flour by ¼ cup (or decrease the liquids a little) and check the result.
- If you're baking a large loaf (more than 1 pound), let it rest and bake longer.
- Be sure not to overwork dough when shaping, or you will compress the gas bubbles.

One final word of advice if you're finding the breads just a little gummy: **Don't slice or eat your loaves when they're still warm.** We know, hot bread has a certain romance, so it's hard to wait for them to cool. But waiting will improve the texture—breads are at their peak two hours after they come out of the oven. Hot or warm bread cuts poorly and dries out quickly. When cool, loaves don't compress so easily when cut. Once the bread has cooled, use a sharp serrated bread knife, which will go right through the crisp crust and soft crumb.

Having said that, sometimes we just can't resist, especially with rolls or very small loaves where gumminess is less likely to be a problem.

The top crust won't crisp and brown nicely:

- Be sure you're using a baking stone where called for, and preheat it for at least 30 minutes, in an oven whose temperature has been checked with a thermometer.
- Bake with steam when called for. Use one of the methods described on pages 27 and 28.
- Try the shelf switcheroo: If you're a crisp crust fanatic, we'll give you one ultimate approach to baking the perfect crust, but it takes a little extra work (remember, this does not apply to egg-enriched breads). First off, place the stone on the bottom shelf, not on a middle shelf as specified in the recipes, and start the loaf there. Two-thirds of the way through baking, transfer the loaf from the stone directly to a rack on the top shelf of the oven (leave the stone where it is). Top crusts brown best near the top of the oven, and bottom crusts brown best near the bottom. This approach works beautifully with free-form loaves, but also helps crisp the crust of hard-crusted loaf-pan breads, where popping the bread out of the pan and transferring shelves makes a big difference. With this approach, you can permanently park your baking stone on the very lowest rack, where it will help even out the heat for everything you bake, not just bread. Then there'll be no need to shift around the stone or racks just because you're baking bread.

Overbaking Problems, Dryness

The crust is great, but the crumb (interior) is dry:

- The bread may be overbaked. Again, make sure your oven is calibrated properly using an oven thermometer.
- Another possibility is that the dough was dry to begin with. In traditional recipes, there's usually an instruction that reads something like "knead thoroughly, until mass of dough is smooth, elastic, and less sticky, adding flour as needed." This often means too much flour gets added. Be careful not to work in much additional flour when shaping.

Flour blobs in the middle of the bread: Be sure to completely mix the initial batch. Using wet hands to incorporate the last bits of flour will often take care of this. This can also be caused when shaping the loaves, with extra flour that gets tucked up under the loaf.

Varying the Grain That Covers the Pizza Peel

Most of our breads are baked right on a hot baking stone, after having been rested and slid off a pizza peel. Cornmeal was the usual "lubricant" in our first book. It prevents the loaf from sticking to either the pizza peel or the hot stone. But cornmeal is only one of many options. We tend to use cornmeal for the more rustic, full-flavored loaves, and whole wheat flour for the more delicate breads, like the French baguette. Even white flour works for the purpose (as in pita and pizza). But coarser grains like cornmeal are the most slippery, and fine-ground wheat flours may require a heavier coating to prevent sticking (sometimes you'll have to nudge the loaves off with a dough scraper (see Equipment, page 32), especially for pita bread). Mostly, though, the choice of grain on the pizza peel is a matter of taste. We've used Malt-O-Meal cereal or oatmeal in a pinch, and Zoë's mom once used grits! Rice flour, commonly used in gluten-free baking, is particularly slippery and makes a great choice. And you can substitute parchment paper for any of these grains, provided that you peel it off for the last third of the baking time (see page 30).

Problems and Frequently Asked Questions from Readers

"MY LOAVES AREN'T RISING MUCH ON THE COUNTER AFTER SHAPING."

After being shaped, our breads don't rise as much on the counter as loaves made from traditional (nonstored) dough. The success of our approach depends on keeping the dough wet (so it doesn't resist bubble expansion as much), and handling the dough as little as possible to preserve the bubbles created in the initial rise in the bucket at room temperature. Our loaves get proportionally more rise from "oven spring" than from "proofing" (proofing is the rise you see while the formed loaves are resting/rising at room temperature). Oven spring is the sudden expansion of gas bubbles in the dough during the first minutes in the oven. You can almost see the loaf popping up if you have a glass window in your oven. So, if you're disappointed in how much (or how little) rise you get on the counter from formed loaves, don't despair! Oven spring will make up for the difference. If you aren't getting good oven spring, check your dough consistency (page 39) and rise time (page 41).

"MY LOAVES STUCK TO THE PIZZA PEEL WHEN I TRIED TO SLIDE THEM OFF."

Sometimes a loaf, pizza, or flatbread will stick to the peel, especially if it has rested too long (pizzas in particular should not sit for long before sliding into the oven). There's a simple solution. Before attempting a slide, we always shake the peel a bit to be sure that nothing is stuck. If it moves well, you'll be fine when you slide it into the oven. If it's not moving well, sprinkle flour or cornmeal around the edge of the loaf and use a dough scraper to nudge some of it under the loaf, unsticking the stuck area. Now you should be able to slide the loaf easily into the oven. To prevent this, increase the amount of cornmeal or flour you're using under your loaves, or switch to parchment paper, which is easier on cleanup. This will also help if you're having trouble with smoking cornmeal on the stone or at the bottom of the oven. The paper slides into the oven with the bread and is peeled off two-thirds of the way through baking for best bottom crust results. We peel the paper off because most parchment products have a silicone coating that partially prevents the escape of moisture from the bottom crust into the stone, and that moisture can prevent crisping.

"MY LOAVES ARE ODDLY SHAPED."

The loaf flattens and spreads sideways while resting on the pizza peel: Sometimes loaves expand well while resting, but too much of the expansion is sideways rather than up. If every loaf is ending up as flatbread, there are several possible explanations.

- The dough is *too* wet: Make sure you're using the right amounts of liquid and dry ingredients.
- Not enough flour was dusted onto the dough while shaping the loaf: The flour helps effective shaping.
- You're using flour with a low-protein content: Be sure to use *unbleached* all-purpose flour; bleaching removes some of the protein from flour. Protein in wheat flour is mostly gluten, which is essential for providing good structure to the loaf. If the gluten content is too low, you'll have trouble getting high, domed loaves. If you want to use bleached or other low-protein flour, you need to increase vital wheat gluten in the recipes.
- The dough is a little too old: When the dough becomes "weepy," with liquid separating out from the dough, it's probably lost too much rising power to produce beautiful domed loaves. It still tastes great, but it may be best used as flatbread, or baked in a loaf pan. You can also work in a little more flour and allow it to sit for at least 2 hours (see also page 50).

Odd-shaped loaves: If you haven't used enough cornmeal or flour on the pizza peel, a spot of dough may stick to it. As the loaf slides off the peel, the spot pulls, causing an odd-shaped loaf. Solution: Use more cornmeal or flour on the pizza peel, or switch to parchment paper, especially if the dough is particularly sticky. You can also add flour to the dough during the stretching and shaping step, which will require your loaf to rest longer before baking.

Another cause of odd-shaped loaves is ineffective slashing—slash at least a quarter-inch deep and keep the blade perpendicular to the crust. If you don't cut deeply enough, the bread will burst open oddly.

"I LIVE 4,000 FEET ABOVE SEA LEVEL AND MY BREAD IS COMING OUT FLAT!"

There can be a big difference in how yeast behaves if you live above 4,000 feet. With less air pressure constraining the rising dough, it rises too quickly, and then collapses abruptly, giving you a dense result. The following changes can help you avoid that:

- Decrease the yeast to 2 teaspoons.
- Increase the vital wheat gluten in the recipes. You may need a little more water to keep the dough at its usual consistency.
- Use more salt, up to an extra half tablespoon if you like the flavor and aren't on a low-salt diet. This slows the effect of the yeast.
- Do the initial rise overnight in the refrigerator (see the refrigerator-rise trick, page 48), and consider mixing the dough with cold liquids.

Each of these techniques allows the dough to rise more slowly, giving it more time to achieve full height.

"THE CRUMB OF MY BREAD IS DENSE WITH SMALL HOLES, HOW DO I FIX IT?"

The following tips can help you to achieve a crumb with a nice open hole structure.

1. Make sure that your dough is not too wet or too dry, as both extremes will result in a dense crumb. Double-check the recipe to see if you are using the right amount of water for the type of flour you use. The most common problem we hear about is too-dry dough made with higher protein flours such as King Arthur All-Purpose or any bread flour. These are fine, but they absorb more liquid than typical all-purpose flours. To account for the difference, you will need to increase the water by up to ¼ cup.

2. Handle your dough very gently. We find that people often want to knead the dough at least a little, especially if they are experienced bread bakers. This knocks gas out of the dough and can give you a dense crumb. When shaping the dough, be very careful with it in order to leave as many of the air bubbles intact as possible. These bubbles create the holes in the bread. Shape the dough for only 20 to 40 seconds.

3. Kitchen temperature, loaf size, and rest time: If your kitchen is much cooler than 68 degrees, or your loaf is larger than 1 pound, you may need to let the dough rest for more time than specified in the recipe.

4. Batch age: If you are using dough that is close to two weeks old, you may want to stick to pizza, pita, or another flatbread. The yeast will not have its full power, and if baked as a high loaf it may come out denser than you want. Another option is to use overstored dough to start a new batch, using the "old-dough" method (see Lazy Sourdough Shortcut, page 51). This will really jump-start the complex flavors of your next batch.

5. The refrigerator-rise trick: Shape your dough into a loaf, free-form or loaf-pan, cover loosely with plastic, and let the pre-shaped loaf rise in the refrigerator for 8 to 14 hours. Allow it to rest at room temperature during the short oven preheat, and then it is ready to bake. Here's one way to do it that allows you to have the dough risen and ready for the oven pretty much as soon as you walk through the door after work.

- The first thing in the morning, cut off a piece of dough and shape it as you normally would. Place the dough on a sheet of parchment paper, cover it loosely with plastic wrap, and put it back in the refrigerator, where it will sit for at least 8 hours and up to 14 hours. The dough will spread slightly, and may not seem to have risen at all. Don't panic, it will still have lovely oven spring. Because you don't handle the dough at all after the refrigerator rise, the bubbles in the dough will remain intact.
- **Right before dinner,** uncover your dough and allow it to rest at room temperature while your oven preheats to the recommended temperature with a stone set on the middle rack. When the oven is hot, slash the loaf as you normally would, and bake as directed in the recipe.

"MY BREAD IS EITHER TOO SALTY OR NOT SALTY ENOUGH! HOW DO I ADJUST THE RECIPES?"

The recipes in the book were tested with Morton brand kosher salt (see page 17 for adjustments if you use other kinds of salt; it's the coarseness that varies). Readers of our first book will notice that the recipes are a little less salty than they were in *Artisan Bread in Five Minutes a Day.* The amounts we settled on were pleasing to us and to our testers, with a fairly typical salt level compared to most of the recipes used by home bakers. But you can adjust the salt to suit your own taste. If you find our recipes too salty, decrease the salt by 25 to 50 percent and see what you think. Below that threshold most but not all people will find the bread flat-tasting (the texture will be different as well). People accustomed to a low-salt diet can decrease the salt all the way to zero (or use potassium-based salt substitutes—see page 17).

If you find our recipes too bland, you can adjust the salt upward, by 25 to 50 percent. Beyond that the salt will begin to inhibit the action of the yeast and your breads won't rise well.

"CAN I DECREASE THE YEAST IN THE RECIPES?"

Some readers asked us whether our technique works with less yeast. Why? Experienced sourdough bakers sometimes prefer the more delicate flavor of a dough risen with less packaged yeast. Some traditionalists believe that rising the dough very slowly, with very little packaged yeast, builds better flavor.

We weren't convinced of this when we wrote *Artisan Bread in Five Minutes a Day*—many of our busy readers value the quicker rise that you get when you use the 1½ tablespoons of yeast called for in our recipes. And we think that our flavor is pretty darn good, especially when the dough ages a day or two.

But if you have more time, our recipes work beautifully with less yeast. We tested two ways, first halving the yeast (about ¾ tablespoon), and then dropping it way down to ½ teaspoon for a whole batch. Both work, but they work slowly. For the ½ teaspoon version, you need to give the dough 6 to 12 hours for its initial rise in the bucket (4 to 5 hours for the ¾ tablespoon version). But the dough will not need additional time after shaping; the 90-minute rest worked just as well for low-yeast dough as for high-yeast dough. *Active* time is still 5 minutes a loaf—it's just the passive resting and rising times that escalate when you switch to the low-yeast version. See what you think and have fun by experimenting.

If you do this with egg-enriched dough, to be on the safe side, do the rise in the refrigerator (see page 48). A long countertop rise could be risky due to spoilage of the eggs.

Visit www.healthybreadinfive.com, where you'll find recipes, photos, videos, and instructional material.

"MY LOAF-PAN BREAD STUCK TO THE PAN—WHAT DO I DO?"

When making breads in a loaf pan using high-moisture dough, we recommend nonstick pans, but even then, we always coat with a thin layer of oil, butter, margarine, or shortening. Wet dough tends to behave like glue during the resting/rising period for loaf-pan breads. Occasionally, a loaf will stick to a pan, but there's an easy way to get it out. After baking, simply wait about 10 minutes, and the loaf will steam free of the pan and you should be able to nudge it out easily. The crust that was in contact with the pan will be a bit moist and soft but it should dry out nicely, or you can put it back into the oven (out of the pan) for 3 to 5 minutes. Whatever you do, don't try to wrestle a hot bread out of a stuck pan, or you'll end up tearing it.

"WHAT DO I DO ABOUT CHANGES IN THE DOUGH TOWARD THE END OF THE STORAGE LIFE?"

Some testers found that toward the end of the storage life of a batch of dough, part of the batch turned sticky and liquidy, and smelled overly fermented. If that happens, don't throw away the dough, just work in enough flour to absorb the excess moisture, and wait at least 2 hours at room temperature before using. If you are not using it right away, refrigerate it again; you can keep it until the end of the dough's recommended life. And if your long-stored dough isn't holding its shape, it will still make great flatbread or loaf-pan bread.

Discard any dough that develops mold on its surface, identified as dark or light patches on the surface of any food, with or without a fuzzy appearance. **Dark liquid collecting above the dough does *not* indicate mold,** simply pour it off and the dough underneath will be fine for use.

"WHAT'S THE BEST WAY TO STORE BAKED BREAD?"

The best way to keep cut bread in good condition is to store it cut-side down on a nonporous flat surface like a plate or a clean countertop. Don't use foil, plastic wrap, or bags, which create a humid environment. This wrecks the crust by allowing it to absorb water. An exception is pita bread, which is supposed to have a soft crust and can be stored in a plastic bag after it cools completely.

Breads made with dough that has been well aged stay fresh the longest, because by-products of fermentation are natural preservatives. Keep that in mind if you would prefer to bake every other day. Use day-old bread for making bread crumbs in the food processor or recycle it into new loaves as *"altus"* (see sidebar, page 115).

∽

LAZY SOURDOUGH SHORTCUT: When your dough bucket is finally empty, or nearly so, don't wash it! Immediately re-mix another batch in the same container. In addition to saving the cleanup step, the aged dough stuck to the sides of the container will give your new batch a headstart on sourdough flavor. Just scrape it down and it will hydrate and incorporate into the new dough. Don't do this with egg-enriched dough; the container should be washed after use.

You can take that even further, by adding a more sizable amount of old dough from your last batch. You can use up to 2 cups of old dough in the batch; just mix it in with the water for your new batch and let it stand until it becomes soupy before you start mixing the new recipe. An immersion blender can be particularly helpful for blending the old dough with water. Add this liquid to your dry ingredients as in the recipe. Professionals call the old dough that you add to a new batch *pâte fermentée* (paht fair-mon-táy), which means nothing more than "fermented dough." **See safety note on immersion blenders, page 34.**

5

THE MASTER RECIPE

A Whole Grain Artisan Free-Form Loaf

We're showcasing a free-form loaf that's rich in whole wheat, shaped as an elongated oval, and topped with a delicious and nutritious seed mixture (if you'd like to start with a 100% whole wheat recipe, apply these directions to "100% Whole Wheat Bread, Plain and Simple" on page 79). It bakes easily and makes terrific sandwiches. Our wet dough develops sourdough character over 2 weeks of storage in the refrigerator. By mixing dough in bulk without kneading and using it as it's needed, you'll truly be able to make this bread in 5 minutes a day (excluding  resting and oven time). Vital wheat gluten (page 8) helps the whole grain dough rise and keeps the mix resilient and storable. The best way to get vital wheat gluten into the dough is by mixing it with the dry ingredients first. So you will start with the dry ingredients and then add in the liquids. This easy recipe and the variations that follow (pages 59 through 74) will give you the basic skills you need to complete the recipes in the rest of the book.

Makes enough dough for at least four 1-pound loaves. The recipe is easily doubled or halved.

INGREDIENT	VOLUME (U.S.)	WEIGHT (U.S.)	WEIGHT (METRIC)
Whole wheat flour*	5½ cups	1 pound, 9 ounces	720 grams
All-purpose flour, unbleached	2 cups	10 ounces	270 grams
Granulated yeast†	1½ tablespoons (2 packets)	0.55 ounces	15 grams
Kosher salt††	1 tablespoon	0.55 ounces	15 grams
Vital wheat gluten	¼ cup	1⅜ ounces	35 grams
Lukewarm water	4 cups	2 pounds	900 grams
Cornmeal or parchment paper for the pizza peel			
1 to 2 tablespoons of whole seed mixture for sprinkling on top crust: sesame, flaxseed, caraway, raw sunflower, poppy, and/or anise (optional)			

*Can use interchangeably with White Whole Wheat Flour (see page 10).
†Can decrease to taste (see page 15).
††Can increase or decrease to taste (see page 17).

WEIGHING YOUR INGREDIENTS

We've included equivalents for weight for this recipe. Many of our testers found it easier to weigh ingredients using digital scales, which are becoming less expensive all the time. Simply press the "tare" (zeroing) button before adding an ingredient, then "tare" again to add the next ingredient. To convert other recipes, see our weight conversion table on page 36–38.

Mixing and Storing the Dough

1. **Measure the dry ingredients:** Use dry-ingredient measuring cups (avoid 2-cup measures, which compress the flour) to gently scoop up flour from a bin, then sweep the top level with a knife or spatula (you can also weigh your ingredients using the equivalents provided). Whisk together the flours, yeast, salt, and vital wheat gluten in a 5-quart bowl, or, preferably, in a resealable, lidded plastic food container or food-grade bucket (not airtight).

2. **Mix with water—kneading is unnecessary:** Warm the water until it feels slightly warmer than body temperature (about 100°F). Add all at once to the dry ingredients and mix without kneading, using a spoon, a 14-cup food processor (with dough attachment), or a heavy-duty stand mixer (with paddle). You might need to use wet hands to get the last bit of flour to incorporate if you're not using a machine. Using warm water will allow the dough to rise fully in about 2 hours. **Don't knead!** It isn't necessary. You're finished when everything is uniformly moist, without dry patches. This step is done in a matter of minutes, and will yield a dough that is wet and remains loose enough to conform to the shape of its container.

3. **Allow to rise:** Cover the dough with a lid (not airtight) that fits well to the container. If you are using a bowl, cover it loosely with plastic wrap. Lidded (or even vented) plastic buckets designed for dough storage are readily available

(page 29); leave it open a crack for the first 48 hours to prevent buildup of gases; after that you can usually seal it. Allow the mixture to rise at room temperature until it begins to collapse (or at least flattens on the top), approximately 2 hours, depending on the room's temperature and the initial water temperature. Longer rising times, even overnight, will not harm the result. After rising, refrigerate in the lidded (not airtight) container and use over the next 14 days. Fully refrigerated wet dough is less sticky and is easier to work with than dough at room temperature. So, the first time you try our method, it's best to refrigerate the dough overnight (or at least 3 hours), before shaping a loaf. Once refrigerated, the dough will seem to have shrunk back upon itself. It will never rise again in the bucket, which is normal for our dough. Whatever you do, **do not punch down this dough!** With our method, you're trying to retain as much gas in the dough as possible, and punching it down knocks gas out and will make your loaves denser.

WHAT WE STILL *DON'T* HAVE TO DO: STEPS FROM TRADITIONAL ARTISAN BAKING THAT WE OMITTED

1. Mix a new batch of dough every time we want to make bread

2. Proof yeast

3. Knead dough

4. Rest/rise the loaves in a draft-free location—it doesn't matter!

5. Fuss over doubling or tripling of dough volume

6. Punch down and re-rise: ***Never*** punch down stored dough!

7. Poke rising loaves, thereby leaving indentations to be sure they've proofed.

Now you know why it only takes five minutes a day, not including resting and baking time.

On Baking Day

4. **Shape a loaf in 20 to 40 seconds.** First, prepare a pizza peel by sprinkling it liberally with cornmeal (or lining it with parchment paper, or use a silicone mat) to prevent your loaf

from sticking to it when you slide it into the oven. Dust the surface of your refrigerated dough with flour. Pull up and cut off a 1-pound (grapefruit-size) piece of dough, using a serrated knife or kitchen shears. Hold the mass of dough in your hands and add a little more flour as needed so it won't stick to your hands. Gently stretch the sur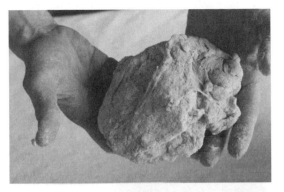face of the dough around to the bottom on all four sides, rotating a quarter-turn as you go to form a ball. Most of the dusting flour will fall off; it's not intended to be incorporated into the dough. The bottom of the ball may appear to be a collection of bunched ends, but it will flatten out and adhere during resting and baking. The correctly shaped final product will be smooth and cohesive. The entire process should take no more than 20 to 40 seconds. If you work the dough longer than this, it might make your loaf dense.

5. **Form a narrow oval-shaped loaf and let it rest:** Stretch the ball gently to elongate it, and taper the ends by rolling them between your palms and pinching them (for a really professional result, use the letter-fold method on page 68).

6. **Allow the loaf to rest,** loosely covered with plastic wrap, on the prepared pizza peel for 90 minutes (40 minutes if you're using fresh, unrefrigerated dough). Alternatively, you can rest the loaf on a silicone mat or on a greased cookie sheet without using a pizza peel. Depending on the age of the dough, you might not see much rise during this period; instead, it will spread sideways. More rising will occur during baking (oven spring).

7. **Thirty minutes before baking, preheat the oven to 450°F,** with a baking stone placed on the middle rack. Place an empty metal broiler tray for holding water on any other rack that won't interfere with the rising bread.

8. **Paint and slash:** Just before baking, use a pastry brush to paint the top with water. Sprinkle with the seed mixture if desired. Slash the loaf with ¼-inch-deep parallel cuts across the top. Use a serrated bread knife held perpendicularly to the bread.

◔◦

THE BROILER TRAY: Never use a glass pan to catch water for steam, or it will shatter!

9. **Baking with steam:** After a 30-minute preheat, you're ready to bake, even though your oven thermometer might not yet be up to full temperature. With a quick forward-jerking motion of the wrist, slide the loaf off the pizza peel and onto the preheated baking stone. If you used parchment paper instead of cornmeal, it will slide onto the stone with the loaf, and if you used a silicone mat or cookie sheet, just place it on the stone. Quickly but carefully pour about 1 cup of hot water from the tap into the broiler tray and close the oven door to trap the steam (or use an alternative method to bake with steam; see pages 27 and 28). Bake for about 30 minutes, or until the crust is richly browned and firm to the touch (smaller or larger loaves will require adjustments in resting and baking time). If you used parchment paper, a silicone mat, or a cookie sheet under the loaf, carefully remove it and bake the loaf directly on the stone or on an oven rack two-thirds of the way through baking. When you remove the loaf from

the oven, it may audibly crackle, or "sing," when initially exposed to room-temperature air. Allow the bread to cool completely, preferably on a wire cooling rack, for best flavor, texture, and slicing. The perfect crust may initially soften, but will firm up again when cooled (see cover photo).

〜

RELAX! You do not need to monitor doubling or tripling of volume as in traditional recipes. Our dough will not double in size once shaped and rested, but when it goes into the oven you will see "oven spring."

10. **Store the remaining dough in the refrigerator in your lidded (not air-tight) container and use it over the next 14 days.** You'll notice throughout the book that certain ingredients mean a shorter shelf life. You'll find that even 24 hours of storage improves the flavor and texture of your bread. The dough begins to ferment and take on sourdough characteristics.

VARIATION: Herb Bread
This simple recipe shows off the versatility of our approach. Herb-scented breads are great favorites for appetizers and snacks. Follow the directions for mixing the Master Recipe dough and add 1 teaspoon dried thyme leaves (2 teaspoons fresh) and ½ teaspoon dried rosemary leaves (1 teaspoon fresh) to the water mixture. You can also use herbs with the other bread recipes in this chapter. This also works with sliced olives, chopped garlic, onions, seeds, nuts, or any other of your favorite ingredients

Moon and Stars Bread (with Sesame Seeds)

"I make this bread for my family when we're on vacation and have the time and open spaces to notice the night sky. We never seem to track the phases of the moon when we're home in the city. But out in the country, a full moon is a special cause for excitement. Granted, this loaf is really a crescent moon, not a full moon, but it's a pretty dramatic shape, with lots of crisp crust formed at the edge from the cuts, and sesame seeds for stars (see photo, page 61)."—Jeff

Makes one 1-pound loaf

1 pound (grapefruit-size portion) Master Recipe dough (page 53)
Sesame seeds for sprinkling on top crust
Cornmeal, parchment paper, or silicone mat for the pizza peel

1. **On baking day,** dust the surface of the refrigerated dough with flour and cut off a 1-pound (grapefruit-size) piece. Dust the piece with more flour and quickly shape it into a ball by stretching the surface of the dough around to the bottom on all four sides, rotating the ball a quarter-turn as you go. Stretch the ball gently to elongate it, and taper the ends by rolling them between your palms and pinching them (or use the letter-fold method for a really professional result, page 68). Bend it into a semicircle—this will become your moon shape.

2. Allow the loaf to rest and rise on a pizza peel prepared with cornmeal or lined with parchment paper for 90 minutes (40 minutes if you're using fresh, unrefrigerated dough), loosely covered with plastic wrap. Alternatively, you can rest the loaf on a silicone mat or a greased cookie sheet without using a pizza peel.

3. **Thirty minutes before baking time, preheat the oven to 450°F,** with a baking stone placed on the middle rack. Place an empty metal broiler tray for holding water on any other rack that won't interfere with the rising bread.

4. Just before baking, use a pastry brush to paint the top with water, and sprinkle with the sesame seeds. Then use kitchen shears to snip 1- to 2-inch deep cuts into the bread on the outside of the curve (see photo). There is no need to slash this loaf.

5. Slide the loaf directly onto the hot stone (or place the silicone mat or cookie sheet on the stone if you used one). Pour 1 cup of hot tap water into the broiler tray and quickly close the oven door (see pages 27 and 28 for steam alternatives). Bake for about 30 minutes, until richly browned and firm. If you used parchment paper, a silicone mat, or a cookie sheet under the loaf, carefully remove it and bake the loaf directly on the stone or on an oven rack two-thirds of the way through baking. Smaller or larger loaves will require adjustments in resting and baking time.

6. Allow the bread to cool on a rack before slicing and eating.

Hearty Whole Wheat Sandwich Loaf

For our money, the best artisan loaves are shaped free-form and baked directly on a stone—the result is super-crusty. But especially for children, sometimes a sandwich loaf is exactly what's needed. So here's a basic sandwich loaf from the whole grain master recipe.

Makes one 2-pound loaf

2 pounds (cantaloupe-size portion) Master Recipe dough (page 53)

1. **On baking day,** lightly grease an 8½×4½-inch nonstick loaf pan. Dust the surface of the refrigerated dough with flour and cut off a 2-pound (cantaloupe-size) piece. Dust with more flour and quickly shape it into a ball by stretching the surface of the dough around to the bottom on all four sides, rotating the ball a quarter-turn as you go.

2. **Elongate the ball into an oval** and place it into the loaf pan; your goal is to fill the pan about three-quarters full. Cover loosely with plastic wrap. Allow the loaf to rest and rise for 1 hour and 45 minutes (60 minutes if you're using fresh, unrefrigerated dough).

3. **Thirty minutes before baking time, preheat the oven to 450°F,** with a baking stone placed on the middle rack. Place an empty metal broiler tray for holding water on any other rack that won't interfere with the rising bread. The baking stone is not essential for loaf-pan breads; if you omit it, the preheat can be as short as 5 minutes.

4. Just before baking, use a pastry brush to paint the top with water. Slash the loaf diagonally with ¼-inch-deep parallel cuts, using a serrated bread knife.

5. Place the loaf on a rack near the center of the oven. Pour 1 cup of hot tap water into the broiler tray and quickly close the oven door (see pages 27 and 28 for steam alternatives). Bake for about 40 to 45 minutes, or until brown and firm.

6. Remove the loaf from the pan and allow it to cool completely on a rack before slicing or eating. If the loaf is difficult to remove despite going around the edge with a spatula, allow it to sit in the pan for 10 minutes. The heat of the loaf will "steam" the stuck parts from the pan. If the crust seems soft or overly damp where it was in contact with the pan, you can return it to the oven, out of the loaf pan, for about 5 minutes to crisp the crust.

7. Allow the bread to cool on a rack before slicing and eating.

DON'T WASH THE CONTAINER, UNLESS IT'S EGGY: If you mixed your dough in a storage container, you've avoided some cleanup. Cut off and shape more loaves as you need them. We often have several types of dough stored in the refrigerator at once. The dough can also be frozen in 1-pound portions in an airtight container and defrosted overnight in the refrigerator prior to baking day; this works particularly well for egg-enriched doughs, which have shorter refrigerator life.

Whole Grain Garlic Knots with Parsley and Olive Oil

Olive oil is our favorite oil. It's rich in healthy monounsaturated fat and is an authentically Italian way to enrich bread. Combined with parsley, garlic, and Parmigiano Reggiano cheese, it's the essence of the Mediterranean.

Makes 5 garlic knots

1 pound (grapefruit-size portion) Master Recipe dough (page 53)
¼ cup olive oil, extra virgin if possible
½ cup finely minced parsley
4 cloves garlic, finely minced
2 tablespoons grated Parmigiano-Reggiano cheese

∽

GARLIC: Eat this and you won't just ward off werewolves—garlic is full of calcium, potassium, and vitamin C. **Parsley** is a Mediterranean herb that's high in vitamins A, C, and K, as well as folic acid. Anything this green must be high in antioxidants, too—it is!

1. In a skillet, sauté the parsley and garlic in olive oil for about 4 minutes over medium heat, until the garlic is soft and the mixture is aromatic. Add more olive oil if mixture looks too dry, because you'll need to be able to drizzle this over the knots.

2. **On baking day,** dust the surface of the refrigerated dough with flour and divide the dough into 3-ounce pieces (about the size of small peaches). Dust each one with more flour and quickly shape into a ball by stretching the surface of the dough around to the bottom on all four sides, rotating each ball a quarter-turn as you go.

3. Elongate each ball into a rope a little less than ½ inch in diameter, and tie it into a knot. Allow the knots to rest for 30 minutes, loosely covered with

plastic wrap, on an olive oil–greased cookie sheet, or a cookie sheet lined with a silicone mat or parchment paper.

4. **Thirty minutes before baking time, preheat the oven to 450°F,** with a baking stone placed on the middle rack. Place an empty metal broiler tray for holding water on any other rack that won't interfere with the rising knots.

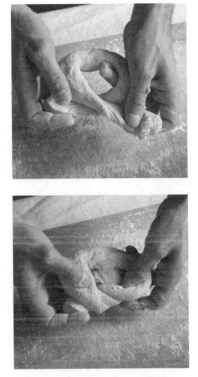

5. Drizzle the knots with the olive oil, garlic, and parsley mixture; you may have some left over for another batch.

6. Place the cookie sheet on the stone, pour 1 cup of hot tap water into the broiler tray, and quickly close the oven door. Bake for about 20 minutes, until browned and firm.

7. Serve slightly warm.

Turkish-Style Pita Bread with Black Sesame Seeds

Turkish and Greek pita bread differ from Israeli/Palestinian pita in two very important ways: First, it doesn't puff, and second, it's enriched, either by mixing butter or oil into the dough, or by brushing it on after the loaves are formed. We avoid puffing here by rolling it a little thicker, "docking" (perforating) the surface with a fork, and baking it at a lower temperature. We've topped the pita with the traditional black sesame seeds, which you can buy at most Asian groceries, or through mail order at Penzeys Spices (see page 311). The seeds create a great flavor combination with the olive oil or butter. Somehow, it both crunches *and* melts in your mouth. You'll see. Serve it with Turkish or Greek dips and appetizers, like *taramasalata* (fish roe spread), feta cheese, and olives.

If you want classically puffed Middle Eastern pita, try the Seed-Encrusted Pita on page 223. Turkish-style pita also works beautifully when baked on a gas grill outdoors (see Whole Grain Pizza on the Gas Grill, page 210).

Makes 1 pita

1 pound (grapefruit-size portion) Master Recipe dough (page 53)
2 teaspoons black sesame seeds for sprinkling
1 tablespoon olive oil or melted butter

1. **Thirty minutes before baking time, preheat the oven to 450°F,** with a baking stone placed on the middle rack. Place an empty metal broiler tray on any other rack that won't interfere with the bread.

2. Just before baking, dust the surface of the refrigerated dough with flour and cut off a 1-pound (grapefruit-size) piece. Dust the piece with more flour and quickly shape it into a ball by stretching the surface of the dough around to the bottom on all four sides, rotating the ball a quarter-turn as you go. Place the ball on a flour-dusted pizza peel.

3. Use your hands to stretch the dough into a round, then roll out to a uniform thickness of ¼ inch. Sprinkle with more flour as needed to prevent sticking.

4. Brush the surface with oil or melted butter, dock (puncture) the dough all over with a fork, and sprinkle it with sesame seeds.

5. Slide the loaf directly onto the hot stone. Pour 1 cup of hot tap water into the broiler tray, and quickly close the oven door. Bake for about 15 to 20 minutes, until golden brown. Use the fork to dock (puncture) again if large bubbles form or if puffing begins.

6. Cut into wedges with kitchen shears or a serrated bread knife. Serve warm or at room temperature.

French Shapes Based on the Letter-Fold

We covered French bread shapes in our first book, but we simplified them so that no one would be intimidated. Some days, it just doesn't matter if the shape is perfect, so for our first book, we had people roughly elongate the dough into pretty much whatever shape they wanted. You can continue to make baguettes and *ficelles* by just elongating an oval of dough, and rolling it between your palms to thin it out. The ends may be a bit knobby, but the taste will be scrumptious. Here's a more polished, professional way of doing it so that yours will look just like the ones in the pictures. In addition to using it for the skinny baguettes and *ficelles*, you can use it to get professional tapered ends with your basic oval loaves, such as in the Master Recipe (page 53).

Baguettes and Ficelles with Beautiful Tapers

Baguettes are a universal symbol of artisan bread, and *ficelles* (fee-séll) are nothing more than really skinny baguettes. They're not at all hard to make, and using the letter-fold technique makes a big difference in getting a professional look.

Makes 1 baguette or 2 (ficelles)

½ pound (orange-size portion) Master Recipe dough (page 53)
Egg white wash (1 egg white mixed with 1 teaspoon water)

1. **Thirty minutes before baking time, preheat the oven to 450°F,** with a baking stone placed on the middle rack. Place an empty metal broiler tray on any other rack that won't interfere with the rising bread.

2. Dust the surface of the refrigerated dough with flour and cut off a ½-pound (orange-size piece) for a baguette, and about half that for a *ficelle*. Dust the piece with more flour and quickly shape it into a ball by stretching the surface of the dough around to the bottom on all four sides, rotating the ball a quarter-turn as you go.

3. Gently stretch the dough into an oval. Fold the dough in thirds, like a letter. Bring in one side and gently press it into the center, taking care not to compress the dough too much.

4. Bring up the other side and pinch the seam closed. The letter-fold technique puts less dough into the ends and that's what gives you the nice taper.

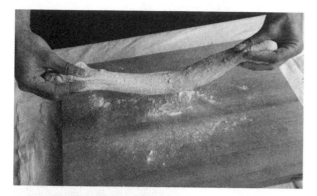

5. Stretch very gently into a log, working the dough until you have a thin baguette. Don't compress the air out of the dough. If the dough resists pulling, let it rest for a moment to relax the gluten, then continue to stretch. Don't fight the dough. You can continue to stretch the dough during the 40-minute rest, until you achieve the desired thin result. Final width for a baguette should be about 1½ inches; for a *ficelle*, ¾ inch.

6. Allow the loaf to rest, loosely covered with plastic wrap, on a pizza peel prepared with cornmeal or lined with parchment paper for 40 minutes (or just 20 minutes if you're using fresh, unrefrigerated dough). Alternatively, you can rest the loaf on a silicone mat, a greased cookie sheet, or perforated baguette pan without using a pizza peel.

7. Just before baking, use a pastry brush to paint the loaf with egg white wash or water. Slash the loaf with 3 slightly diagonal cuts ¼ inch deep, using a serrated bread knife.

8. Slide the loaf directly onto the hot stone (or place the silicone pad, cookie sheet, or baguette pan on the stone if you used one). Pour 1 cup of hot tap water into the metal broiler tray, and quickly close the oven door (see pages 27 and 28 for steam alternatives). Bake for about 25 minutes for a baguette, or 15 to 20 minutes for a *ficelle*, until richly browned and firm.

9. Allow the bread to cool on a rack before slicing and eating.

Epí

If you start with a letter-folded baguette (page 69), you can create an *epi* (wheat stalk–shaped bread) with perfectly tapered "grains" of wheat that are the hallmark of this loaf. This classic wheat stalk–shaped bread is impressive and somewhat intimidating, until you see how easy it is to make. We love the *epi* not only for its gorgeous appearance but also because it's the crustiest loaf there is. All of those cuts and angles offer more surface to crisp in the oven. It's a little more sophisticated to serve with dinner than ordinary rolls, and believe it or not, it's even easier to make!

***Makes 1* epí**

½ pound (orange-size portion) Master Recipe dough (page 53)
Parchment paper to line the pizza peel

1. **Thirty minutes before baking time, preheat the oven to 450°F,** with a baking stone placed on the middle rack. Place an empty metal broiler tray on any other rack that won't interfere with the rising bread.

2. Dust the surface of the refrigerated dough with flour and cut off a ½-pound (orange-size) piece. Dust the piece with more flour and quickly shape it into a ball by stretching the surface of the dough around to the bottom on all four sides, rotating the ball a quarter-turn as you go.

3. To form the *epi*, gently stretch the dough into an oval. Fold the dough in thirds, like a letter. Bring in one side and gently press it into the center (see page 69).

4. Bring up the other side and pinch the seam closed. This will help you produce tapered ends.

5. Stretch very gently into a log, working the dough until you have a nice thin baguette about 1½ inches in diameter (see page 70). If the dough resists

pulling, let it rest for a moment to relax the gluten, then continue to stretch. Don't fight the dough.

6. Lay the baguette on the edge of a prepared pizza peel. For the *epi*, parchment paper is preferred because it will allow the formed loaf to slide into the oven with a minimum of distortion and sticking. Allow the loaf to rest, loosely covered with plastic wrap, for 40 minutes (or just 20 minutes if you're using fresh, unrefrigerated dough).

7. Dust the loaf with flour and then, using kitchen shears and starting at one end of the loaf, cut into the dough at a very shallow angle. If you cut too vertically, the "wheat grains" won't be nice and pointy. Cut with a single snip all the way down to a quarter-inch from the cutting board, but be careful not to cut all the way through the dough or you'll end up with individual rolls. Kitchen shears with long blades are best for this task.

8. Lay each piece that you've cut over to one side, alternating sides with each cut. Continue to cut in this fashion until you've reached the other end.

9. Slide the loaf directly onto the hot stone (or place the silicone mat or cookie sheet on the stone if you used one). Pour 1 cup of hot tap water into the metal broiler tray, and quickly close the oven door (see pages 27 and 28 for steam alternatives). Bake for about 25 minutes, until richly browned and firm. Peel off the parchment paper and finish the loaf directly on the stone or on an oven rack two-thirds of the way through baking.

10. Allow the bread to cool on a rack before slicing and eating.

Other French Shapes

Boule or Couronne

These are not based on the letter-fold. They're even easier because they're just shaped balls of dough: If you stop there, that's a boule (pronounced bool), a ball-shaped bread. If you poke your thumbs through, you end up with a *couronne*, the crown-shaped bread of Lyon, France (if truth be told, it resembles a large bagel). Use your hands to stretch the hole open so that it's about triple the width of the wall of the ring. Rest and bake the boule as detailed on pages 79–80 (see photo, color insert). For the *couronne*, follow resting and baking instructions for the baguette (page 69).

Wreath Bread

This is a gorgeous loaf to make during the holiday season. Start with a *couronne* (above), and then make cuts as for the *epi* (page 72) all the way around, to create a festive wreath shape with dramatic points. You can use enriched dough to make a wreath bread as well (see photo, color insert).

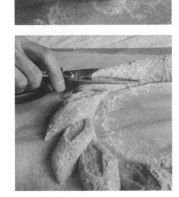

Cinnamon–Raisin Whole Wheat Bagels

"Two things that a transplanted New York bagel–snob like me doesn't like to admit are: 1) New York bagels aren't quite what they used to be, and 2) I like cinnamon-raisin bagels, even though they're newfangled. Just as French readers of our blog tell us that baguettes in France aren't what they used to be, many New York bagels have become mass-produced and bland, without the chew and crispy crust that I remember (there are exceptions but you have to seek them out). So here's how to hand-shape, boil, and bake your own. If you're really a traditionalist, don't bother adding the cinnamon, sugar, and raisins and you'll have a terrific plain whole grain bagel (see photo, color insert)."—Jeff

Makes about 10 bagels

2 pounds (cantaloupe-size portion) Master Recipe dough (page 53)
2 tablespoons sugar (brown or white)
1½ teaspoons ground cinnamon
¾ cup raisins

The Boiling-Pot
8 quarts boiling water
¼ cup sugar
1 teaspoon baking soda

1. Mix the sugar and cinnamon in a small bowl. Using your hands and a rolling pin, flatten the dough to a thickness of ¼ inch. Sprinkle the dough with the cinnamon-sugar and raisins. Roll up the dough, jelly-roll style, to incorporate the raisins. Shape into a ball and dust with flour.

2. Cut off a 3-ounce piece of dough from the ball (about the size of a small peach). Dust the piece with flour and quickly shape it into a ball by stretching the surface of the dough around to the bottom on all four sides, rotating the ball a quarter-turn as you go.

3. Punch your thumb through a dough ball to form the hole. Stretch it open with your fingers until the hole's diameter is about triple the width of the bagel wall (see photo). Repeat with the rest of the dough balls, cover them loosely with plastic wrap, and allow them to rest at room temperature for 20 minutes.

4. **Thirty minutes before baking time, preheat the oven to 425°F,** with a baking stone placed on the middle rack. Place an empty metal broiler tray on any other rack that won't interfere with the rising bagels.

5. **Prepare the boiling-pot:** Bring a large saucepan or stockpot full of water to a boil. Reduce to a simmer and add the sugar and baking soda.

6. Drop the bagels into the simmering water one at a time, making sure they are not crowding one another. They need enough room to float without touching or they will be misshapen. Let them simmer for 2 minutes, flip them over with a slotted spoon, and simmer for another minute on the other side.

7. Remove them from the water, using the slotted spoon, and place them on a clean kitchen towel that has been lightly dusted with whole wheat flour. This will absorb some of the excess water from the bagels. Then place them on a peel covered with whole wheat flour. Alternatively, you can place the bagels on a silicone mat or a greased cookie sheet without using a pizza peel.

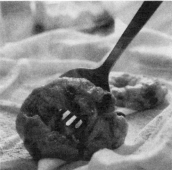

8. Slide the bagels directly onto the hot stone. Pour 1 cup of hot tap water into the broiler tray,

and quickly close the oven door. (see pages 27 and 28 for steam alternatives). Bake for about 20 to 25 minutes, until deeply browned and firm.

9. Serve these a bit warm—they're fantastic!

6

WHOLE GRAIN BREADS

Whole grains are better for you than white flour. They're loaded with fiber that comes from bran, the fibrous coating on the seeds that are ground to make flour. Whole grain flour also includes the germ, which contains a wealth of vitamins, antioxidants, and a little vegetable-based fat, all destined to nourish the newly sprouted plant; that nourishment ends up in our bread when we leave it in the flour. White flour milling discards the two nutritionally crucial parts of the grain—the bran and the germ.

About bran: Somewhere in history, cultures decided that the inner white part of the grain was where the nutrition lived and that eating it was somehow more "refined." They decided that the outer shell (the bran), should be eaten only when we couldn't afford to throw it away and needed something to fill up on. Well, they were partly right. There's little protein, calories, or vitamins in bran. But bran is fiber, and a healthy digestive system requires it to function properly. Adults need about 30 grams of fiber per day, and our 100% Whole Wheat Bread provides over 2 grams per 1½-ounce slice. White bread, on the other hand, contains less than ½ gram per slice, and near zero in most cases.

About the germ: Unlike bran, wheat germ contains nutritious vitamins and antioxidants. But before we even start on those, remember that wheat germ has fiber as well, over 14 grams per cup, which is more than whole wheat flour. In addition, a 2-tablespoon portion contains 20 percent of the recommended daily allowance (RDA) of vitamin E and folic acid, 15 percent of the thiamine, and 10 percent of the magnesium, phosphorus, and zinc. Not bad for something that people used to feed to farm animals.

100% Whole Wheat Bread, Plain and Simple

This is for all the purists, who want nothing to get in the way of the flavor and goodness of whole wheat. We've added vital wheat gluten to give the dough a better rise, but it's otherwise simple and delicious. Try it with whole grain spelt instead of whole wheat if you like.

Makes enough dough for at least four 1-pound loaves. The recipe is easily doubled or halved.

7 cups whole wheat flour (or substitute whole grain spelt flour, see page 12)
1½ tablespoons granulated yeast, or 2 packets (decrease to taste, page 15)
1 tablespoon kosher salt (increase or decrease to taste, page 17)
¼ cup vital wheat gluten
3¾ cups lukewarm water

1. **Mixing and storing the dough:** Whisk together the flour, yeast, salt, and vital wheat gluten in a 5-quart bowl, or a lidded (not airtight) food container.

2. Add the water and mix without kneading, using a spoon, a 14-cup food processor (with dough attachment), or a heavy-duty stand mixer (with paddle). You might need to use wet hands to get the last bit of flour to incorporate if you're not using a machine.

3. Cover (not airtight), and allow the dough to rest at room temperature until it rises and collapses (or flattens on top), approximately 2 hours.

4. The dough can be used immediately after the initial rise, though it is easier to handle when cold. Refrigerate it in a lidded (not airtight) container and use it over the next 10 days.

5. **On baking day,** dust the surface of the refrigerated dough with flour and cut off a 1-pound (grapefruit-size) piece. Dust the piece with more flour and

quickly shape it into a ball by stretching the surface of the dough around to the bottom on all four sides, rotating the ball a quarter-turn as you go.

6. Allow the loaf to rest, loosely covered with plastic wrap, on a pizza peel prepared with cornmeal or lined with parchment paper for 90 minutes (40 minutes if you're using fresh, unrefrigerated dough). Alternatively, you can rest the loaf on a silicone mat or greased cookie sheet without using a pizza peel.

7. **Thirty minutes before baking time, preheat the oven to 450°F,** with a baking stone placed on the middle rack. Place an empty metal broiler tray on any other rack that won't interfere with the rising bread.

8. Just before baking, use a pastry brush to paint the top with water. Slash the loaf with ¼-inch-deep parallel cuts, using a serrated bread knife.

9. Slide the loaf directly onto the hot stone (or place the silicone mat or cookie sheet on the stone if you used one). Pour 1 cup of hot tap water into the broiler tray, and quickly close the oven door (see pages 27 and 28 for steam alternatives). Bake for about 30 to 35 minutes, until richly browned and firm. If you used parchment paper, a silicone mat, or a cookie sheet under the loaf, carefully remove it and bake the loaf directly on the stone or an oven rack two-thirds of the way through baking. Smaller or larger loaves will require adjustments in resting and baking time.

10. Allow the bread to cool on a rack before slicing and eating.

VARIATION: Traditional American-Style Honey Whole Wheat Bread
Add ½ cup of honey, and decrease the water by ½ cup (you don't need to carefully dissolve it in the water before mixing). The result will be a more tender, kid-friendly loaf that is very traditional in the United States. Bake in a lightly greased loaf pan, using a 2-pound (cantaloupe-size) piece of dough. Decrease the temperature to 350°F, and increase baking time to 50 to 60 minutes.

100% Whole Wheat Bread with Olive Oil

Olive oil and whole wheat are perfect partners in bread. The oil is rich in mo-nounsaturates, so it's a great way for healthy fats to complement the nutrients in whole wheat. The dough makes marvelous free-form loaves, pizza, and an Algerian flatbread that is unlike anything you've ever tried (page 228).

Makes enough dough for at least four 1-pound loaves. The recipe is easily doubled or halved.

7 cups whole wheat flour
1½ tablespoons granulated yeast, or 2 packets (decrease to taste, page 15)
1 tablespoon kosher salt (increase or decrease to taste, page 17)
¼ cup vital wheat gluten
3½ cups lukewarm water
½ cup olive oil

1. **Mixing and storing the dough:** Whisk together the flour, yeast, salt, and vital wheat gluten in a 5-quart bowl, or a lidded (not airtight) food container.

2. Add the liquid ingredients and mix without kneading, using a spoon, a 14-cup food processor (with dough attachment), or a heavy-duty stand mixer (with paddle). You might need to use wet hands to get the last bit of flour to incorporate if you're not using a machine.

3. Cover (not airtight), and allow the dough to rest at room temperature until it rises and collapses (or flattens on top), approximately 2 hours.

4. The dough can be used immediately after the initial rise, though it is easier to handle when cold. Refrigerate it in a lidded (not airtight) container and use it over the next 7 days.

5. **On baking day,** dust the surface of the refrigerated dough with flour and cut off a 1-pound (grapefruit-size) piece. Dust the piece with more flour and quickly shape it into a ball by stretching the surface of the dough around to the bottom on all four sides, rotating the ball a quarter-turn as you go.

6. Elongate the ball into a narrow oval. Allow the loaf to rest, loosely covered with plastic wrap, on a pizza peel prepared with cornmeal or lined with parchment paper for 90 minutes (40 minutes if you're using fresh, unrefrigerated dough). Alternatively, you can rest the loaf on a silicone mat or greased cookie sheet without using a pizza peel.

7. **Thirty minutes before baking time, preheat the oven to 450°F,** with a baking stone placed on the middle rack. Place an empty metal broiler tray on any other rack that won't interfere with the rising bread.

8. Just before baking, use a pastry brush to paint the top with water. Slash the loaf with ¼-inch-deep parallel cuts, using a serrated bread knife.

9. Slide the loaf directly onto the hot stone (or place the silicone mat or cookie sheet on the stone if you used one). Pour 1 cup of hot tap water into the broiler tray, and quickly close the oven door (see pages 27 and 28 for steam alternatives). Bake for about 30 minutes, until richly browned and firm. If you used parchment paper, a silicone mat, or a cookie sheet under the loaf, carefully remove it and bake the loaf directly on the stone or an oven rack two-thirds of the way through baking. Smaller or larger loaves will require adjustments in resting and baking time.

10. Allow the bread to cool on a rack before slicing and eating.

Vollkornbrot: 100% Whole Grain

Vollkornbrot is German for "whole kernel bread," so to make an authentic one, you need to find some wheat or rye berries—the whole, unbroken kernels of grain (they're not really berries). Rye berries are hard to find, but natural foods co-ops often carry wheat berries and whole rye flakes (flattened-out rye berries), or you can order these ingredients from King Arthur Flour. The result is a 100% whole grain loaf that is rustic, hearty, and moist—perfect when sliced thinly, slathered with butter, and topped with smoked fish, cold cuts, or cheese.

Because of the high quantity of grains, this dough is not worked like most. The dough has little resiliency, and you can't tightly shape it; just press the dough into the shape you want. Don't expect a lot of rising during the long (2-hour) resting time after shaping.

"German bread is among the best in the world even though much of it is sold in supermarkets today. Even there, everything's baked on the premises according to methods that haven't really changed much since the days of the corner bakery. So on my first day as a tourist in Germany, off I went into a supermarket to buy a loaf of vollkornbrot. One semester of college German sufficed to make the precious loaf appear, but unfortunately a friend traveling with me turned to ask me quietly, 'Is that one FRESH?' Not quietly enough—the words are pretty much the same in German. The now-crabby bakery lady withered us with an outraged 'Ja, das ist FRISCH!' "—Jeff

Makes enough dough for at least two 2-pound loaves. The recipe is easily doubled or halved. Any leftover dough can be made into buns (see page 180).

5 cups whole wheat flour
1 cup wheat berries
1 cup rye flakes
1½ tablespoons granulated yeast, or 2 packets (decrease to taste, page 15)
1 tablespoon kosher salt (increase or decrease to taste, page 17)

¼ cup vital wheat gluten
3¾ cups lukewarm water
2 tablespoons molasses

1. **Mixing and storing the dough:** Whisk together the flour, wheat berries, rye flakes, yeast, salt, and vital wheat gluten in a 5-quart bowl, or a lidded (not airtight) food container.

2. Combine the water and molasses and mix them with the dry ingredients without kneading, using a spoon, a 14-cup food processor (with dough attachment), or a heavy-duty stand mixer (with paddle). You might need to use wet hands to get the last bit of flour to incorporate if you're not using a machine.

3. Cover (not airtight), and allow the dough to rest at room temperature until dough rises and collapses (or flattens on top), approximately 2 hours.

4. Refrigerate it in a lidded (not airtight) container and use over the next 7 days, but **do not use the dough until it has aged at least 24 hours (to give the whole kernels a chance to absorb water).**

5. **On baking day,** lightly grease an 8½ × 4½-inch nonstick loaf pan. Dust the surface of the refrigerated dough with flour and cut off a 2-pound (cantaloupe-size) piece. Dust the piece with more flour and quickly shape it into a ball by stretching the surface of the dough around to the bottom on all four sides, rotating the ball a quarter-turn as you go.

6. Elongate the ball into an oval and place it into a loaf pan; your goal is to fill the pan about three-quarters full. Cover loosely with plastic wrap. Allow the loaf to rest for 2 hours.

7. **Thirty minutes before baking time, preheat the oven to 450°F,** with a baking stone placed on the middle rack. Place an empty metal broiler tray on any other rack that won't interfere with the rising bread.

8. Just before baking, use a pastry brush to paint the top with water.

9. Place the loaf on a rack near the center of the oven. Pour 1 cup of hot tap water into the broiler tray, and quickly close the oven door (see pages 27 and 28 for steam alternatives). Bake for about 45 minutes, until richly browned and firm.

10. Remove the loaf from the pan (see page 50) and allow the bread to cool on a rack before slicing thinly and eating.

100% Whole Wheat and Flaxseed Bread

"Wherever flaxseed becomes a regular food item among the people, there will be better health."—Mahatma Gandhi

This is a book about healthy breads, and we would be remiss not to include those made with flax, which has some powerful health effects (see sidebar) and a mild and nutty flavor. If you'd rather downplay the flavor of flax, try our aromatic Rosemary Flax Baguette (page 89), in which the herb dominates the grain flavors.

~

OMEGA-3 FATTY ACIDS are a super-healthy type of polyunsaturated fat. The Inuit peoples of Alaska experience low levels of heart disease, and some researchers have suggested that it may result from their high intake of fish and marine animals rich in omega-3 fatty acids. This despite an otherwise high-calorie, high-fat, and high-cholesterol diet. But some of our readers don't like fish, and others are vegans. People have also told us that they just can't eat enough fish to provide much of an omega-3 boost in their diets.

So, short of moving to Alaska and gorging on the local cuisine, how can we help you get more omega-3 fatty acids in your diet? One word: **flaxseed!** It's a concentrated vegetarian source of omega-3. Not very Inuit, but very effective.

Makes enough dough for at least four 1-pound loaves. The recipe is easily doubled or halved.

½ cup ground flaxseed
7 cups whole wheat flour
1½ tablespoons granulated yeast, or 2 packets (decrease to taste, page 15)
1 tablespoon kosher salt (increase or decrease to taste, page 17)
¼ cup vital wheat gluten
3¾ cups lukewarm water

1. **Mixing and storing the dough:** Whisk together the flaxseed, flour, yeast, salt, and vital wheat gluten in a 5-quart bowl, or a lidded (not airtight) food container.

2. Add the water and mix without kneading, using a spoon, a 14-cup food processor (with dough attachment),

or a heavy-duty stand mixer (with paddle). You might need to use wet hands to get the last bit of flour to incorporate if you're not using a machine.

3. Cover (not airtight), and allow the dough to rest at room temperature until it rises and collapses (or flattens on top), approximately 2 hours.

4. The dough can be used immediately after its initial rise, though it is easier to handle when cold. Refrigerate it in a lidded (not airtight) container and use over the next 10 days. The flavor will be best if you wait for at least 24 hours of refrigeration.

5. **On baking day,** dust the surface of the refrigerated dough with flour and cut off a 1-pound (grapefruit-size) piece. Dust the piece with more flour and quickly shape it into a ball by stretching the surface of the dough around to the bottom on all four sides, rotating the ball a quarter-turn as you go.

6. Allow the loaf to rest, loosely covered with plastic wrap, on a pizza peel prepared with cornmeal or lined with parchment paper for 90 minutes (40 minutes if you're using fresh, unrefrigerated dough). Alternatively, you can rest the loaf on a silicone mat or a greased cookie sheet without using a pizza peel.

7. **Thirty minutes before baking time, preheat the oven to 450°F,** with a baking stone placed on the middle rack. Place an empty metal broiler tray on any other rack that won't interfere with the rising bread.

8. Just before baking, dust the top of the loaf with flour and then slash the loaf with ¼-inch-deep parallel cuts, using a serrated bread knife.

9. Slide the loaf directly onto the hot stone (or place the silicone mat or cookie sheet on the stone if you used one). Pour 1 cup of hot tap water into the broiler tray, and quickly close the oven door (see pages 27 and 28 for steam

alternatives). Bake for about 30 to 35 minutes, until richly browned and firm. If you used parchment paper, a silicone mat, or a cookie sheet, carefully remove it and bake the loaf directly on the hot stone or an oven rack two-thirds of the way through baking. Smaller or larger loaves will require adjustments in resting and baking time.

10. Allow the bread to cool on a rack before slicing or eating.

Rosemary Flax Baguette

Flax has a strong flavor that some people love, but it is an acquired taste for others. For those folks, we wanted to create something that had all the health benefits without an obvious flax flavor (see sidebar on page 86). The addition of rosemary and olive oil makes this an aromatic and absolutely delicious loaf. To accentuate the rosemary's presence in the bread we added a few sprigs to the outside of the baguette—gorgeous! For those of you who love the taste of flax, you can add a couple more tablespoons to the dough without throwing off the recipe.

Makes enough dough for at least eight ½-pound loaves. The recipe is easily doubled or halved.

½ cup ground flaxseed

3 cups whole wheat flour

4 cups unbleached all-purpose flour

½ cup wheat germ

1½ tablespoons granulated yeast, or 2 packets (decrease to taste, page 15)

1 tablespoon kosher salt (increase or decrease to taste, page 17)

¼ cup vital wheat gluten

3½ cups lukewarm water

½ cup olive oil

3 tablespoons fresh rosemary, minced, plus sprigs to decorate the top

Egg white wash (1 egg white beaten with 1 teaspoon water)

1. **Mixing and storing the dough:** Whisk together the flaxseed, flours, wheat germ, yeast, salt, and

Like turmeric (see sidebar, page 228), rosemary contains antioxidants, and has been studied as an ingredient in marinades for protein-rich grilled foods. So this is delicious news—Indian spices and Mediterranean herbs both have health benefits in addition to great flavors. Kansas State University researchers found that naturally occurring rosmarinic acid in rosemary (and other herbs) inhibits the formation of heterocyclic amines (HCAs) that build up in food during grilling. HCAs have been implicated as carcinogenic (cancer-causing) agents. Leave it to Kansas to discover yet another benefit of the Mediterranean diet!

vital wheat gluten in a 5-quart bowl, or a lidded (not airtight) food container.

2. Add the water, olive oil, and minced rosemary and mix without kneading, using a spoon, a 14-cup food processor (with dough attachment), or a heavy-duty stand mixer (with paddle). You might need to use wet hands to get the last bit of flour to incorporate if you're not using a machine.

3. Cover (not airtight), and allow the dough to rest at room temperature until it rises and collapses (or flattens on top), approximately 2 hours.

4. The dough can be used immediately after its initial rise, though it is easier to handle when cold. Refrigerate it in a lidded (not airtight) container and use over the next 10 days. The flavor will be best if you wait for at least 24 hours of refrigeration.

5. **On baking day,** dust the surface of the refrigerated dough with flour and cut off a ½-pound (orange-size) piece. Dust the piece with more flour and quickly shape it into a ball by stretching the surface of the dough around to the bottom on all four sides, rotating the ball a quarter-turn as you go.

6. Elongate the ball into a baguette shape, or use the letter-fold technique to get a perfect tapered result (see page 68). Allow to rest, loosely covered with plastic wrap, on a pizza peel prepared with cornmeal or lined with parchment paper for 40 minutes (20 minutes if you're using fresh, unrefrigerated dough). Alternatively, you can rest the loaf on a silicone mat, a greased cookie sheet, or a baguette pan (see chapter 3, Equipment, page 31), without using a pizza peel.

7. **Thirty minutes before baking time, preheat the oven to 450°F,** with a baking stone placed on the middle rack. Place an empty metal broiler tray on any other rack that won't interfere with the rising bread.

8. Just before baking, use a pastry brush to paint the top with egg white wash and then slash the loaf with ¼-inch-deep parallel cuts, using a serrated bread knife. Decorate the top of the loaf by poking a few rosemary sprigs into the cut part of the dough, laying them flat against the loaf.

9. Slide the loaf directly onto the hot stone (or place the silicone mat or cookie sheet on the stone if you used one). Pour 1 cup of hot tap water into the broiler tray, and quickly close the oven door (see pages 27 and 28 for steam alternatives). Bake for about 25 minutes, until richly browned and firm. If you used parchment paper, a silicone mat, or a cookie sheet, carefully remove it and bake the loaf directly on the stone or an oven rack two-thirds of the way through baking. Smaller or larger loaves will require adjustments in resting and baking time.

10. Allow the bread to cool on a rack before slicing or eating.

Soft Whole Wheat Sandwich Bread

This is the bread your kids will want in their school lunch boxes every day. It's nice and soft, with just a touch of sweetness from honey. You'll love that it is made with whole wheat and your kids will think it's perfect with everything from peanut butter and jelly to ham and cheese. When formed into flat buns and sprinkled with sesame seeds it makes the best hamburger buns ever; see page 94 for instructions.

Makes enough dough for at least two 2-pound loaves. The recipe is easily doubled or halved.

5 cups whole wheat flour
2½ cups unbleached all-purpose flour
1½ tablespoons granulated yeast, or 2 packets
1 tablespoon kosher salt (increase or decrease to taste, page 17)
¼ cup vital wheat gluten
2½ cups lukewarm water
½ cup honey
5 large eggs
⅔ cup neutral-flavored oil, or unsalted butter, melted, or zero trans fat, zero hydrogenated oil margarine, melted

1. **Mixing and storing the dough:** Whisk together the flours, yeast, salt, and vital wheat gluten in a 5-quart bowl, or a lidded (not airtight) food container.

2. Combine the liquid ingredients and mix them with the dry ingredients without kneading, using a spoon, a 14-cup food processor (with dough attachment), or a heavy-duty stand mixer (with paddle). You might need to use wet hands to get the last bit of flour to incorporate if you're not using a machine.

3. Cover (not airtight), and allow the dough to rest at room temperature until it rises and collapses (or flattens on top), approximately 2 hours.

4. The dough can be used immediately after its initial rise, though it is easier to handle when cold. Refrigerate it in a lidded (not airtight) container and use over the next 5 days. The flavor will be best if you wait for at least 24 hours of refrigeration.

5. **On baking day,** lightly grease an 8 ½ × 4½-inch nonstick loaf pan. Dust the surface of the refrigerated dough with flour and cut off a 2-pound (cantaloupe-size) piece. Dust the piece with more flour and quickly shape it into a ball by stretching the surface of the dough around to the bottom on all four sides, rotating the ball a quarter-turn as you go.

6. Elongate the ball into an oval and place it into the loaf pan; your goal is to fill the pan about three-quarters full. Cover it loosely with plastic wrap. Allow the loaf to rest for 90 minutes (40 minutes if you're using fresh, unrefrigerated dough).

7. **Thirty minutes before baking time, preheat the oven to 350°F,** with a baking stone placed on the middle rack. The baking stone is not essential for loaf-pan breads; if you omit it, the preheat can be as short as 5 minutes.

8. Place the loaf on a rack near the center of the oven and bake for about 45 to 50 minutes, or until golden brown. Smaller or larger loaf pans will require adjustments in baking time.

9. Remove the bread from the pan (see page 50) and allow it to cool completely on a rack before slicing and eating.

Hamburger (or Hot Dog) Buns

Hamburger and hot dog buns present a special challenge for home artisan bakers. We're always going for the perfect crisp crust in our breads. But we really don't want a crisp or firm crust in hamburger or hot dog buns. If you make these buns with a hard or crisp crust, you can really bruise the top of your mouth! What to do? There are two choices: You can either stick with enriched dough, and the oil or butter will soften the crust. Or, you can use non-enriched ("lean") dough, but don't omit the egg wash or melted butter before baking.

Makes 6 buns

Use any of these refrigerated pre-mixed doughs: Soft Whole Wheat Sandwich Bread dough is our first choice (page 92), or any of the enriched doughs (Chapter 10, page 257)

1½ pounds (small cantaloupe-size portion) of any pre-mixed dough listed above

Egg wash (1 egg beaten with 1 tablespoon water) or melted butter

Sesame seeds (optional)

1. **On baking day,** dust the surface of the refrigerated dough with flour and cut off a 1½-pound (small cantaloupe-size) piece. Dust the piece with more flour and quickly shape it into a ball by stretching the surface of the dough around to the bottom on all four sides, rotating the ball a quarter-turn as you go.

2. **To form hamburger buns,** divide the ball into 6 roughly equal portions (each about the size of a plum). Shape each one into a smooth ball as you did above. Place the buns at least 2 inches apart on two cookie sheets lined with parchment paper. Press them so that they are slightly flattened. Allow to rest, loosely covered with plastic wrap, for 40 minutes (20 minutes if you're using fresh, unrefrigerated dough). Alternatively, you can rest the buns on a silicone mat or a greased cookie sheet.

3. **To form hot dog buns,** divide the ball into 6 roughly equal portions (each about the size of a plum). Shape each one into a smooth ball. Stretch each ball into a 6-inch-long rope. Allow to rest as above.

4. **Thirty minutes before baking time, preheat the oven to 350°F.** The baking stone is not essential for this recipe; if you omit it, the preheat can be as short as 5 minutes.

5. Just before baking, use a pastry brush to paint the tops of the buns with egg wash or melted butter, and sprinkle with sesame seeds if desired. Slide the cookie sheet into the oven. Bake for about 20 minutes, until richly browned and firm.

6. Allow the buns to cool on a rack before slicing and eating.

Olive Spelt Bread

This is one of our favorite breads in the book. We've fallen in love with spelt flour and it's made all the better here by the addition of yogurt. It gives the bread a tanginess right from the start that we've waited days for in other doughs. We've used a whole milk yogurt, which gives the bread richness, but the bread is also excellent with a nonfat version.

∽

ZINC: Yogurt is a terrific source of the trace element zinc, but its real claim to fame is its **calcium** content. It's the most calcium-rich dairy food. Between zinc and calcium, yogurt may be the mineral king!

Makes enough dough for at least four 1-pound loaves. The recipe is easily doubled or halved.

4 cups spelt flour
2 cups unbleached all-purpose flour
1½ tablespoons granulated yeast, or
    2 packets (decrease to taste,
    page 15)
1 tablespoon kosher salt (increase or
    decrease to taste, page 17)

¼ cup vital wheat gluten
2 cups lukewarm water
2 cups plain whole milk yogurt (or nonfat)
1 cup pitted green olives, chopped

1. **Mixing and storing the dough:** Whisk together the flours, yeast, salt, and vital wheat gluten in a 5-quart bowl, or a lidded (not airtight) food container.

2. Combine the water, yogurt, and olives and mix them with the dry ingredients without kneading, using a spoon, a 14-cup food processor (with dough attachment), or a heavy-duty stand mixer (with paddle). You might need to use wet hands to get the last bit of flour to incorporate if you're not using a machine.

3. Cover (not airtight), and allow the dough to rest at room temperature until it rises and collapses (or flattens on top), approximately 2 hours.

4. The dough can be used immediately after its initial rise, though it is easier to handle when cold. Refrigerate it in a lidded (not airtight) container and use over the next 7 days. The flavor will be best if you wait for at least 24 hours of refrigeration.

5. **On baking day,** dust the surface of the refrigerated dough with flour and cut off a 1-pound (grapefruit-size) piece. Dust the piece with more flour and quickly shape it into a ball by stretching the surface of the dough around to the bottom on all four sides, rotating the ball a quarter-turn as you go.

6. Allow the loaf to rest, loosely covered with plastic wrap, on a pizza peel prepared with cornmeal or lined with parchment paper for 90 minutes (40 minutes if you're using fresh, unrefrigerated dough). Alternatively, you can rest the loaf on a silicone mat or a greased cookie sheet without using a pizza peel.

7. **Thirty minutes before baking time, preheat the oven to 450°F,** with a baking stone placed on the middle rack. Place an empty metal broiler tray on any other rack that won't interfere with the rising bread.

8. Just before baking, dust the top with flour. Slash the loaf diagonally with ¼-inch-deep parallel cuts, using a serrated bread knife.

9. Slide the loaf directly onto the hot stone (or place the silicone mat or cookie sheet on the stone if you used one). Pour 1 cup of hot tap water into the broiler tray, and quickly close the oven door (see pages 27 and 28 for steam alternatives). Bake for about 35 minutes, until richly browned and firm. If you used parchment paper, a silicone mat, or a cookie sheet under the loaf, carefully remove it and bake the loaf directly on the stone or an oven rack two-thirds of the way through baking. Smaller or larger loaves will require adjustments in resting and baking time.

10. Allow the bread to cool on a rack before slicing and eating.

Pesto and Pine Nut Bread

"The basil, cheese, and pine nuts are so fragrant while this bread is baking that it's a chore to wait for it to cool down and cut into it. I've made this dough with both fresh pesto that my stepmother, Patricia, makes from her garden, and the jarred stuff. My stepmother's is to die for, but in a pinch the store-bought is a great substitute. Serve the bread with fresh mozzarella, a drizzle of olive oil, and a really great red wine. Bellissimo!"—Zoë

Makes enough dough for at least four 1-pound loaves. The recipe is easily doubled or halved.

2 cups spelt flour
2 cups white whole wheat flour
3 cups unbleached all-purpose flour
1½ tablespoons granulated yeast, or 2 packets (decrease to taste, page 15)
1 tablespoon kosher salt (increase or decrease to taste, page 17)
2 tablespoons vital wheat gluten
3½ cups lukewarm water
¾ cup pesto (for homemade, see Pesto Pizza, page 213, or use a jarred variety)
½ cup pine nuts

1. **Mixing and storing the dough:** Whisk together the flours, yeast, salt, and vital wheat gluten in a 5-quart bowl, or a lidded (not airtight) food container.

2. Combine the water, pesto, and pine nuts and mix them with the dry ingredients without kneading, using a spoon, a 14-cup food processor (with dough attachment), or a heavy-duty stand mixer (with paddle). You might need to use wet hands to get the last bit of flour to incorporate if you're not using a machine.

3. Cover (not airtight), and allow the dough to rest at room temperature until it rises and collapses (or flattens on top), approximately 2 hours.

4. The dough can be used immediately after its initial rise, though it is easier to handle when cold. Refrigerate it in a lidded (not airtight) container and use over the next 10 days. The flavor will be best if you wait for at least 24 hours of refrigeration.

5. **On baking day,** dust the surface of the refrigerated dough with flour and cut off a 1-pound (grapefruit-size) piece. Dust the piece with more flour and quickly shape it into a ball by stretching the surface of the dough around to the bottom on all four sides, rotating the ball a quarter-turn as you go.

6. Elongate the ball into a narrow oval. Allow the loaf to rest, loosely covered with plastic wrap, on a pizza peel prepared with cornmeal or lined with parchment paper for 90 minutes (40 minutes if you're using fresh, unrefrigerated dough). Alternatively, you can rest the loaf on a silicone mat or a greased cookie sheet without using a pizza peel.

7. **Thirty minutes before baking time, preheat the oven to 450°F,** with a baking stone placed on the middle rack. Place an empty metal broiler tray on any other shelf that won't interfere with the rising bread.

8. Just before baking, use a pastry brush to paint the top crust with water. Slash the loaf diagonally with ¼-inch-deep parallel cuts, using a serrated bread knife.

9. Slide the loaf directly onto the hot stone (or place the silicone mat or cookie sheet on the stone if you used one). Pour 1 cup of hot tap water into the broiler tray, and quickly close the oven door (see pages 27 and 28 for steam alternatives). Bake for about 30 minutes, until richly browned and firm. If you used parchment paper, a silicone mat, or a cookie sheet under the loaf, carefully remove it and bake it directly on the stone or an oven shelf two-thirds of the way through baking. Smaller or larger loaves will require adjustments in resting and baking time.

10. Allow the bread to cool on a rack before slicing and eating.

Roasted Garlic Bread

Spelt flour, ground flaxseed, and *lots* of garlic are not only good for you, but create an incredible flavor. For the best garlic bread of your life, split the loaf lengthwise after baking and fill it with parsley butter. Two heads of garlic might sound like a lot, but roasting mellows garlic's pungent bite.

Makes enough dough for at least four 1-pound loaves. The recipe is easily doubled or halved.

> ∾
>
> **GARLIC WON'T WARD OFF VAMPIRES,** but it might ward off some troublesome health problems. It's a terrific source of the minerals manganese and selenium, plus vitamins B_6 and C. Other phytochemicals (beneficial plant chemicals) in garlic appear to lower cholesterol and prevent heart disease.

2 heads garlic
¼ cup ground flaxseed
3½ cups spelt flour
4 cups unbleached all-purpose flour
1½ tablespoons granulated yeast, or 2 packets (decrease to taste, page 15)
1 tablespoon kosher salt (increase or decrease to taste, page 17)
2 tablespoons vital wheat gluten
4 cups lukewarm water

The Parsley Butter (optional)

4 tablespoons unsalted butter, softened, or zero trans fat, zero hydrogenated oil margarine, softened
2 tablespoons finely chopped parsley
Salt and freshly ground black pepper to taste

1. **Roasting the garlic:** Wrap the garlic heads in aluminum foil and bake for 45 minutes at 400°F. Allow to cool, and cut off the tops of the heads. Squeeze out the roasted garlic and set aside.

2. **Mixing and storing the dough:** Whisk together the flaxseed, flours, yeast, salt, and vital wheat gluten in a 5-quart bowl, or a lidded (not airtight) food container.

3. Add the water and roasted garlic and mix without kneading, using a spoon, a 14-cup food processor (with dough attachment), or a heavy-duty stand mixer (with paddle). You might need to use wet hands to get the last bit of flour to incorporate if you're not using a machine.

4. Cover (not airtight), and allow the dough to rest at room temperature until it rises and collapses (or flattens on top), approximately 2 hours.

5. The dough can be used immediately after its initial rise, though it is easier to handle when cold. Refrigerate it in a lidded (not airtight) container and use over the next 10 days. The flavor will be best if you wait for at least 24 hours of refrigeration.

6. **On baking day,** dust the surface of the refrigerated dough with flour and cut off a 1-pound (grapefruit-size) piece. Dust the piece with more flour and quickly shape it into a ball by stretching the surface of the dough around to the bottom on all four sides, rotating the ball a quarter-turn as you go.

7. Elongate the ball into a narrow oval. Allow the loaf to rest, loosely covered with plastic wrap, on a pizza peel prepared with cornmeal or lined with parchment paper for 90 minutes (40 minutes if you're using fresh, unrefrigerated dough). Alternatively, you can rest the loaf on a silicone mat or a greased cookie sheet without using a pizza peel.

8. **Thirty minutes before baking time, preheat the oven to 450°F,** with a baking stone placed on the middle rack. Place an empty metal broiler tray on any other rack that won't interfere with the rising bread.

9. Just before baking, use a pastry brush to paint the top crust with water. Slash the loaf diagonally with ¼-inch-deep parallel cuts, using a serrated bread knife.

10. Slide the loaf directly onto the hot stone (or place the silicone mat or cookie sheet on the stone if you used one). Pour 1 cup of hot tap water into the broiler tray, and quickly close the oven door (see pages 27 and 28 for steam alternatives). Bake for about 30 to 35 minutes, until richly browned and firm. If you used parchment paper, a silicone mat, or a cookie sheet under the loaf, carefully remove it and bake the loaf directly on the stone or an oven rack two-thirds of the way through baking. Smaller or larger loaves will require adjustments in resting and baking time.

11. *Optional parsley butter.* Mix together the ingredients for the parsley butter. Set aside.

12. Allow the bread to cool on a rack before slicing and eating. Split the loaf while slightly warm and fill with parsley butter, if desired. Wrap in foil, and return to the oven for 10 minutes.

Herbed Potato and Roasted Garlic Bread

This fragrant loaf is made with an entire head of roasted garlic and herbed potatoes. The potatoes add moistness to the bread, and leaving the skins on increases their fiber and nutrient content. This bread is perfect for soups and salads or dipped in olive oil.

Makes enough dough for at least 4 1-pound loaves. The recipe is easily doubled or halved.

1 head garlic

3½ cups spelt flour

3 cups whole wheat flour

¼ cup ground flaxseed

1 teaspoon *herbes de Provence* (use a prepared herb mix or make your own with an equal mixture of dried marjoram, thyme, rosemary, basil, and savory, plus a little lavender if it's available)

1½ tablespoons granulated yeast, or 2 packets (decrease to taste, page 15)

1 tablespoon kosher salt (increase or decrease to taste, page 17)

¼ cup vital wheat gluten

1 large raw potato, cut into ¼-inch cubes (clean but don't peel potato)

3½ cups lukewarm water

POTATOES, WITH SKINS, PLEASE: Potatoes are terrifically high in the essential mineral potassium, which may help control blood pressure, especially for those eating too much salt. But leave the skin on the potatoes—most of the potato's fiber is in the skin.

1. **Roasting the garlic:** Wrap the garlic head in aluminum foil and bake for 45 minutes at 400°F. Allow to cool and cut off the top of the head. Squeeze out the roasted garlic and set aside.

2. **Mixing and storing the dough:** Whisk together the flours, flaxseed, *herbes de Provence*, yeast, salt, and vital wheat gluten in a 5-quart bowl, or a lidded (not airtight) food container.

3. Add the potato, water, and roasted garlic and mix without kneading, using a spoon, a 14-cup food processor (with dough attachment), or a heavy-duty stand mixer (with paddle). You might need to use wet hands to get the last bit of flour to incorporate if you're not using a machine.

4. Cover (not airtight), and allow the dough to rest at room temperature until it rises and collapses (or flattens on top), approximately 2 hours.

5. The dough can be used immediately after its initial rise, though it is easier to handle when cold. Refrigerate it in a lidded (not airtight) container and use over the next 10 days. The flavor will be best if you wait for at least 24 hours of refrigeration.

6. **On baking day,** dust the surface of the refrigerated dough with flour and cut off a 1-pound (grapefruit-size) piece. Dust the piece with more flour and quickly shape it into a ball by stretching the surface of the dough around to the bottom on all four sides, rotating the ball a quarter-turn as you go.

7. Elongate the ball into a narrow oval. Allow the loaf to rest, loosely covered with plastic wrap, on a pizza peel prepared with cornmeal or lined with parchment paper for 90 minutes (40 minutes if you're using fresh, unrefrigerated dough). Alternatively, you can rest the loaf on a silicone mat or a greased cookie sheet without using a pizza peel.

8. **Thirty minutes before baking time, preheat the oven to 450°F,** with a baking stone placed on the middle rack. Place an empty metal broiler tray on any other rack that won't interfere with the rising bread.

9. Just before baking, use a pastry brush to paint the top crust with water. Slash the loaf diagonally with ¼-inch-deep parallel cuts, using a serrated bread knife.

10. Slide the loaf directly onto the hot stone (or place the silicone mat or a cookie sheet on the stone if you used one). Pour 1 cup of hot tap water into the broiler tray, and quickly close the oven door (see pages 27 and 28 for

steam alternatives). Bake for about 30 to 35 minutes, until richly browned and firm. If you used parchment paper, a silicone mat, or a cookie sheet under the loaf, carefully remove it and bake the loaf directly on the stone or an oven rack two-thirds of the way through baking. Smaller or larger loaves will require adjustments in resting and baking time.

11. Allow the bread to cool on a rack before slicing and eating.

Emmer Bread

Emmer (see page 12) is a marvelous ancient grain with a great flavor, but it can be dense in bread. We developed terrific flavor by adding a small amount of white vinegar and beer to the mix. Sesame seeds in the crumb itself make a nice counterpoint to the flavors that develop in the dough. Emmer flour can be ordered from Bluebird Grain Farms (see page 311). Be sure to order the fine-milled emmer flour (which is milled from whole grain), not "whole grain emmer," which is the unground whole kernel of emmer.

∽

EMMER is hot among adventurous chefs at top restaurants, who are using it in its whole-kernel form to create incredible pilaf dishes (it's usually known by the Italian *farro* when used this way). Bluebird Grain Farms (see page 311) also sells emmer in its whole-kernel, unground form; it can be cooked like rice into a pilaf, or tossed into salads. The flavor is marvelous, and the grain is much higher in protein than wheat is—16 to 18 percent compared with wheat's 9 to 12 percent. Emmer contains gluten, so it can't be eaten by people with celiac disease, but the gluten content is much lower than that of wheat.

Makes enough dough for at least five 1-pound loaves. The recipe is easily doubled or halved.

4½ cups fine-milled whole grain emmer flour
4½ cups unbleached all-purpose flour
⅛ cup sesame seeds, plus additional for sprinkling on top crust
1½ tablespoons granulated yeast, or 2 packets (decrease to taste, page 15)
1 tablespoon kosher salt (increase or decrease to taste, page 17)
¼ cup vital wheat gluten
4 cups lukewarm water
½ cup any beer except porter, stout, or other strongly flavored brew
2 tablespoons white vinegar

1. **Mixing and storing the dough:** Whisk together the flours, sesame seeds, yeast, salt, and

vital wheat gluten in a 5-quart bowl, or a lidded (not airtight) food container.

2. Combine the liquid ingredients and mix them with the dry ingredients without kneading, using a spoon, a 14-cup food processor (with dough attachment), or a heavy-duty stand mixer (with paddle). You might need to use wet hands to get the last bit of flour to incorporate if you're not using a machine.

3. Cover (not airtight), and allow the dough to rest at room temperature until it rises and collapses (or flattens on top), approximately 2 hours.

4. The dough can be used immediately after its initial rise, though it is easier to handle when cold. Refrigerate it in a lidded (not airtight) container and use over the next 7 days. The flavor will be best if you wait for at least 24 hours of refrigeration.

5. **On baking day,** dust the surface of the refrigerated dough with flour and cut off a 1-pound (grapefruit-size) piece. Dust the piece with more flour and quickly shape it into a ball by stretching the surface of the dough around to the bottom on all four sides, rotating the ball a quarter-turn as you go.

6. Elongate the ball into a narrow oval. Allow the loaf to rest, loosely covered with plastic wrap, on a pizza peel prepared with cornmeal or lined with parchment paper for 90 minutes (40 minutes if you're using fresh, unrefrigerated dough). Alternatively, you can rest the loaf on a silicone mat or a greased cookie sheet without using a pizza peel.

7. **Thirty minutes before baking time, preheat the oven to 450°F,** with a baking stone placed on the middle rack. Place an empty metal broiler tray on any other rack that won't interfere with the rising bread.

8. Just before baking, use a pastry brush to paint the top crust with water. Slash the loaf diagonally with ¼-inch-deep parallel cuts, using a serrated bread knife.

9. Slide the loaf directly onto the hot stone (or place the silicone mat or cookie sheet on the stone if you used one). Pour 1 cup of hot tap water into the broiler tray, and quickly close the oven door (see pages 27 and 28 for steam alternatives). Bake for about 30 minutes, until richly browned and firm. If you used parchment paper, a silicone mat, or a cookie sheet under the loaf, carefully remove it and bake the loaf directly on the stone or an oven rack two-thirds of the way through baking. Smaller or larger loaves will require adjustments in resting and baking time.

10. Allow the loaf to cool on a rack before slicing and eating.

Cracked Wheat Bread

This bread is all about whole wheat in its many forms. By blending crunchy cracked wheat with white whole wheat and traditional whole wheat, we produced a bread with wonderful texture, great flavor, and lots of nutrition. Because we don't soak the cracked whole wheat, you must let this dough sit for at least 8 hours before using it. This allows the cracked wheat to soften, and gives the dough more complexity and the desired sourdough characteristics.

Makes enough dough for at least four 1-pound loaves. The recipe is easily doubled or halved.

4 cups white whole wheat flour
2 cups unbleached all-purpose flour
1 cup cracked whole wheat
1½ tablespoons granulated yeast, or 2 packets (decrease to taste, page 15)
1 tablespoon kosher salt (increase or decrease to taste, page 17)
¼ cup vital wheat gluten
4¼ cups lukewarm water

1. **Mixing and storing the dough:** Whisk together the flours, cracked wheat, yeast, salt, and vital wheat gluten in a 5-quart bowl, or a lidded (not airtight) food container.

2. Add the water and mix without kneading, using a spoon, a 14-cup food processor (with dough attachment), or a heavy-duty stand mixer (with paddle). You might need to use wet hands to get the last bit of flour to incorporate if you're not using a machine.

3. Cover (not airtight), and allow the dough to rest at room temperature until it rises and collapses (or flattens on top), approximately 2 hours.

4. Refrigerate it in a lidded (not airtight) container and use over the next 10 days. **Wait at least 8 hours to use the dough because the cracked wheat needs to absorb water before it is baked.**

5. **On baking day,** dust the surface of the refrigerated dough with flour and cut off a 1-pound (grapefruit-size) piece. Dust the piece with more flour and quickly shape it into a ball by stretching the surface of the dough around to the bottom on all four sides, rotating the ball a quarter-turn as you go, then elongate into an oval.

6. Allow the loaf, to rest, loosely covered with plastic wrap, on a pizza peel prepared with cornmeal or lined with parchment paper for 90 minutes. Alternatively, you can rest the loaf on a silicone mat or a greased cookie sheet without using a pizza peel.

7. **Thirty minutes before baking time, preheat the oven to 450°F,** with a baking stone placed on the middle rack. Place an empty metal broiler tray on any other rack that won't interfere with the rising bread.

8. Just before baking, use a pastry brush to paint the top with water. Slash the loaf with ¼-inch-deep parallel cuts, using a serrated bread knife.

9. Slide the loaf directly onto the hot stone (or place the silicone mat or cookie sheet on the stone if you used one). Pour 1 cup of hot tap water into the broiler tray, and quickly close the oven door (see pages 27 and 28 for steam alternatives). Bake for about 30 minutes, until richly browned and firm. If you used parchment paper, a silicone mat, or a cookie sheet under the loaf, carefully remove it and bake the loaf directly on the stone or an oven rack two-thirds of the way through baking. Smaller or larger loaves will require adjustments in resting and baking time.

10. Allow the loaf to cool on a rack before slicing and eating.

Ten-Grain Bread

We both developed a ten-grain bread, at exactly the same time, completely by accident. But whose version to use? We didn't end up clopping each other over the head with rolling pins. Instead, we combined the two recipes and came up with something we really love. For the ten-grain product, we decided on a nationally available ten-grain hot cereal from Bob's Red Mill, rather than the harder-to-find ten-grain flours stocked by natural food co-ops. Either will work, but you have to adjust the water if you use something other than the Bob's Red Mill product.

Makes enough dough for at least four 1-pound loaves. The recipe is easily doubled or halved.

2 cups ten-grain hot cereal (Bob's Red Mill brand), uncooked
3 cups white whole wheat flour
2 cups unbleached all-purpose flour
1½ tablespoons granulated yeast, or 2 packets (decrease to taste, page 15)
1 tablespoon kosher salt (increase or decrease to taste, page 17)
¼ cup vital wheat gluten
3½ cups lukewarm water
1 to 2 tablespoons of seed mixture for sprinkling on the top crust: sesame, flaxseed, caraway, raw sunflower, poppy, and/or anise

1. **Mixing and storing the dough:** Whisk together the cereal, flours, yeast, salt, and vital wheat gluten in a 5-quart bowl, or a lidded (not airtight) food container.

2. Add the water and mix without kneading, using a spoon, a 14-cup food processor (with dough attachment), or a heavy-duty stand mixer (with paddle). You might need to use wet hands to get the last bit of flour to incorporate if you're not using a machine.

3. Cover (not airtight), and allow the dough to rest at room temperature until it rises and collapses (or flattens on top), approximately 2 hours.

4. The dough can be used immediately after the initial rise, though it is easier to handle when cold. Refrigerate it in a lidded (not airtight) container and use over the next 10 days.

5. **On baking day,** dust the surface of the refrigerated dough with flour and cut off a 1-pound (grapefruit-size) piece. Dust the piece with more flour and quickly shape it into a ball by stretching the surface of the dough around to the bottom on all four sides, rotating the ball a quarter-turn as you go.

6. Elongate the ball into an oval. Allow the loaf to rest, loosely covered with plastic wrap, on a pizza peel prepared with cornmeal or lined with parchment paper for 90 minutes (40 minutes if you're using fresh, unrefrigerated dough). Alternatively, you can rest the loaf on a silicone mat or a greased cookie sheet without using a pizza peel.

7. **Thirty minutes before baking time, preheat the oven to 450°F**, with a baking stone placed on the middle rack. Place an empty metal broiler tray on any other rack that won't interfere with the rising bread.

8. Just before baking, use a pastry brush to paint the top crust with water. Sprinkle with the seed mixture and slash the loaf with ¼-inch-deep parallel cuts, using a serrated bread knife.

9. Slide the loaf directly onto the hot stone (or place the silicone mat or cookie sheet on the stone if you used one). Pour 1 cup of hot tap water into the broiler tray, and quickly close the oven door (see pages 27 and 28 for steam alternatives). Bake for about 30 minutes, until richly browned and firm. If you used parchment paper, a silicone mat, or a cookie sheet under the loaf, carefully remove it and bake the loaf directly on the stone or an oven rack two-thirds of the way through baking. Smaller or larger loaves will require adjustments in resting and baking time.

10. Allow to cool on a rack before slicing or eating.

Whole Grain Rye Bread

This loaf is not your grandmother's rye bread, delicious as it was. Most of us who grew up with great fresh rye were eating bread that was very low in whole grains. Our version is bursting with whole grain flavors; it's a much heartier product than Grandma's was. These days, U.S. shoppers will find only high-bran rye in stores. Avoid "light" or "medium" rye (which are only available through mail order anyway), and you'll end up with the very high whole grain result we have in mind here.

Makes enough dough for at least four 1-pound loaves. The recipe is easily doubled or halved.

2½ cups whole wheat flour
2¾ cups rye flour
2½ cups unbleached all purpose flour
1½ tablespoons granulated yeast, or 2 packets (decrease to taste, page 15)
1 tablespoon kosher salt (increase or decrease to taste, page 17)
1½ tablespoons caraway seeds, plus additional for sprinkling on top crust
¼ cup vital wheat gluten
4 cups lukewarm water

1. **Mixing and storing the dough:** Whisk together the flours, yeast, salt, caraway, and vital wheat gluten in a 5-quart bowl, or a lidded (not airtight) food container.

2. Add the water and mix without kneading, using a spoon, a 14-cup food processor (with dough attachment), or a heavy-duty stand mixer (with paddle). You might need to use wet hands to get the last bit of flour to incorporate if you're not using a machine.

3. Cover (not airtight), and allow the dough to rest at room temperature until it rises and collapses (or flattens on top), approximately 2 hours.

4. The dough can be used immediately after the initial rise, though it is easier to handle when cold. Refrigerate it in a lidded (not airtight) container and use over the next 7 days. *The flavor will be better if you wait for at least 24 hours of refrigeration.*

5. **On baking day,** dust the surface of the refrigerated dough with flour and cut off a 1-pound (grapefruit-size) piece. Dust the piece with more flour and quickly shape it into a ball by stretching the surface of the dough around to the bottom on all four sides, rotating the ball a quarter-turn as you go.

6. Elongate the ball into a narrow oval. Allow the loaf to rest, loosely covered with plastic wrap, on a pizza peel prepared with cornmeal or lined with parchment paper for 90 minutes (40 minutes if you're using fresh, unrefrigerated dough). Alternatively, you can rest the loaf on a silicone mat or a greased cookie sheet without using a pizza peel.

7. **Thirty minutes before baking time, preheat the oven to 450°F,** with a baking stone placed on the middle rack. Place an empty metal broiler tray on any other rack that won't interfere with the rising bread.

8. Just before baking, use a pastry brush to paint the top with water, and then sprinkle with the additional caraway seeds. Slash the loaf with ¼-inch-deep parallel cuts, using a serrated bread knife.

9. Slide the loaf directly onto the hot stone (or place the silicone mat or cookie sheet on the stone if you used one). Pour 1 cup of hot tap water into the broiler tray, and quickly close the oven door. Bake for about 30 to 35 minutes, until richly browned and firm. If you used parchment paper, a silicone mat, or a cookie sheet under the loaf, carefully remove it two-thirds of the way through baking and bake the loaf directly on the stone or an oven rack. Smaller or larger loaves will require adjustments in resting and baking time.

10. Allow the bread to cool on a rack before slicing and eating.

Bavarian-Style Whole Grain Pumpernickel Bread

On our Web site, people asked us whether they could use wicker rising baskets (*banneton* in French, or *brotform* in German) to contain the dough and prevent it from spreading sideways during prolonged rising. We were a bit skeptical, fearing that dough this wet might stick to the wicker. But so long as you coat the wicker heavily with white flour, it's not a problem. And it can be a gorgeous solution when you've mixed the dough a little too wet, or it's near the end of its storage life (see page 31). The traditional Bavarian-style pumpernickel rises in a *brotform*, and it's designed to be a very rustic bread, ringed with scorched flour. It's perfect with butter or for dipping into hearty soups. The smaller *bannetons* are a bit difficult to find, but it's worth seeking out a 6½-inch one. If you use a larger *banneton* (like the commonly available 9-inch model), it's going to take 3 pounds of dough and require a very long baking time (at least an hour). If you don't have a *banneton*, this dough bakes up beautifully as a free-form or loaf bread.

Makes enough dough for at least four 1-pound loaves. The recipe is easily doubled or halved.

2½ cups whole wheat flour

2¾ cups rye flour

2½ cups unbleached all-purpose flour

1½ tablespoons granulated yeast, or 2 packets (decrease to taste, page 15)

1 tablespoon kosher salt (increase or decrease to taste, page 17)

1 tablespoon caramel color powder or ¼ cup of homemade liquid caramel color (see chapter 2, page 23)

ALTUS: Traditional pumpernickel recipes call for the addition of "*altus,*" which is stale rye or pumpernickel bread crumbs, soaked in water, squeezed dry, and blended into the dough. If you want to find a use for some stale rye or pumpernickel bread, you can experiment with this approach, which some say adds moisture and flavor to many traditional rye breads. Add up to a cup of *altus* with the liquid ingredients. You may need to adjust flour to end up with dough of your usual consistency.

¼ cup vital wheat gluten
1 tablespoon caraway seeds
2 tablespoons molasses
4 cups lukewarm water

1. **Mixing and storing the dough:** Whisk together the flours, yeast, salt, caramel color, vital wheat gluten, and caraway seeds in a 5-quart bowl, or a lidded (not airtight) food container. If you make your own caramel, it's going to be a liquid, so add it in step 2 and decrease water by ¼ cup.

2. Combine the water and molasses, and your own caramel if using, and mix them with the dry ingredients without kneading, using a spoon, a 14-cup food processor (with dough attachment), or a heavy-duty stand mixer (with paddle). You might need to use wet hands to get the last bit of flour to incorporate if you're not using a machine.

3. Cover (not airtight), and allow the dough to rest at room temperature until it rises and collapses (or flattens on top), approximately 2 hours.

4. The dough can be used immediately after the initial rise, though it is easier to handle when cold. Refrigerate it in a lidded (not airtight) container and use over the next 7 days.

5. **On baking day,** prepare a 6½-inch *banneton/brotform* by generously sprinkling it with flour; shake it all around so it coats the sides. **Be generous with the flour.** Dust the surface of the pumpernickel dough with flour and cut off a 1-pound (grapefruit-size) piece of dough. Dust the piece with more flour and quickly shape it into a ball by stretching the surface of the dough around to the bottom on all four sides, rotating the ball a quarter-turn as you go.

6. Place the loaf into the *banneton* **with the irregular side up;** the smooth, tightly shaped side stays in contact with the basket. The dough should come about two-thirds of the way up the sides of the *banneton.* Cover the *ban-*

neton loosely with plastic wrap and allow the loaf to rest at room temperature for 90 minutes (40 minutes if you are using fresh, unrefrigerated
dough). You might not see impressive rising during this time.

7. **Thirty minutes before baking time, preheat the oven to 450°F,** with a baking
stone placed on the middle rack. Place an empty metal broiler tray on any
other rack that won't interfere with the rising bread.

8. After the dough is rested, gently use your fingers to be sure that it isn't sticking to the *banneton*. Don't dig way down or you may deflate the loaf. Gently
turn the basket over onto your preheated stone; it should unmold and drop
gently. If it doesn't, help it out with your fingers and make the best of it **(be
careful; don't burn yourself on the hot stone).** It should be fine even if it de-
flates a bit, thanks to oven spring. Using a serrated knife, make ¼-inch-deep
slashes in a cross pattern, which will create a beautiful effect with the con-
centric circles of flour (see, page 32).

9. Pour 1 cup of hot tap water into the broiler tray, and quickly close the oven
door (see pages 27 and 28 for steam alternatives). Bake for about 30 minutes, until firm. Smaller or larger loaves will require adjustments in resting
and baking time.

10. Allow the bread to cool on a rack before slicing or eating.

Black-and-White Braided Pumpernickel and Rye Loaf

This festive loaf is a New York classic. Pumpernickel and rye doughs are braided together to create a delicious showpiece that is great for sandwiches, or just "shmeared" with butter (see photo, color insert).

Makes one braided 1-pound loaf

½ pound (orange-size portion) Bavarian-Style Whole Grain Pumpernickel Bread dough (page 115)
½ pound (orange-size portion) Whole Grain Rye Bread dough (page 113)
Caraway seeds for sprinkling on top crust

1. Dust the surface of the pumpernickel dough with flour and cut off an orange-size piece. Dust the piece with more flour and quickly shape it into a ball by stretching the surface of the dough around to the bottom on all four sides, rotating the ball a quarter-turn as you go.

2. Dust the surface of the rye dough with flour and cut off an orange-size piece. Dust the piece with more flour and quickly shape it into a ball by stretching the surface of the dough around to the bottom on all four sides, rotating the ball a quarter-turn as you go. Cut the ball in half and form 2 balls.

3. Roll each ball between your hands (or on a board), stretching to form 3 long ropes of equal length (the pumpernickel rope will be thicker because its dough ball was twice as large). If the balls resist shaping, let them rest for 5 minutes and try again—don't fight the dough.

4. Line up the 3 ropes, keeping the pumpernickel rope in the center. Braid the ropes, starting from the center and working to one end. If you've never done a 3-stranded braid before, it's simple—just remember to drape one of the outside strands over the center one, then do the same with the other

outside strand (see challah photo, page 259). Repeat till you reach the end and then pinch the strands together. Flip the loaf over, rotate it, braid from the center out to the remaining end, and pinch the ends of the strands together. This produces a loaf with a more uniform thickness than when braided from end to end.

5. Allow the loaf to rest, loosely covered with plastic wrap, on a pizza peel prepared with cornmeal or lined with parchment paper for 90 minutes (40 minutes if you're using fresh, unrefrigerated dough). Alternatively, you can rest the loaf on a silicone mat or a greased cookie sheet without using a pizza peel.

6. **Thirty minutes before baking time, preheat the oven to 450°F**, with a baking stone placed on the middle rack. Place an empty metal broiler tray on any other rack that won't interfere with the rising bread.

7. Just before baking, use a pastry brush to paint the loaf with water, and then sprinkle with the caraway seeds.

8. Slide the loaf directly onto the hot stone (or place the silicone mat or cookie sheet directly on the stone if you used one). Pour 1 cup of hot tap water into the broiler tray, and quickly close the oven door (see pages 27 and 28 for steam alternatives). Bake for about 35 minutes, until richly browned and firm. If you used parchment paper, a silicone mat, or a cookie sheet under the loaf, carefully remove it and bake the loaf directly on the stone or an oven rack two-thirds of the way through baking. Smaller or larger loaves will require adjustments in resting and baking time.

9. Allow the bread to cool on a rack before slicing and eating.

Bradley Benn's Beer Bread

"My friend Bradley Benn is a talented potter in Minneapolis, and, as it turns out, an accomplished bread baker. Much to my surprise and delight, he delivered a fabulous loaf of bread to my home. He had adapted his favorite beer bread for the Artisan Bread in Five Minutes a Day *quick method and used white whole wheat flour. The flavor had sourdough characteristics, the crumb was wonderful, and the onions and walnuts added the perfect touch. The whole wheat beer dough makes a wonderful loaf without the addition of the onions and walnuts as well. He was kind enough not only to share the bread, but also his recipe, which I deliver to you. Thank you, Bradley!"*—Zoë

The fats in walnuts have a terrific beneficial effect on cholesterol, plus they're loaded with fiber and vitamin E. But eat them in moderation, because they're high in calories.

Makes enough dough for at least three 1-pound loaves. The recipe is easily doubled or halved.

¾ cup rye flour

5 cups white whole wheat flour

1½ tablespoons granulated yeast, or 2 packets (decrease to taste, page 15)

1 tablespoon kosher salt (increase or decrease to taste, page 17)

¼ cup vital wheat gluten

1¼ cups water

1½ cups beer

¼ cup neutral-flavored oil

1 tablespoon honey

The Onion Mixture, per loaf

½ medium sweet onion, chopped

2 tablespoons olive oil

Salt and pepper to taste

1 teaspoon fresh rosemary (½ teaspoon dried)

½ cup walnuts, chopped

½ teaspoon fresh rosemary (¼ teaspoon dried) for sprinkling on the top crust

½ teaspoon coarse salt for sprinkling on the top crust

1. **Mixing and storing the dough:** Whisk together the flours, yeast, salt, and vital wheat gluten in a 5-quart bowl, or a lidded (not airtight) food container.

2. Combine the water, beer, ¼ cup oil, and honey and mix them with the dry ingredients without kneading, using a spoon, a 14-cup food processor (with dough attachment), or a heavy-duty stand mixer (with paddle). You might need to use wet hands to get the last bit of flour to incorporate if you're not using a machine.

3. Cover (not airtight), and allow the dough to rest at room temperature until it rises and collapses (or flattens on top), approximately 2 hours.

4. The dough can be used immediately after initial rise, though it is easier to handle when cold. Refrigerate it in a lidded (not airtight) container and use over the next 10 days. The flavor will be best if you wait for at least 24 hours of refrigeration.

5. **Preparing the onions:** In a sauté pan over medium heat cook the onions, olive oil, salt, pepper, and rosemary until the onions are wilted, but not darkened. Remove from heat and set aside.

6. **On baking day,** dust the surface of the refrigerated dough with flour and cut off a 1-pound (grapefruit-size) piece. Dust with more flour and quickly shape it into a ball by stretching the surface of the dough around to the bottom on all four sides, rotating the ball a quarter-turn as you go.

7. With a rolling pin, roll out the dough until it is a ¼-inch-thick rectangle. As you roll out the dough, use enough flour to prevent it from sticking to the work surface, but not so much as to make the dough dry.

8. Spread the sautéed onion mixture and walnuts evenly over the rolled-out dough, leaving a ½-inch border all around. Roll the dough into a log starting at the long end. Pinch the ends closed. Allow the loaf to rest, loosely covered with plastic wrap, and rise on a pizza peel prepared with cornmeal or lined with parchment paper for 90 minutes (40 minutes if you're using fresh, un-refrigerated dough). Alternatively, you can rest the loaf on a silicone mat or a greased cookie sheet without using a pizza peel.

9. **Thirty minutes before baking time, preheat the oven to 400°F,** with a baking stone placed on the middle rack. Place an empty metal broiler tray on any other rack that won't interfere with the rising bread.

10. Just before baking, use a pastry brush to paint the top with water, and then sprinkle with additional rosemary and coarse salt. Slash the loaf with ¼-inch-deep parallel cuts, using a serrated bread knife.

11. Slide the loaf directly onto the hot stone. Pour 1 cup of hot tap water into the broiler tray, and quickly close the oven door (see pages 27 and 28 for steam alternatives). Bake for about 45 minutes, until deeply browned and firm. If you used parchment paper, a silicone mat, or a cookie sheet under the loaf, carefully remove it and bake the loaf directly on the stone or an oven rack two-thirds of the way through baking. Smaller or larger loaves will require adjustments in resting and baking time.

12. Allow the bread to cool on a rack before slicing or eating.

Dilled Rye with White Whole Wheat

Dill is a traditional ingredient in Scandinavian-style breads, and we decided to showcase it in a rye that contains white whole wheat flour. White whole wheat products are marvelous for kids who don't like the slightly bitter flavor of traditional whole wheat. It's as rich in bran and wheat germ as traditional whole wheat, but the flavor is mild and the color is a lighter brown.

Makes enough dough for at least four 1-pound loaves. The recipe is easily doubled or halved.

2¾ cups rye flour
2½ cups white whole wheat flour
2½ cups unbleached all-purpose flour
1½ tablespoons granulated yeast, or 2 packets (decrease to taste, page 15)
1 tablespoon kosher salt (increase or decrease to taste, page 17)
¼ cup vital wheat gluten
2 tablespoons chopped fresh dill (2 teaspoons dried), plus additional for sprinkling on crust
4 cups lukewarm water

1. **Mixing and storing the dough:** Whisk together the flours, yeast, salt, and vital wheat gluten in a 5-quart bowl, or a lidded (not airtight) food container.

2. Add the dill and water and mix without kneading, using a spoon, a 14-cup food processor (with paddle), or a heavy-duty stand mixer (with paddle). You might need to use wet hands to get the last bit of flour to incorporate if you're not using a machine.

3. Cover (not airtight), and allow the dough to rest at room temperature until it rises and collapses (or flattens on top), approximately 2 hours.

4. The dough can be used immediately after the initial rise, though it is easier to handle when cold. Refrigerate it in a lidded (not airtight) container and use over the next 7 days.

5. **On baking day,** dust the surface of the refrigerated dough with flour and cut off a 1-pound (grapefruit-size piece). Dust the piece with more flour and quickly shape it into a ball by stretching the surface of the dough around to the bottom on all four sides, rotating the ball a quarter-turn as you go.

6. Elongate the ball into an oval. Allow the loaf to rest, loosely covered with plastic wrap, on a pizza peel prepared with cornmeal or lined with parchment paper for 90 minutes (40 minutes if you're using fresh, unrefrigerated dough). Alternatively, you can rest the loaf on a silicone mat or a greased cookie sheet without using a pizza peel.

7. **Thirty minutes before baking time, preheat the oven to 450°F,** with a baking stone placed on the middle rack. Place an empty metal broiler tray on any other rack that won't interfere with the rising bread.

8. Just before baking, use a pastry brush to paint the top with water, and then sprinkle with the additional dill. Slash the loaf with ¼-inch-deep parallel cuts, using a serrated bread knife.

9. Slide the loaf directly onto the hot stone (or place the silicone mat or cookie sheet on the stone if you used one.). Pour 1 cup of hot tap water into the broiler tray, and quickly close the oven door (see pages 27 and 28 for steam alternatives). Bake for about 30 minutes, until richly browned and firm. If you used parchment paper, a silicone mat, or a cookie sheet under the loaf, carefully remove it and bake the loaf directly on the stone or an oven rack two-thirds of the way through baking. Smaller or larger loaves will require adjustments in resting and baking time.

10. Allow the bread to cool on a rack before slicing or eating.

100% Whole Grain Rosemary Potato Dinner Rolls with a Salt Crust

These crusty whole grain rosemary rolls (with soy flour for extra protein) have a lovely soft-textured crumb because of the potatoes. We admit that our inspiration for these salty rolls are French fries. Not everyone loves salt as much as we do, so feel free to cut back. This is also true for anyone on a low-sodium diet— you can eliminate the salt crust altogether.

Makes enough dough for at least five batches of 8 rolls (40 rolls)

5 cups whole wheat flour
1 cup rye flour
¼ cup soy flour
1½ tablespoons granulated yeast, or 2 packets (decrease to taste, page 15)
1 tablespoon kosher salt (increase or decrease to taste, page 17)
¼ cup vital wheat gluten
2 tablespoons fresh rosemary, chopped fine
3 cups lukewarm water
¼ cup olive oil
3 cups diced raw potatoes, in ¼-inch cubes (clean the potatoes but don't peel them)
1 teaspoon coarse sea salt for the top crust
1 tablespoon coarsely chopped rosemary for the top crust

1. **Mixing and storing the dough:** Whisk together the flours, yeast, salt, vital wheat gluten, and 2 tablespoons rosemary in a 5-quart bowl, or a lidded (not airtight) food container.

2. Add the liquid ingredients and potatoes and mix without kneading, using a spoon, a 14-cup food processor (with dough attachment), or a heavy-duty stand mixer (with paddle). You might need to use wet hands to get the last bit of flour to incorporate if you're not using a machine.

3. Cover (not airtight), and allow the dough to rest at room temperature until it rises and collapses (or flattens on top), approximately 2 hours.

4. The dough can be used immediately after its initial rise, though it is easier to handle when cold. Refrigerate it in a lidded (not airtight) container and use over the next 7 days. The flavor will be best if you wait for at least 24 hours of refrigeration.

5. **On baking day,** dust the surface of the refrigerated dough with flour and cut off a 1-pound (grapefruit-size) piece. Dust the piece with more flour and quickly shape it into a ball by stretching the surface of the dough around to the bottom on all four sides, rotating the ball a quarter-turn as you go.

6. **To form the rolls:** Divide the ball into 8 roughly equal portions (each about the size of a golf ball). Shape each one into a smooth ball. Allow them to rest, loosely covered with plastic wrap, on a cookie sheet lined with parchment paper for 40 minutes (20 minutes if you're using fresh, unrefrigerated dough). Alternatively, you can rest the rolls on a silicone pad–lined cookie sheet or on a greased cookie sheet.

7. **Thirty minutes before baking time, preheat the oven to 450°F,** with a baking stone placed on the middle rack. Place an empty metal broiler tray on any other rack that won't interfere with the rising rolls.

8. Just before baking, use a pastry brush to paint the top crusts of the rolls with water, and sprinkle the rolls with the sea salt and chopped rosemary.

9. Slide the cookie sheet directly onto the hot stone. Pour 1 cup of hot tap water into the broiler tray, and quickly close the oven door (see pages 27 and 28 for steam alternatives). Bake for about 20 minutes, until richly browned and firm.

10. Allow the rolls to cool on a rack before eating.

Buckwheat Bread

"The flavor of buckwheat reminds me of being freezing cold and soaked to the bone. My husband and I were in Normandy, touring the magical Mont-Saint-Michel in spring. It was glorious but rainy and cold. We found comfort in a café with Calvados and buckwheat crêpes. The flavor of the grain is so wonderful in this bread that you won't mind what weather conditions you may find yourself in while you eat. The unground buckwheat groats add a lovely texture to the bread. You can find them in your local co-op or on the Internet."—Zoë

Makes enough dough for at least four 1-pound loaves. The recipe is easily doubled or halved.

½ cup buckwheat groats
1 cup buckwheat flour
2 cups unbleached all-purpose flour
4 cups whole wheat flour
1½ tablespoons granulated yeast, or 2 packets (decrease to taste, page 15)
1 tablespoon kosher salt (increase or decrease to taste, page 17)
¼ cup vital wheat gluten
4½ cups lukewarm water

1. Soak the groats in 1 cup of the lukewarm water for 30 minutes.

2. **Mixing and storing the dough:** Whisk together the flours, yeast, salt, and vital wheat gluten in a 5-quart bowl, or a lidded (not airtight) food container.

3. Add the groats (including the soaking water) and the remaining 3½ cups water and mix without kneading, using a spoon, a 14-cup food processor (with dough attachment), or a heavy-duty stand mixer (with paddle). You might need to use wet hands to get the last bit of flour to incorporate if you're not using a machine.

4. Cover (not airtight), and allow the dough to rest at room temperature until it rises and collapses (or flattens on top), approximately 2 hours.

5. The dough can be used immediately after the initial rise, though it is easier to handle when cold. Refrigerate it in a lidded (not airtight) container and use over the next 10 days. The flavor will be best if you wait for at least 24 hours of refrigeration.

6. **On baking day,** dust the surface of the refrigerated dough with flour and cut off a 1-pound (grapefruit-size) piece. Dust with more flour and quickly shape it into a ball by stretching the surface of the dough around to the bottom on all four sides, rotating the ball a quarter-turn as you go.

7. Allow the loaf to rest, loosely covered with plastic wrap, on a pizza peel prepared with cornmeal or lined with parchment paper for 90 minutes (40 minutes if you're using fresh, unrefrigerated dough). Alternatively, you can rest the loaf on a silicone mat or a greased cookie sheet without using a pizza peel.

8. **Thirty minutes before baking time, preheat the oven to 450°F,** with a baking stone placed on the middle rack. Place an empty metal broiler tray on any other rack that won't interfere with the rising bread.

9. Just before baking, use a pastry brush to paint the top with water. Slash the loaf with ¼-inch-deep parallel cuts across the top, using a serrated bread knife.

10. Slide the loaf directly onto the hot stone (or place the silicone mat or cookie sheet on the stone if you used one). Pour 1 cup of hot tap water into the broiler tray, and quickly close the oven door (see pages 27 and 28 for steam alternatives). Bake for about 30 minutes, until richly browned and firm. If you used parchment paper, a silicone mat, or a cookie sheet under the loaf, carefully remove it and bake the loaf directly on the stone or an oven rack two-thirds of the way through baking. Smaller or larger loaves will require adjustments in resting and baking time.

11. Allow the bread to cool on a rack before slicing or eating.

Anadama Corn Bread

Pretty much every traditional American cookbook we own contains a recipe for this bread, a Native American–inspired loaf sweetened with molasses. The corn and molasses are perfect at Thanksgiving or served with a hearty stew. Newer books seem to ignore anadama bread, and that's a shame, because this classic is a winner. This loaf spreads and bakes flatter than most.

Molasses is an unrefined sweetener that imparts a complexity that white sugar lacks. There are actually some bitter and caramel notes to savor—it beautifully rounds out the whole wheat we used to boost the fiber and vitamin content of the bread.

Makes enough dough for at least four 1-pound loaves. The recipe is easily doubled or halved.

1½ cups cornmeal
¼ cup wheat germ
2¼ cups whole wheat flour
3 cups unbleached all-purpose flour
1½ tablespoons granulated yeast, or 2 packets (decrease to taste, page 15)
1 tablespoon kosher salt (increase or decrease to taste, page 17)
¼ cup vital wheat gluten
3½ cups lukewarm water
½ cup molasses

1. **Mixing and storing the dough:** Whisk together the cornmeal, wheat germ, flours, yeast, salt, and vital wheat gluten in a 5-quart bowl, or a lidded (not airtight) food container.

2. Combine the water and molasses and mix them with the dry ingredients without kneading, using a spoon, a 14-cup food processor (with dough attachment), or a heavy-duty stand mixer (with paddle). You might need to

use wet hands to get the last bit of flour to incorporate if you're not using a machine.

3. Cover (not airtight), and allow the dough to rest at room temperature until it rises and collapses (or flattens on top), approximately 2 hours.

4. The dough can be used immediately after the initial rise, though it is easier to handle when cold. Refrigerate it in a lidded (not airtight) container and use over the next 7 days.

5. **On baking day,** dust the surface of the refrigerated dough with flour and cut off a 1-pound (grapefruit-size) piece. Dust the piece with more flour and quickly shape it into a ball by stretching the surface of the dough around to the bottom on all four sides, rotating the ball a quarter-turn as you go.

6. Allow the loaf to rest, loosely covered with plastic wrap, on a pizza peel prepared with cornmeal or lined with parchment paper for 90 minutes (40 minutes if you're using fresh, unrefrigerated dough). Alternatively, you can rest the loaf on a silicone mat or a greased cookie sheet without using a pizza peel.

7. **Thirty minutes before baking time, preheat the oven to 450°F**, with a baking stone placed on the middle rack. Place an empty metal broiler tray on any other rack that won't interfere with the rising bread.

8. Just before baking, use a pastry brush to paint the top crust with water. Slash the loaf with ¼-inch-deep parallel cuts, using a serrated bread knife.

9. Slide the loaf directly onto the hot stone (or place the silicone mat or cookie sheet on the stone if you used one). Pour 1 cup of hot tap water into the broiler tray, and quickly close the oven door (see pages 27 and 28 for steam alternatives). Bake for about 30 minutes, until richly browned and firm. If you used parchment paper, a silicone mat, or a cookie sheet

under the loaf, carefully remove it and bake the loaf directly on the stone or an oven rack two-thirds of the way through baking. Smaller or larger loaves will require adjustments in resting and baking time.

10. Allow the bread to cool on a rack before slicing or eating.

Quinoa Bread

Quinoa (pronounced *keen-wah*) is something of a wonder grain. It's high in protein, calcium, and fiber. Native cultures of South America made this grain a staple millennia ago, and it's been rediscovered by natural food fans after years of neglect.

Makes enough dough for at least four 1-pound loaves. The recipe is easily doubled or halved.

3 cups white whole wheat flour
3½ cups unbleached all-purpose flour
1 cup whole grain quinoa, uncooked
1½ tablespoons granulated yeast, or 2 packets (decrease to taste, page 15)
1 tablespoon kosher salt (increase or decrease to taste, page 17)
¼ cup vital wheat gluten
3¾ cups lukewarm water

1. **Mixing and storing the dough:** Whisk together the flours, quinoa, yeast, salt, and vital wheat gluten in a 5-quart bowl, or a lidded (not airtight) food container.

2. Add the water and mix without kneading, using a spoon, a 14-cup food processor (with dough attachment), or a heavy-duty stand mixer (with paddle). You might need to use wet hands to get the last bit of flour to incorporate if you're not using a machine.

3. Cover (not airtight), and allow the dough to rest at room temperature until it rises and collapses (or flattens on top), approximately 2 hours.

4. The dough can be used immediately after the initial rise, though it is easier to handle when cold. Refrigerate it in a lidded (not airtight) container and

use over the next 10 days. The flavor will be best if you wait for at least 24 hours of refrigeration.

5. **On baking day,** dust the surface of the refrigerated dough with flour and cut off a 1-pound (grapefruit-size) piece. Dust the piece with more flour and quickly shape it into a ball by stretching the surface of the dough around to the bottom on all four sides, rotating the ball a quarter-turn as you go.

6. Elongate the ball into a narrow oval. Allow the loaf to rest on a pizza peel prepared with cornmeal or lined with parchment paper for 90 minutes (40 minutes if you're using fresh, unrefrigerated dough). Alternatively, you can rest the loaf on a silicone mat or a greased cookie sheet without using a pizza peel.

7. **Thirty minutes before baking time, preheat the oven to 450°F,** with a baking stone placed on the middle rack. Place an empty metal broiler tray on any other rack that won't interfere with the rising bread.

8. Just before baking, use a pastry brush to paint the top with water. Slash the loaf with ¼-inch-deep parallel cuts, using a serrated bread knife.

9. Slide the loaf directly onto the hot stone (or place the silicone mat or cookie sheet on the stone if you used one). Pour 1 cup of hot tap water into the broiler tray, and quickly close the oven door (see pages 27 and 28 for steam alternatives). Bake for about 30 minutes, until richly browned and firm. If you used parchment paper, a silicone mat, or a cookie sheet under the loaf, carefully remove it and bake the loaf directly on the stone or an oven rack two-thirds of the way through baking. Smaller or larger loaves will require adjustments in resting and baking time.

10. Allow the bread to cool on a rack before slicing or eating.

Toasted Millet and Fruit Bread

"I got the idea for this bread after eating a memorable millet cookie my friend and pastry chef Michelle Gayer serves at the Salty Tart, her bakery in Minneapolis. I loved the crunch and the earthiness mixed with the sweet."—Zoë

Millet has a very subtle flavor, so we like to toast it first. This gives the grain a more complex taste that comes through in the bread. Because the dough is quite wet and will be refrigerated (giving the millet a chance to absorb water), there's no need to pre-cook this hard grain; it will soften just enough. The chewy sweetness of all the dried fruit adds a wonderful contrast to the crunch of the millet, but you can make a plain millet version by leaving out the fruit if you like.

Makes enough dough for at least five 1-pound loaves. The recipe is easily doubled or halved.

1 cup millet
4 cups whole wheat flour
2 cups unbleached all-purpose flour
½ cup brown sugar
1½ tablespoons granulated yeast, or 2 packets (decrease to taste, page 15)
1½ tablespoons kosher salt (increase or decrease to taste, page 17)
¼ cup vital wheat gluten
3¾ cups lukewarm water
3 cups mixed dried fruit (raisins, dried cranberries, dried cherries, dried currants)

1. **Mixing and storing the dough:** Before mixing, toast the millet in a dry skillet over medium heat, stirring and shaking

∾

MILLET is a major component of bird seed. Birds just seem to love it, and the tiny, beadlike grains are great for adorable songbirds. Tweet tweet.* But it turns out that millet is very nutritious for humans as well, with as much protein as wheat, and it's particularly high in niacin, vitamin B_6, folic acid, calcium, iron, potassium, magnesium, and zinc. Because it's a drought-resistant crop, it's important for basic survival all over arid parts of the African continent.

*Speaking of which, follow us on Twitter at http://twitter.com/ArtisanBreadIn5.

constantly until it turns golden brown. Whisk together the millet, flours, brown sugar, yeast, salt, and vital wheat gluten in a 5-quart bowl, or a lidded (not airtight) food container.

2. Add the water and fruit and mix without kneading, using a spoon, a 14-cup food processor (with dough attachment), or a heavy-duty stand mixer (with paddle). You might need to use wet hands to get the last bit of flour to incorporate if you're not using a machine.

3. Cover (not airtight), and allow the dough to rest at room temperature until it rises and collapses (or flattens on top), approximately 2 hours.

4. The dough must be refrigerated for at least 24 hours before use. Refrigerate it in a lidded (not airtight) container and use over the next 7 days.

5. **On baking day,** dust the surface of the refrigerated dough with flour and cut off a 1-pound (grapefruit-size) piece. Dust with more flour and quickly shape it into a ball by stretching the surface of the dough around to the bottom on all four sides, rotating the ball a quarter-turn as you go. Because of the millet and dried fruit the loaf will never be perfectly smooth.

6. Elongate the ball into a narrow oval. Allow the loaf to rest, loosely covered with plastic wrap, on a pizza peel prepared with flour or lined with parchment paper for 90 minutes. Alternatively, you can rest the loaf on a silicone mat or a greased cookie sheet without using a pizza peel.

7. **Thirty minutes before baking time, preheat the oven to 375°F,** with a baking stone placed on the middle rack. Place an empty metal broiler tray on any other rack that won't interfere with the rising bread.

8. Just before baking, use a pastry brush to paint the top with water. Slash the loaf with ¼-inch-deep parallel cuts, using a serrated bread knife.

9. Slide the loaf directly onto the hot stone (or place the silicone mat or cookie sheet on the stone if you used one). Pour 1 cup of hot tap water into the broiler tray, and quickly close the oven door (see pages 27 and 28 for steam alternatives). Bake for about 40 minutes, until richly browned and firm. If you used parchment paper, a silicone mat, or a cookie sheet under the loaf, carefully remove it and bake the loaf directly on the stone or an oven rack two-thirds of the way through baking. Smaller or larger loaves will require adjustments in resting and baking time.

10. Allow the loaf to cool on a rack before slicing and eating.

Red Wine and Cheese Bread

The flavors of red wine and cheese make such a natural combination, and they're often served with a nice crusty bread. So, why not put them both *in* the bread? It turns out to be a fabulously tasty loaf. The bread goes beautifully with hearty stews like beef bourguignon.

Makes enough dough for at least four 1-pound loaves. The recipe is easily doubled or halved.

½ cup rye flour
1 cup whole wheat flour
5½ cups unbleached all-purpose flour
1½ tablespoons granulated yeast, or 2 packets (decrease to taste, page 15)
1 tablespoon kosher salt (increase or decrease to taste, page 17)
1½ cups lukewarm water
1½ cups red wine
1 cup grated sharp cheddar cheese, or your favorite hard cheese

1. **Mixing and storing the dough:** Whisk together the flours, yeast, and salt in a 5-quart bowl, or a lidded (not airtight) food container.

RED WINE MAY BE GOOD FOR YOUR HEALTH (IN MODERATION): Red wine may help prevent premature hardening of the arteries (atherosclerosis), which causes heart attack and stroke. **Resveratrol** is the phytochemical (plant-based chemical) that provides the happy effect, coming mainly from the grape skin; this explains the higher resveratrol dose from red wine, which is fermented in contact with the highly colored skin for a much longer time than white wine. Harvard scientists recently linked resveratrol with protection of cells from the aging process and even from radiation damage. So red wine may become the new Botox. Maybe.

Speaking of happy effects, don't expect to get tipsy from eating winey bread. Alcohol boils off at oven temperature and virtually none of it is left in the finished product.

Pharmaceutical companies are hard at work trying to isolate resveratrol for

(continued)

(continued)

nutritional supplements, but we'd much prefer to get our daily dose in bread or liquid form (raisins, which are dried grapes, have it, too).

2. Add the liquid ingredients and cheese to the dry ingredients and mix without kneading, using a spoon, a 14-cup food processor (with dough attachment), or a heavy-duty stand mixer (with paddle). You might need to use wet hands to get the last bit of flour to incorporate if you're not using a machine.

3. Cover (not airtight), and allow the dough to rest at room temperature until it rises and collapses (or flattens on top), approximately 2 hours.

4. The dough can be used immediately after its initial rise, though it is easier to handle when cold. Refrigerate it in a lidded (not airtight) container and use over the next 7 days. The flavor will be best if you wait for at least 24 hours of refrigeration.

5. **On baking day,** dust the surface of the refrigerated dough with flour and cut off a 1-pound (grapefruit-size) piece. Dust the piece with more flour and quickly shape it into a ball by stretching the surface of the dough around to the bottom on all four sides, rotating the ball a quarter-turn as you go.

6. Elongate the ball into a narrow oval. Allow the dough to rest, loosely covered with plastic wrap, on a pizza peel prepared with cornmeal or lined with parchment paper for 90 minutes (40 minutes if you're using fresh, unrefrigerated dough). Alternatively, you can rest the loaf on a silicone mat or a greased cookie sheet without using a pizza peel.

7. **Thirty minutes before baking time, preheat the oven to 450°F,** with a baking stone placed on the middle rack. Place an empty metal broiler tray on any other rack that won't interfere with the rising bread.

8. Just before baking, use a pastry brush to paint the top crust with water. Slash the loaf diagonally with ¼-inch-deep parallel cuts, using a serrated bread knife.

9. Slide the loaf directly onto the hot stone (or place the silicone mat or cookie sheet on the stone if you used one). Pour 1 cup of hot tap water into the broiler tray, and quickly close the oven door (see pages 27 and 28 for steam alternatives). Bake for about 30 minutes, until richly browned and firm. If you used parchment paper, a silicone mat, or a cookie sheet under the loaf, carefully remove it and bake it directly on the stone or an oven rack two-thirds of the way through baking. Smaller or larger loaves will require adjustments in resting and baking time.

10. Allow the loaf to cool on a rack before slicing and eating.

100% Whole Grain Brown Rice Bread (Get Rid of Those Leftovers!)

"I grew up on brown rice. When I cook with it today, I am transported straight back to Mullen Hill, the commune where I grew up in Vermont. Back then it was pure hippie fare, but today you find it everywhere, and for good reason—it's good for you, and it tastes great. The nutty flavor and chewy texture are so much richer and more complex than white rice."—Zoë

Makes enough dough for at least four 1-pound loaves. The recipe is easily doubled or halved.

5½ cups whole wheat flour
½ cup ground flaxseed
1½ tablespoons granulated yeast, or 2 packets (decrease to taste, page 15)
1 tablespoon kosher salt (increase or decrease to taste, page 17)
¼ cup vital wheat gluten
3½ cups lukewarm water
1 cup cooked brown rice

1. **Mixing and storing the dough:** Whisk together the flour, flaxseed, yeast, salt, and vital wheat gluten in a 5-quart bowl, or a lidded (not airtight) food container.

2. Combine the water and rice and mix into the dry ingredients without kneading, using a spoon, a 14-cup food processor (with dough attachment), or a heavy-duty stand mixer (with paddle). You might need to use wet hands to get the last bit of flour to incorporate if you're not using a machine.

3. Cover (not airtight), and allow the dough to rest at room temperature until it rises and collapses (or flattens on top), approximately 2 hours.

4. The dough can be used immediately after its initial rise, though it is easier to handle when cold. Refrigerate it in a lidded (not airtight) container and use over the next 10 days. The flavor will be best if you wait for at least 24 hours of refrigeration.

5. **On baking day,** dust the surface of the refrigerated dough with flour and cut off a 1-pound (grapefruit-size) piece. Dust the piece with more flour and quickly shape it into a ball by stretching the surface of the dough around to the bottom on all four sides, rotating the ball a quarter-turn as you go.

6. Elongate the ball into a narrow oval. Allow to rest, loosely covered with plastic wrap, on a pizza peel prepared with cornmeal or lined with parchment paper for 90 minutes (40 minutes if you're using fresh, unrefrigerated dough). Alternatively, you can rest the loaf on a silicone mat or a greased cookie sheet without using a pizza peel

7. **Thirty minutes before baking time, preheat the oven to 450°F,** with a baking stone placed on the middle rack. Place an empty metal broiler tray for water on any other rack that won't interfere with the rising bread.

8. Just before baking, use a pastry brush to paint the top with water. Slash the loaf with ¼-inch-deep parallel cuts, using a serrated bread knife.

9. Slide the loaf directly onto the hot stone (or place the silicone mat or cookie sheet on the stone if you used one). Pour 1 cup of hot tap water into the broiler tray, and quickly close the oven door (see pages 27 and 28 for steam alternatives). Bake for about 35 to 40 minutes, until richly browned and firm. If you used parchment paper, a silicone mat, or a cookie sheet under the loaf, carefully remove it and bake the loaf directly on the stone or an oven rack two-thirds of the way through baking. Smaller or larger loaves will require adjustments in resting and baking time.

10. Allow the bread to cool on a rack before slicing and eating.

Wild Rice Pilaf Bread

Wild rice is a North Woods staple, an ancient Native American crop that is still traditionally grown in paddies in Minnesota and Wisconsin, and sometimes gathered by hand. It is the gluten-free seed of a wild North American grass. Cultivated varieties available in supermarkets are a less expensive alternative to the wild product and work well in this recipe. A classic Minnesota side dish is a delicious pilaf made with wild rice, mushrooms and onions—that mixture inspired this bread.

WILD RICE is a great source of the minerals potassium and phosphorous and the B vitamins. **Mushrooms** are incredibly rich in **niacin,** but are also a great source of potassium, an essential mineral that may lower blood pressure. **Onions** are a good source of antioxidant flavonoids.

You must fully cook the wild rice according to its package directions before using it in the recipe, or you'll end up with rock-hard uncooked grains!

Makes enough dough for at least five 1-pound loaves. The recipe is easily doubled or halved.

2 medium onions, chopped coarsely
½ cup olive oil
1½ cups thinly sliced mushrooms
½ teaspoon dried thyme (or 1 teaspoon fresh)
4½ cups whole wheat flour
4 cups unbleached all-purpose flour
1½ tablespoons granulated yeast, or 2 packets (decrease to taste, page 15)
1 tablespoon kosher salt (increase or decrease to taste, page 17)
¼ cup vital wheat gluten
2 large eggs
3½ cups lukewarm water
1 cup cooked wild rice, drained, or with cooking liquid fully absorbed

1. **Preparing the vegetables:** In a skillet, sauté the onions in the olive oil over medium-high heat until lightly browned; add the mushrooms and thyme and continue until the mushrooms give off their liquid. Allow to cool.

2. **Mixing and storing the dough:** Whisk together the flours, yeast, salt, and vital wheat gluten in a 5-quart bowl, or a lidded (not airtight) food container.

3. Add the liquid ingredients, the onion/mushroom mixture, and the wild rice and mix without kneading, using a spoon, a 14-cup food processor (with dough attachment), or a heavy-duty stand mixer (with paddle). You might need to use wet hands to get the last bit of flour to incorporate if you're not using a machine.

4. Cover (not airtight), and allow the dough to rest at room temperature until it rises and collapses (or flattens on top), approximately 2 hours. The flavor will be best if you wait for at least 24 hours of refrigeration.

5. The dough can be used immediately after its initial rise, though it is easier to handle when cold. Refrigerate it in a lidded (not airtight) container and use over the next 5 days.

6. **On baking day,** dust the surface of the refrigerated dough with flour and cut off a 1-pound (grapefruit-size) piece. Dust the piece with more flour and quickly shape it into a ball by stretching the surface of the dough around to the bottom on all four sides, rotating the ball a quarter-turn as you go.

7. Elongate the ball into a narrow oval. Allow the loaf to rest, loosely covered with plastic wrap, on a pizza peel prepared with cornmeal or lined with parchment paper for 90 minutes (40 minutes if you're using fresh, unrefrigerated dough). Alternatively, you can rest the loaf on a silicone mat or a greased cookie sheet without using a pizza peel.

8. **Thirty minutes before baking time, preheat the oven to 450°F,** with a baking stone placed on the middle rack. Place an empty metal broiler tray on any other rack that won't interfere with the rising bread.

9. Just before baking, use a pastry brush to paint the top crust with water. Slash the loaf diagonally with ¼-inch-deep parallel cuts, using a serrated bread knife.

10. Slide the loaf directly onto the hot stone. Pour 1 cup of hot tap water into the broiler tray, and quickly close the oven door (see pages 27 and 28 for steam alternatives). Bake for about 35 minutes, until richly browned and firm. If you used parchment paper, a silicone mat, or a greased cookie sheet under the loaf, carefully remove it and bake it directly on the stone or an oven rack two-thirds of the way through baking. Smaller or larger loaves will require adjustments in resting and baking time.

11. Allow the bread to cool on a rack before slicing and eating.

100% Whole Grain Maple Oatmeal Bread

This version of our favorite oatmeal bread has the sweet flavor of maple and cinnamon together with the hearty warm comfort of wheat and oats. You will love it toasted with jam or with your favorite sandwich fillings.

Makes enough dough for at least two 2-pound loaves. The recipe is easily doubled or halved. Use any leftover dough to make muffins (page 199).

5 cups white whole wheat flour
2 cups old-fashioned rolled oats
½ cup wheat germ
1½ tablespoons granulated yeast, or 2 packets (decrease to taste, page 15)
1 tablespoon kosher salt (increase or decrease to taste, page 17)
¼ cup vital wheat gluten
1 teaspoon ground cinnamon
2½ cups lukewarm water
1 cup buttermilk
¾ cup maple syrup
¼ cup neutral-flavored oil
Egg wash (1 egg beaten with 1 tablespoon water) for brushing on the top crust
Raw sugar for sprinkling on top

1. **Mixing and storing the dough:** Whisk together the flour, oats, wheat germ, yeast, salt, vital wheat gluten, and cinnamon in a 5-quart bowl, or a lidded (not airtight) food container.

2. Add the liquid ingredients and mix without kneading, using a spoon, a 14-cup food processor (with dough attachment), or a heavy-duty stand mixer (with paddle). You might need to use wet hands to get the last bit of flour to incorporate if you're not using a machine.

3. Cover (not airtight), and allow the dough to rest at room temperature until it rises and collapses (or flattens on top), approximately 2 hours.

4. The dough can be used immediately after its initial rise, though it is easier to handle when cold. Refrigerate it in a lidded (not airtight) container and use over the next 7 days.

5. **On baking day,** lightly grease an 8½×4½-inch nonstick loaf pan. Dust the surface of the refrigerated dough with flour and cut off a 2-pound (cantaloupe-size) piece. Dust with more flour and quickly shape it into a ball by stretching the surface of the dough around to the bottom on all four sides, rotating the ball a quarter-turn as you go.

6. Elongate the ball into an oval and place it into the loaf pan; your goal is to fill the pan about three-quarters full. Cover loosely with plastic wrap. Allow the loaf to rest and rise for 1 hour 45 minutes (60 minutes if you're using fresh, unrefrigerated dough).

7. **Thirty minutes before baking time, preheat the oven to 375°F,** with a baking stone placed on the middle rack. The baking stone is not essential for loaf pan breads; if you omit it, the preheat can be as short as 5 minutes.

8. Just before baking, use a pastry brush to paint the top crust with egg wash, then sprinkle it with sugar.

9. Slide the loaf directly onto the hot stone or on a rack near the middle of the oven. Bake for about 45 to 50 minutes, until richly browned and firm.

10. Remove the bread from pan (see page 50) and allow to cool on a rack before slicing and eating.

Betsy's Seeded Oat Bread

This bread was developed for Betsy, whom we met on our Web site. She requested a hearty loaf full of tasty and nutritious seeds. We loved the idea and came up with a recipe. We figured there was no one better to test it than Betsy herself. We wanted to make sure it was just what she wanted. Together we fine-tuned it and came up with a fabulous bread packed with pumpkin, sunflower, sesame, and flaxseeds. These seeds are sometimes called "brain food" because of their high content of vitamin B (see Appendix, page 307, for more on the B vitamins). They are also an excellent source of omega-3 oils and protein. All that, combined with rolled oats and whole grains, makes this bread seriously delicious and seriously good for you.

> **SEEDS ARE NATURE'S PERFECT PACKAGING FOR VITAMINS AND HEALTHY OILS:** The oils in seeds are packed into the seed's skin, which protects them from spoilage. The oil is high in healthy monounsaturated and polyunsaturated fats.

Makes enough dough for at least four 1-pound loaves. The recipe is easily doubled or halved.

2 cups whole wheat flour

3 cups unbleached all-purpose flour

1½ cups old-fashioned rolled oats

2 tablespoons ground flaxseed

¾ cup pumpkin seeds, plus more for sprinkling on top crust

¾ cup sunflower seeds, plus more for sprinkling on top crust

¼ cup sesame seeds, plus more for sprinkling on top crust

1½ tablespoons granulated yeast, or 2 packets (decrease to taste, page 15)

1 tablespoon kosher salt (increase or decrease to taste, page 17)
¼ cup vital wheat gluten
3 cups lukewarm water
½ cup barley malt syrup, honey, or agave syrup
¼ cup neutral-flavored oil

1. **Mixing and storing the dough:** Whisk together the flours, rolled oats, seeds, yeast, salt, and vital wheat gluten in a 5-quart bowl, or a lidded (not airtight) food container.

2. Combine the liquid ingredients and mix them with the dry ingredients without kneading, using a spoon, a 14-cup food processor (with dough attachment), or a heavy-duty stand mixer (with paddle). You might need to use wet hands to get the last bit of flour to incorporate if you're not using a machine.

3. Cover (not airtight), and allow the dough to rest at room temperature until it rises and collapses (or flattens on top), approximately 2 hours.

4. The dough can be used immediately after its initial rise, though it is easier to handle when cold. Refrigerate it in a lidded (not airtight) container and use over the next 7 days. The flavor will be best if you wait for at least 24 hours of refrigeration.

5. **On baking day,** dust the surface of the refrigerated dough with flour and cut off a 1-pound (grapefruit-size) piece. Dust the piece with more flour and quickly shape it into a ball by stretching the surface of the dough around to the bottom on all four sides, rotating the ball a quarter-turn as you go.

6. Elongate the ball into a narrow oval. Allow the loaf to rest, covered loosely with plastic wrap, on a pizza peel prepared with cornmeal or lined with parchment paper for 90 minutes (40 minutes if you're using fresh, unrefrigerated dough). Alternatively, you can rest the loaf on a silicone mat or a greased cookie sheet without using a pizza peel.

7. **Thirty minutes before baking time, preheat the oven to 400°F**, with a baking stone placed on the middle rack. Place an empty metal broiler tray on any other rack that won't interfere with the rising bread.

8. Just before baking, use a pastry brush to paint the top crust with water. Sprinkle with the seeds and slash the loaf diagonally with ¼-inch-deep parallel cuts, using a serrated bread knife.

9. Slide the loaf directly onto the hot stone (or place the silicone mat or cookie sheet on the stone if you used one). Pour 1 cup of hot tap water into the broiler tray, and quickly close the oven door (see pages 27 and 28 for steam alternatives). Bake for about 40 minutes, until richly browned and firm. If you used parchment paper, a silicone mat, or a cookie sheet under the loaf, carefully remove it and bake the loaf directly on the stone or an oven rack two-thirds of the way through baking. Smaller or larger loaves will require adjustments in resting and baking time.

10. Allow the bread to cool on a rack before slicing and eating.

7

BREADS WITH HIDDEN FRUITS AND VEGETABLES

There's been a lot written lately about sneaking healthy fruits and vegetables into cooked foods to boost nutrients in kids' meals (and in our own). In this chapter, we fortify our breads with vegetables and fruits rich in phytochemicals (beneficial plant chemicals), vitamins, and antioxidants. The United States Department of Agriculture now recommends that adults consume nine half cup servings of fruits and vegetables every day. We have a friend who says that he cannot even name nine fruits and vegetables. He has a point. It's not easy to get that much fruit and vegetable every day, and it's especially challenging for children. Don't expect bread, or any single food, to meet all dietary requirements. Just remember that every little bit helps. Here are some recipes that give you one extra chance to get kids to eat healthier foods. And don't forget pizzas with healthy ingredients like Whole Grain Pizza with Roasted Red Peppers and Fontina (page 205), Zucchini Flatbread (page 208), or Pesto Pizza with Chicken (page 213). You can also try some unorthodox pizza crusts with some of the vegetable and fruit-enriched doughs in this chapter.

So make the most of the pretty colors, and let the kids help with their favorite recipes from this chapter. Who knows, in a few years, they may be the ones baking the daily bread. Your goal might be to get kids to eat their recommended nine servings, but often, the beautiful color will sell the kids on healthy food all by itself (red, green, blue; you'll see).

Tabbouleh Bread with Parsley, Garlic, and Bulgur

People don't usually think of parsley as a vegetable, because it's almost always used as a garnish. But the herb's bright flavor works beautifully with wheat; we got the idea by eating lots of Turkish tabbouleh salad one summer—the dominant flavors in tabbouleh are bulgur wheat, garlic, parsley, and lemon zest.

Makes enough dough for at least four 1-pound loaves. The recipe is easily doubled or halved.

3 tablespoons olive oil

2 medium garlic cloves, chopped fine

5½ cups unbleached all-purpose flour

1 cup whole wheat flour

1½ tablespoons granulated yeast, or 2 packets (decrease to taste, page 15)

1 tablespoon kosher salt (increase or decrease to taste, page 17)

½ cup whole grain bulgur, soaked at least 2 hours (or overnight) in 1 cup water (will make 2 cups of bulgur—do not drain if liquid isn't completely absorbed)

1 bunch parsley, tough stems removed, chopped (about 1½ cups loosely packed)

2 teaspoons lemon zest (or more, to taste)

3 cups lukewarm water

1. Heat the olive oil over medium heat in a heavy skillet large enough to hold the parsley comfortably. Sauté the garlic until fragrant and then add the parsley; continue to sauté for approximately 5 minutes.

2. **Mixing and storing the dough:** Whisk together the flours, yeast, and salt in a 5-quart bowl, or a lidded (not airtight) food container.

3. Combine the sautéed parsley, bulgur, zest, and water and mix them with the dry ingredients without kneading, using a spoon, a 14-cup food processor (with dough attachment), or a heavy-duty stand mixer (with paddle). You

might need to use wet hands to get the last bit of flour to incorporate if you're not using a machine.

4. Cover (not airtight), and allow the dough to rest at room temperature until it rises and collapses (or flattens on top), approximately 2 hours.

5. The dough can be used immediately after its initial rise, though it is easier to handle when cold. Refrigerate it in a lidded (not airtight) container and use over the next 10 days. The flavor will be best if you wait for at least 24 hours of refrigeration.

6. **On baking day,** dust the surface of the refrigerated dough with flour and cut off a 1-pound (grapefruit-size) piece. Dust the piece with more flour and quickly shape it into a ball by stretching the surface of the dough around to the bottom on all four sides, rotating the ball a quarter-turn as you go.

7. Elongate the ball into a narrow oval. Allow to the loaf to rest, loosely covered with plastic wrap, on a pizza peel prepared with cornmeal or lined with parchment paper for 90 minutes (40 minutes if you're using fresh, unrefrigerated dough). Alternatively, you can rest the loaf on a silicone mat or greased cookie sheet without using a pizza peel.

8. **Thirty minutes before baking time, preheat the oven to 450°F,** with a baking stone placed on the middle rack. Place an empty metal broiler tray on any other rack that won't interfere with the rising bread.

9. Just before baking, use a pastry brush to paint the top crust with water. Slash the loaf diagonally with ¼-inch-deep parallel cuts, using a serrated bread knife.

10. Slide the loaf directly onto the hot stone (or place the silicone mat or cookie sheet on the stone if you used one). Pour 1 cup of hot tap water into the broiler tray, and quickly close the oven door (see pages 27 and 28 for steam

alternatives). Bake for about 30 minutes, until richly browned and firm. If you used parchment paper, a silicone mat, or a cookie sheet under the loaf, carefully remove it and bake the loaf directly on the stone or an oven rack two-thirds of the way through baking. Smaller or larger loaves will require adjustments in resting and baking time.

11. Allow the bread to cool on a rack before slicing and eating.

Garlic-Studded Baguette

"This is the grown-up, sophisticated version of the garlic bread from my childhood, the one that came wrapped in foil and dripping with butter and garlic salt. Don't get me wrong, as a ten-year-old I could have eaten an entire loaf, but my tastes have changed and now I prefer the flavor of pure unadulterated roasted garlic. In this recipe we bake the raw garlic right on top of the loaf. Once the baguette is baked and crusty, the garlic will be mellow and soft enough to spread on the slices."—Zoë

This recipe also works beautifully with cherry tomatoes pressed into the top of the loaf. Their sweet roasted flesh is also wonderful on the warm sliced bread (see the color insert).

Makes one 16-inch baguette

Use any of these refrigerated pre-mixed doughs: Master Recipe (page 53), 100%
   Whole Wheat Bread with Olive Oil (page 81), or other non-enriched dough
½ pound (orange-size portion) of any pre-mixed dough listed above
4 garlic cloves cut in half (or 6 cherry tomatoes)
Egg white wash (1 egg white beaten with 1 teaspoon water)

1. **Thirty minutes before baking time, preheat the oven to 450°F,** with a baking stone placed on the middle rack. Place an empty metal broiler tray on any other rack that won't interfere with the rising bread.

2. Dust the surface of the refrigerated dough with flour and quickly shape it into a ball by stretching the surface of the dough around to the bottom on all four sides, rotating the ball a quarter-turn as you go.

3. Gently stretch the dough into an oval. Fold the dough in thirds, like a letter. Bring in one side and gently press it into the center (see page 69).

4. Bring up the other side and pinch the seam closed. This will help you to get an evenly shaped baguette and a tapered end.

5. Stretch the dough very gently into a log, working the dough until you have a nice thin baguette. Don't compress the air out of the dough. If it resists pulling, let it rest for a moment to relax the gluten, then come back and continue to stretch. Don't fight the dough. The final width for a baguette should be about 1½ inches.

6. Allow the loaf to rest, loosely covered with plastic wrap, on a pizza peel prepared with cornmeal or lined with parchment paper, for 40 minutes (or just 20 minutes if you're using fresh, unrefrigerated dough). Alternatively, you can rest the loaf on a silicone mat or a perforated baguette pan (see Equipment, page 31) without using a pizza peel. Just before baking, use a pastry brush to paint the top crust with egg white wash. Then use the handle of a wooden spoon to gently make an indentation along the length of the baguette, pressing about halfway through the dough to create a trench. Press the garlic (or cherry tomatoes) into the trench, evenly spacing them along the baguette. Be sure to really press them in so they don't pop out when baking.

7. Slide the loaf directly onto the hot stone (or place the silicone mat or baguette pan on the stone if you used one). Pour 1 cup of hot tap water into the broiler tray, and quickly close the oven door (see pages 27 and 28 for steam alternatives). Bake for about 25 minutes, or until richly browned and firm. If you used parchment paper, a silicone mat, or a baguette pan under the loaf, carefully remove it and bake the loaf directly on the stone or an oven rack two-thirds of the way through baking.

8. Allow the bread to cool on a rack before slicing and eating. Spread the now-roasted garlic on the sliced bread.

Carrot Bread

We adore carrot cake, so why not put all that good stuff into a bread? We like ours packed with carrots, coconut, dried fruit, cinnamon, and a touch of brown sugar. It is not only unbelievably tasty, but it is also gorgeous and the carrots are high in vitamin A. Try this bread toasted with the cream cheese icing from the cinnamon crescent rolls (page 294) or just eat a slice with a nice sharp cheddar cheese for a great contrast.

Makes enough dough for at least two 2-pound loaves. The recipe is easily doubled or halved.

WHAT'S UP, DOC? CARROTS are loaded with vitamin A and beta-carotene. Beta-carotene is the orange pigment that gives carrots and this bread their vibrant color (the body converts beta-carotene into a number of active forms of vitamin A).

Vitamin A is crucial for normal vision, healthy skin, growth in children, and normal reproductive function in both women and men.

3 cups whole wheat flour
3 cups unbleached all-purpose flour
½ cup wheat germ
1 cup finely shredded coconut (both sweetened and unsweetened work well)
2 teaspoons ground cinnamon
½ cup brown sugar
1½ tablespoons granulated yeast, or 2 packets (decrease to taste, page 15)
1 tablespoon kosher salt (increase or decrease to taste, page 17)
¼ cup vital wheat gluten
3½ cups lukewarm water
2 cups well-packed, finely grated carrots, approximately 4 carrots (11 ounces)
½ cup chopped dried fruit (dried pineapple, dried currants, raisins)
½ cup chopped walnuts (optional)
Egg wash (1 egg beaten with 1 tablespoon water) for painting the top crust
Raw sugar for sprinkling on top crust

1. **Mixing and storing the dough:** Whisk together the flours, wheat germ, coconut, cinnamon, brown sugar, yeast, salt, and vital wheat gluten in a 5-quart bowl, or a lidded (not airtight) food container.

2. Add the water, carrots, dried fruit, and walnuts (if you're a nut-lover) and mix without kneading, using a spoon, a 14-cup food processor (with dough attachment), or a heavy-duty stand mixer (with paddle). You might need to use wet hands to get the last bit of flour to incorporate if you're not using a machine.

3. Cover (not airtight), and allow the dough to rest at room temperature until it rises and collapses (or flattens on top), approximately 2 hours.

4. The dough can be used immediately after its initial rise, though it is easier to handle when cold. Refrigerate it in a lidded (not airtight) container and use over the next 5 days.

5. **On baking day,** lightly grease an 8½×4½-inch nonstick loaf pan. Dust the surface of the refrigerated dough with flour and cut off a 2-pound (cantaloupe-size) piece. Dust the piece with more flour and quickly shape it into a ball by stretching the surface of the dough around to the bottom on all four sides, rotating the ball a quarter-turn as you go.

6. Elongate the ball into an oval and place it in the loaf pan; your goal is to fill the pan about three-quarters full. Allow the loaf to rest, loosely covered with plastic wrap, for 1 hour 45 minutes (60 minutes if you're using fresh, unrefrigerated dough).

7. **Thirty minutes before baking time, preheat the oven to 375°F,** with a baking stone placed on the middle rack. The baking stone is not essential for loaf pan breads; if you omit it, the preheat can be as short as 5 minutes.

8. Just before baking, use a pastry brush to paint the top crust with egg wash, then sprinkle it with sugar.

9. Slide the loaf directly onto the hot stone or on a rack near the middle of the oven. Bake for about 45 to 50 minutes, until richly browned and firm.

10. Remove the bread from the pan (see page 50) and allow it to cool on a rack before slicing and eating.

Avocado-Guacamole Bread

Bite into our avocado bread for a smoky sensation. Try it with a bowl of hot chili in the wintertime and you'll forget about the cold.

Makes enough dough for at least four 1-pound loaves. The recipe is easily doubled or halved.

4 cups whole wheat flour (or white whole wheat flour)
3¼ cups unbleached all-purpose flour
1½ tablespoons granulated yeast, or 2 packets, (decrease to taste, page 15)
1½ tablespoons kosher salt (increase or decrease to taste, page 17)
¼ cup vital wheat gluten
3½ cups lukewarm water
1 garlic clove, finely minced
1 ripe medium tomato, cubed, including liquid and seeds
1 ripe avocado, pitted, peeled, and mashed

AVOCADO AND TOMATO IN BREAD: Though avocados are high in calories and fat, the fat is mostly monounsaturated and can improve your cholesterol profile. Just be sure to eat avocados in moderation.

Tomatoes are super-low in calories but rich in **lycopene**, which may offer some protection against certain cancers. Lycopene is a pigment responsible for the beautiful reddish color in tomatoes, guava, papaya, pink grapefruit, and watermelon. It's a potent antioxidant (see page 4). Tomatoes are also rich in iron.

1. **Mixing and storing the dough:** Whisk together the flours, yeast, salt, and vital wheat gluten in a 5-quart bowl, or a lidded (not airtight) food container.

2. Combine the water, garlic, tomato, and avocado, and mix them with the dry ingredients without kneading, using a spoon, a 14-cup food processor (with dough attachment), or a heavy-duty stand mixer (with paddle). You might need to use wet hands to get the last bit of flour to incorporate if you're not using a machine.

3. Cover (not airtight), and allow the dough to rest at room temperature until it rises and collapses (or flattens on top), approximately 2 hours.

4. The dough can be used immediately after its initial rise, though it is easier to handle when cold. Refrigerate it in a lidded (not airtight) container and use over the next 5 days.

5. **On baking day,** dust the surface of the refrigerated dough with flour and cut off a 1 pound (grapefruit-size) piece. Dust the piece with more flour and quickly shape it into a ball by stretching the surface of the dough around to the bottom on all four sides, rotating the ball a quarter-turn as you go.

6. Elongate the ball into a narrow oval. Allow the loaf to rest, loosely covered with plastic wrap, on a pizza peel prepared with cornmeal or lined with parchment paper for 90 minutes (40 minutes if you're using fresh, unrefrigerated dough). Alternatively, you can rest the loaf on a silicone mat or a greased cookie sheet without using a pizza peel.

7. **Thirty minutes before baking time, preheat the oven to 450°F,** with a baking stone placed on the middle rack. Place an empty metal broiler tray on any other rack that won't interfere with the rising bread.

8. Just before baking, use a pastry brush to paint the top crust with water. Slash the loaf diagonally with ¼-inch-deep parallel cuts, using a serrated bread knife.

9. Slide the loaf directly onto the hot stone (or place the silicone mat or cookie sheet on the stone if you used one). Pour 1 cup of hot tap water into the broiler tray, and quickly close the oven door (see pages 27 and 28 for steam alternatives). Bake for about 35 minutes, until richly browned and firm. If you used parchment paper, a silicone mat, or a cookie sheet under the loaf, carefully remove it and bake the loaf directly on the stone or an oven rack two-thirds of the way through baking. Smaller or larger loaves will require adjustments in resting and baking time.

10. Allow the bread to cool on a rack before slicing and eating.

Pain au Potiron (Peppery Pumpkin and Olive Oil Loaf)

Although pumpkin is generally thought of as quintessentially American (Native Americans were the first to cultivate it), there's actually a marvelous French Provençal tradition of bread spiked with peppered pumpkin. Dice the raw pumpkin small so that it will cook through during the baking time. You can substitute raw squash or sweet potato for the pumpkin (see photo, color insert).

∾

PUMPKINS are low in calories and high in fiber and vitamin A.

Makes enough dough for at least four 1-pound loaves. The recipe is easily doubled or halved.

3¾ cups whole wheat flour
3½ cups unbleached all-purpose flour
1½ tablespoons granulated yeast, or 2 packets (decrease to taste, page 15)
1 tablespoon kosher salt (increase or decrease to taste, page 17)
2 tablespoons vital wheat gluten
1¼ cups peeled, ¼-inch-dice raw pie pumpkin (sometimes called "sugar" pumpkin), or substitute squash or sweet potato
Freshly ground black pepper
3½ cups lukewarm water
¼ cup olive oil

1. **Mixing and storing the dough:** Whisk together the flours, yeast, salt, and vital wheat gluten in a 5-quart bowl, or a lidded (not airtight) food container.

2. Generously season the pumpkin, squash, or sweet potato with the pepper.

3. Add the liquid ingredients and pumpkin to the dry ingredients and mix without kneading, using a spoon, a 14-cup food processor (with dough attachment), or a heavy-duty stand mixer (with paddle). You might need to

use wet hands to get the last bit of flour to incorporate if you're not using a machine.

4. Cover (not airtight), and allow the dough to rest at room temperature until it rises and collapses (or flattens on top), approximately 2 hours.

5. The dough can be used immediately after its initial rise, though it is easier to handle when cold. Refrigerate it in a lidded (not airtight) container and use over the next 10 days. The flavor will be best if you wait for at least 24 hours of refrigeration.

6. **On baking day,** dust the surface of the refrigerated dough with flour and cut off a 1-pound (grapefruit-size) piece. Dust with more flour and quickly shape it into a ball by stretching the surface of the dough around to the bottom on all four sides, rotating the ball a quarter-turn as you go.

7. Elongate the ball into a narrow oval. Allow the loaf to rest, loosely covered with plastic wrap, on a pizza peel prepared with cornmeal or lined with parchment paper for 90 minutes (40 minutes if you're using fresh, unrefrigerated dough). Alternatively, you can rest the loaf on a silicone mat or a greased cookie sheet without using a pizza peel.

8. **Thirty minutes before baking time, preheat the oven to 450°F,** with a baking stone placed on the middle rack. Place an empty metal broiler tray on any other rack that won't interfere with the rising bread.

9. Just before baking, use a pastry brush to paint the top crust with water. Slash the loaf diagonally with ¼-inch-deep parallel cuts, using a serrated bread knife.

10. Slide the loaf directly onto the hot stone (or place the silicone mat or cookie sheet on the stone if you used one). Pour 1 cup of hot tap water into the broiler tray, and quickly close the oven door (see pages 27 and 28 for steam alternatives). Bake for about 30 minutes, until richly browned and firm. If

you used parchment paper, a silicone mat, or a cookie sheet under the loaf, carefully remove it and bake the loaf directly on the stone or an oven rack two-thirds of the way through baking. Smaller or larger loaves will require adjustments in resting and baking time.

11. Allow the bread to cool on a rack before slicing and eating.

Provençal Fisherman's Bread (Pain Bouillabaisse)

Bouillabaisse is the delicious fish soup of Provence, France. There's an old Provençal tradition of taking the aromatic flavors from this soup (*herbes de Provence*, saffron, and fennel) and putting them into a bread (leave out the fish). Fresh fennel provides a subtle licorice flavor and sneaks in yet another vegetable. This bread is fantastic for serving with Provençal appetizers and condiments like *aïoli*, Niçoise olives, and of course, *bouillabaisse*.

"Years ago, my wife, Laura, and I bicycled through Provence, the lush and hilly countryside of southern France bordering the Mediterranean. The weather can be extreme, and on one rainy and blustery day, we rode into the medieval town of Uzès, completely soaked, exhausted, and most important, starving. An old façade read "Hostellerie Provençale Restaurant," so we parked our bicycles under an ancient embankment and walked inside for a well-deserved lunch in a charming, unassuming place where the warmth of the hostess made all the difference. Madame's bouillabaisse *was fantastic, and warmed us to the core."*—Jeff

Makes enough dough for at least four 1-pound loaves. The recipe is easily doubled or halved.

3¾ cups whole wheat flour

3½ cups unbleached all-purpose flour

1½ teaspoons *herbes de Provence* (use a prepared herb mix or make your own with an equal mixture of dried marjoram, thyme, rosemary, basil, and savory, plus a little lavender if it's available)

½ teaspoon saffron powder

1½ tablespoons granulated yeast, or 2 packets (decrease to taste, page 15)

USING AUTHENTIC SAFFRON THREADS: Our recipe calls for the widely available and affordable saffron powder, but authentic saffron threads produce a more delicate and delicious flavor. To use it, omit the powder, crumble enough threads to measure ⅛ teaspoon, and simmer gently in the 3½ cups of water for 10 minutes. Remove from heat, re-measure the liquid, and add water if needed to bring back the volume to 3½ cups. Cool to lukewarm before using in the recipe.

1 tablespoon kosher salt (increase or decrease to taste, page 17)
¼ cup vital wheat gluten
2 to 4 garlic cloves, minced (to taste)
1 cup thinly sliced fennel bulb, cut into 1-inch pieces, white parts only
3½ cups lukewarm water
½ cup olive oil

1. **Mixing and storing the dough:** Whisk together the flours, *herbes de Provence*, saffron powder, yeast, salt, and vital wheat gluten in a 5-quart bowl, or a lidded (not airtight) food container.

2. Add the garlic, fennel, and the liquid ingredients and mix without kneading, using a spoon, a 14-cup food processor (with dough attachment), or a heavy-duty stand mixer (with paddle). You might need to use wet hands to get the last bit of flour to incorporate if you're not using a machine.

3. Cover (not airtight), and allow the dough to rest at room temperature until it rises and collapses (or flattens on top), approximately 2 hours.

4. The dough can be used immediately after its initial rise, though it is easier to handle when cold. Refrigerate it in a lidded (not airtight) container and use over the next 10 days. The flavor will be best if you wait for at least 24 hours of refrigeration.

5. **On baking day,** dust the surface of the refrigerated dough with flour and cut off a 1-pound (grapefruit-size) piece. Dust with more flour and quickly shape it into a ball by stretching the surface of the dough around to the bottom on all four sides, rotating the ball a quarter-turn as you go.

6. Elongate the ball into a narrow oval. Allow the loaf to rest, loosely covered with plastic wrap, on a pizza peel prepared with cornmeal or lined with parchment paper for 90 minutes (40 minutes if you're using fresh, unrefrigerated dough). Alternatively, you can rest the loaf on a silicone mat or a greased cookie sheet without using a pizza peel.

7. **Thirty minutes before baking time, preheat the oven to 450°F,** with a baking stone placed on the middle rack. Place an empty metal broiler tray on any other rack that won't interfere with the rising bread.

8. Just before baking, use a pastry brush to paint the top crust with water. Slash the loaf diagonally with ¼-inch-deep parallel cuts, using a serrated bread knife.

9. Slide the loaf directly onto the hot stone (or place the silicone mat or cookie sheet on the stone if you used one). Pour 1 cup of hot tap water into the broiler tray, and quickly close the oven door (see pages 27 and 28 for steam alternatives). Bake for about 30 minutes, until richly browned and firm. If you used parchment paper, a silicone mat, or a cookie sheet under the loaf, carefully remove it and bake the loaf directly on the stone or an oven rack two-thirds of the way through baking. Smaller or larger loaves will require adjustments in resting and baking time.

10. Allow the bread to cool on a rack before slicing and eating.

Lentil Curry Bread

Lentils are a great source of fiber and vitamins, but some kids won't eat curried lentil soup. Here's a great way to get them to try the flavor—we haven't found a kid yet who won't eat this. It's one of our all-time favorites, and lentils are loaded with protein, folic acid, and B vitamins.

Makes enough dough for at least four 1-pound loaves. The recipe is easily doubled or halved.

The Lentils
4¼ cups water
1 cup dried lentils
1 tablespoon curry powder

The Dough
2 cups whole wheat flour
5½ cups unbleached all-purpose flour
1½ tablespoons granulated yeast, or 2 packets (decrease to taste, page 15)
1 tablespoon kosher salt (increase or decrease to taste, page 17)
3 tablespoons vital wheat gluten
2 cups lukewarm water
¼ cup neutral-flavored oil

1. **Preparing the lentils:** Place the water and lentils into a medium-size saucepan, bring to a boil, then cover and reduce to a low simmer for approximately 30 to 60 minutes, or until the lentils are soft. Add small amounts of water to the lentils to keep them just covered during cooking. Remove from heat and allow to cool slightly.

2. Without draining the liquid, pour the mixture into a blender, add the curry powder, and process until smooth.

3. **Mixing and storing the dough:** Whisk together the flours, yeast, salt, and vital wheat gluten in a 5-quart bowl, or a lidded (not airtight) food container.

4. Add the liquid ingredients and the lentils and mix without kneading, using a spoon, a 14-cup food processor (with dough attachment), or a heavy-duty stand mixer (with paddle). You might need to use wet hands to get the last bit of flour to incorporate if you're not using a machine.

5. Cover (not airtight), and allow the dough to rest at room temperature until it rises and collapses (or flattens on top), approximately 2 hours.

6. The dough can be used immediately after its initial rise, though it is easier to handle when cold. Refrigerate it in a lidded (not airtight) container and use over the next 7 days. As the dough ages, its surface might develop a yellow-green color from the curried lentils. This is normal.

7. **On baking day,** dust the surface of the refrigerated dough with flour and cut off a 1-pound (grapefruit-size) piece. Dust the piece with more flour and quickly shape it into a ball by stretching the surface of the dough around to the bottom on all four sides, rotating the ball a quarter-turn as you go.

8. Elongate the ball into a narrow oval. Allow the loaf to rest, loosely covered with plastic wrap, on a pizza peel prepared with cornmeal or lined with parchment paper for 90 minutes (40 minutes if you're using fresh, unrefrigerated dough). Alternatively, you can rest the loaf on a silicone mat or a greased cookie sheet without using a pizza peel.

8. **Thirty minutes before baking time, preheat the oven to 450°F,** with a baking stone placed on the middle rack. Place an empty metal broiler tray on any other rack that won't interfere with the rising bread.

9. Just before baking, use a pastry brush to paint the top crust with water. Slash the loaf diagonally with ¼-inch-deep parallel cuts, using a serrated bread knife.

10. Slide the loaf directly onto the hot stone (or place the silicone mat or cookie sheet on the stone if you used one). Pour 1 cup of hot tap water into the broiler tray, and quickly close the oven door (see pages 27 and 28 for steam alternatives). Bake for about 30 minutes, until richly browned and firm. If you used parchment paper, a silicone mat, or a cookie sheet under the loaf, carefully remove it and bake the loaf directly on the stone or an oven rack two-thirds of the way through baking. Smaller or larger loaves will require adjustments in resting and baking time.

11. Allow the bread to cool on a rack before slicing and eating.

Mesquite Bread

"Zoë and I were privileged to teach at Barbara Fenzl's Les Gourmettes Cooking School in Phoenix. Barbara helped introduce Americans to great Southwestern cooking on her PBS television series Savor the Southwest. *The school is in her lovely home, and we were captivated by the photographs on her kitchen wall. The first ones our eyes fell on were of Julia Child and Jacques Pépin teaching in her kitchen—a bit intimidating, but Barbara immediately put us at ease by digging in and helping us with the prep work.*

"As we left, Barbara pressed a sample of mesquite flour into my hands, and suggested that I might like it in bread. I enhanced the mesquite flavor with a few other Southwestern and Mexican ingredients: agave syrup, hot serrano peppers, masa flour, and cilantro. Flavor aside, hot peppers may have potent health effects, and corn masa is a rich nutrient source (see sidebar). For a great Southwestern flatbread, try this dough in Southwestern Focaccia with Roasted Corn and Goat Cheese (page 220)."— Jeff

Makes enough dough for at least four 1-pound loaves. The recipe is easily doubled or halved.

1 cup mesquite flour (sometimes sold as mesquite powder or meal)
3½ cups unbleached all-purpose flour

HOT PEPPERS CONTAIN CAPSAICIN, A POTENT PHYTOCHEMICAL (BENEFICIAL PLANT CHEMICAL): Capsaicin is what makes spicy peppers hot and it also may decrease the likelihood of blood clots, heart attack, and stroke.

Corn masa, also called *masa harina*, is a Latin American corn product treated with alkali, which produces the distinctive flavor in Latin American dishes like tamales and tortillas; it also releases niacin from nondigestible parts of the corn. Corn, whether alkali-treated or not, is an excellent source of lutein, an antioxidant that may prevent some cancers and some vision problems. If you use mesquite dough for the Southwestern *Focaccia* with Roasted Corn and Goat Cheese (page 220) you'll be getting a good helping of both kinds of corn.

2¼ cups whole wheat flour

½ cup corn masa

1½ tablespoons granulated yeast, or 2 packets (decrease to taste, page 15)

1 tablespoon kosher salt (increase or decrease to taste, page 17)

¼ cup vital wheat gluten

3½ cups lukewarm water

¼ cup agave syrup

2 serrano peppers, finely minced after removing the seeds (use rubber gloves for handling cut hot peppers and substitute jalapeños if you want less heat)

½ cup chopped cilantro

1. **Mixing and storing the dough:** Whisk together the flours, corn masa, yeast, salt, and vital wheat gluten in a 5-quart bowl, or a lidded (not airtight) food container.

2. Add the liquid ingredients, peppers, and cilantro and mix without kneading, using a spoon, 14-cup food processor (with dough attachment), or a heavy-duty stand mixer (with paddle). You might need to use wet hands to get the last bit of flour to incorporate if you're not using a machine.

3. Cover (not airtight), and allow the dough to rest at room temperature until it rises and collapses (or flattens on top), approximately 2 hours.

4. The dough can be used immediately after its initial rise, though it is easier to handle when cold. Refrigerate it in a lidded (not airtight) container and use over the next 7 days. The flavor will be best if you wait for at least 24 hours of refrigeration.

5. **On baking day,** dust the surface of the refrigerated dough with flour and cut off a 1-pound (grapefruit-size) piece. Dust with more flour and quickly shape it into a ball by stretching the surface of the dough around to the bottom on all four sides, rotating the ball a quarter-turn as you go.

6. Elongate the ball into a narrow oval. Allow the loaf to rest, loosely covered

with plastic wrap, on a pizza peel prepared with corn masa or lined with parchment paper for 90 minutes (40 minutes if you're using fresh, unrefrigerated dough). Alternatively, you can rest the loaf on a silicone mat or a greased cookie sheet without using a pizza peel.

7. **Thirty minutes before baking time, preheat the oven to 400°F,** with a baking stone placed on the middle rack. Place an empty metal broiler tray on any other rack that won't interfere with the rising bread.

8. Just before baking, use a pastry brush to paint the top crust with water. Slash the loaf diagonally with ¼-inch-deep parallel cuts, using a serrated bread knife.

9. Slide the loaf directly onto the hot stone (or place the silicone mat or cookie sheet on the stone if you used one). Pour 1 cup of hot tap water into the broiler tray, and quickly close the oven door (see pages 27 and 28 for steam alternatives). Bake for about 35 to 40 minutes, until richly browned and firm. If you used parchment paper, a silicone mat, or a cookie sheet under the loaf, carefully remove it and bake the loaf directly on the stone or an oven rack two-thirds of the way through baking. Smaller or larger loaves will require adjustments in resting and baking time.

10. Allow the bread to cool on a rack before slicing and eating.

Four-Leaf Clover Broccoli and Cheddar Buns

"My seven-year-old son will eat just about anything. Sushi or mussels in white wine sauce are among his favorites—he'll even do liver pâté and recently had escargots. But he won't touch spinach or broccoli. I suppose I could let it go, considering what he is willing to eat, but broccoli is so good for him. It contains vitamins like A, C, and K that I want him to have, not to mention all the fiber. It is good for your eyes, bones, and immune system and even helps to prevent some forms of cancer. So it was very exciting when I made these cute green buns in the shape of four-leaf clovers, packed with broccoli and sprinkled with cheddar cheese—he loved them."—Zoë

Makes at least three batches of 8 buns (24 total)

15 ounces (about 5 cups) raw broccoli florets
1½ cups water for cooking the broccoli
3 cups whole wheat flour
4 cups unbleached all-purpose flour
1½ tablespoons granulated yeast, or 2 packets (decrease to taste, page 15)
1 tablespoon kosher salt (increase or decrease to taste, page 17)
¼ cup vital wheat gluten
1¾ cups lukewarm water
Neutral-flavored oil for greasing the muffin tin
1 cup shredded cheddar cheese for sprinkling on the buns, per batch

1. **Cooking the broccoli**: In a medium-size saucepan, bring water to a boil, add the broccoli, and cook on medium-high heat, with the lid on, for 3 to 4 minutes. It is very important not to overcook the broccoli or it will taste bitter. It should be bright green. Remove from the stove and place the broccoli and the cooking water into a blender to puree. Puree as finely as you can, but don't expect it to be perfectly smooth. This will yield 3 cups of broccoli puree. Set aside to cool slightly.

2. **Mixing and storing the dough:** Whisk together the flours, yeast, salt, and vital wheat gluten in a 5-quart bowl, or in a lidded (not airtight) food container.

3. Add the 1¾ cups lukewarm water and broccoli puree and mix without kneading, using a spoon, a 14-cup food processor (with dough attachment), or a heavy-duty stand mixer (with paddle). You might need to use wet hands to get the last bit of flour to incorporate if you're not using a machine.

4. Cover (not airtight), and allow the dough to rest at room temperature until it rises and collapses (or flattens on top), approximately 2 hours.

5. The dough can be used immediately after its initial rise, although it is easier to handle when cold. Refrigerate it in a non-airtight lidded container and use over the next 7 days.

6. **On baking day,** grease a muffin pan. Dust the surface of the refrigerated dough with flour and cut off a 1½-pound (cantaloupe-size) piece. Dust the piece with more flour and quickly shape it into a loose ball by stretching the surface of the dough around to the bottom on all four sides, rotating the ball a quarter-turn as you go.

7. **To form the rolls,** divide the ball into 8 roughly equal portions (each about the size of a plum). Cut each of the plum-size pieces into 4 smaller pieces. Shape each one into a smooth small ball. Put the 4 rounds together to form the clover leaf and place in the cups of the muffin tin. Allow to rest, loosely covered with plastic wrap, for 40 minutes (20 minutes if you're using fresh, unrefrigerated dough).

8. **Thirty minutes before baking time, preheat the oven to 450°F**, with a baking stone placed on the middle rack. Place an empty metal broiler tray on any other rack that won't interfere with the rising buns.

9. Just before baking, sprinkle the buns with the cheddar cheese, being careful not to get it on the pan.

10. Slide the muffin tin directly onto the hot stone. Pour 1 cup of hot tap water into the broiler tray, and quickly close the oven door (see pages 27 and 28 for steam alternatives). Bake for about 20 to 25 minutes, until richly browned and firm. The cheese will be melted and a bit caramelized.

11. Remove the buns from the pan and allow them to cool slightly before eating.

Sweet Potato and Spelt Bread

Aside from sweet potato's marvelous nutritional content, it is sweet, delicious, and adds gorgeous bright orange flecks throughout this loaf. Working on this bread was our wonderful introduction to spelt flour, an ancient grain whose flavor and texture seem to improve everything we tried it in.

Makes enough dough for at least four 1-pound loaves. The recipe is easily doubled or halved. Any leftover dough can be made into buns (see page 180).

4 cups spelt flour

2 cups unbleached all-purpose flour

1½ tablespoons granulated yeast, or 2 packets (decrease to taste, page 15)

1 tablespoon kosher salt (increase or decrease to taste, page 17)

¼ cup vital wheat gluten

3¼ cups lukewarm water

1 large sweet potato, skin on, cleaned and coarsely shredded (3½ cups, packed)

ဢ

LEAVE THE SKIN ON YOUR SWEET POTATOES: Leaving the skin on ratchets up the fiber in this recipe, but even the soft flesh of the sweet potato is loaded with nutrition. It's a striking source of magnesium and potassium, plus vitamins A and E. Vitamin E is the powerful antioxidant vitamin that works with vitamin C in your diet to round up free radicals and rid them from your body.

1. **Mixing and storing the dough:** Whisk together the flours, yeast, salt, and vital wheat gluten in a 5-quart bowl, or a lidded (not airtight) food container.

2. Add the water and sweet potato and mix without kneading, using a spoon, a 14-cup food processor (with dough attachment), or a heavy-duty stand

mixer (with paddle). You might need to use wet hands to get the last bit of flour to incorporate if you're not using a machine.

3. Cover (not airtight), and allow the dough to rest at room temperature until it rises and collapses (or flattens on top), approximately 2 hours.

4. The dough can be used immediately after its initial rise, though it is easier to handle when cold. Refrigerate it in a lidded (not airtight) container and use over the next 7 days. The flavor will be best if you wait for at least 24 hours of refrigeration.

5. **On baking day,** dust the surface of the refrigerated dough with flour and cut off a 1-pound (grapefruit-size) piece. Dust with more flour and quickly shape it into a ball by stretching the surface of the dough around to the bottom on all four sides, rotating the ball a quarter-turn as you go.

6. Elongate the ball into a narrow oval. Allow the loaf to rest, loosely covered with plastic wrap, on a pizza peel prepared with cornmeal or lined with parchment for 90 minutes (40 minutes if you're using fresh, unrefrigerated dough). Alternatively, you can rest the loaf on a silicone mat or a greased cookie sheet without using a pizza peel.

7. **Thirty minutes before baking time, preheat the oven to 450°F,** with a baking stone placed on the middle rack. Place an empty metal broiler tray on any other rack that won't interfere with the rising bread.

8. Just before baking, use a pastry brush to paint the top crust with water. Slash the loaf diagonally with ¼-inch-deep parallel cuts, using a serrated bread knife.

9. Slide the loaf directly onto the hot stone (or place the silicone mat or cookie sheet on the stone if you used one). Pour 1 cup of hot tap water into the broiler tray, and quickly close the oven door (see pages 27 and 28 for steam

alternatives). Bake for about 30 minutes, until richly browned and firm. If you used parchment paper, a silicone mat, or a cookie sheet under the loaf, carefully remove it two-thirds of the way through baking and bake the loaf directly on the stone or an oven rack. Smaller or larger loaves will require adjustments in resting and baking time.

10. Allow the bread to cool on a rack before slicing and eating.

Red Beet Buns

These are beautiful bright buns, with a crimson crust and a crumb flecked with red. The sweetness of beets adds a wonderful flavor, and the color is glorious (see photo, color insert).

Makes enough dough for five batches of 8 buns (40 total)

BEETS: The root's deep red color comes from beta-cyanin, but this is more than a pretty face. The pigment may help prevent cell mutations that can cause cancer. They're also a rich source of folic acid.

2 cups white whole wheat flour
2 cups unbleached all-purpose flour
3 cups spelt flour
1½ tablespoons granulated yeast, or 2 packets (decrease to taste, page 15)
1 tablespoon kosher salt (increase or decrease to taste, page 17)
¼ cup vital wheat gluten
3¼ cups lukewarm water
3 cups finely shredded peeled raw beets
½ white onion, finely chopped

1. **Mixing and storing the dough:** Whisk together the flours, yeast, salt, and vital wheat gluten in a 5-quart bowl, or a lidded (not airtight) food container.

2. Add the water, beets, and onion and mix without kneading, using a spoon, a 14-cup food processor (with dough attachment), or a heavy-duty stand mixer (with paddle). You might need to use wet hands to get the last bit of flour to incorporate if you're not using a machine.

3. Cover (not airtight), and allow the dough to rest at room temperature until it rises and collapses (or flattens on top), approximately 2 hours.

4. The dough can be used immediately after its initial rise, though it is easier to handle when cold. Refrigerate it in a lidded (not airtight) container and use

over the next 5 days. The flavor will be best if you wait for at least 24 hours of refrigeration.

5. **On baking day,** dust the surface of the refrigerated dough with flour and cut off a 1-pound (grapefruit-size) piece. Dust the piece with more flour and quickly shape it into a ball by stretching the surface of the dough around to the bottom on all four sides, rotating the ball a quarter-turn as you go.

6. **To form the buns:** Divide the ball into 8 roughly equal portions (each about the size of a golf ball). Shape each one into a smooth ball. Allow them to rest, loosely covered with plastic wrap, on a cookie sheet lined with parchment paper for 40 minutes (20 minutes if you're using fresh, unrefrigerated dough). Alternatively, you can rest the buns on a silicone mat–lined cookie sheet or a greased cookie sheet.

7. **Thirty minutes before baking time, preheat the oven to 450°F,** with a baking stone placed on the middle rack. Place an empty metal broiler tray on any other shelf that won't interfere with the rising buns.

8. Just before baking, use a pastry brush to paint the top crusts with water.

9. Slide the cookie sheet directly onto the hot stone. Pour 1 cup of hot tap water into the broiler tray, and quickly close the oven door (see pages 27 and 28 for steam alternatives). Bake for about 20 minutes, until richly browned and firm.

10. Allow the buns to cool on a rack before eating.

Stuffed "Sandwich" Loaf

In our constant attempt to find things for children to bring to school for lunch, we developed a bread with the filling rolled right into the dough. Here are three of our favorite combinations—you should let your imagination run wild and come up with your own versions, to suit your taste.

Makes one 2-pound loaf

Use any lean or enriched dough to your liking
1 pound (grapefruit-size portion) of any pre-mixed dough listed above

The Roasted Vegetable and Chèvre Filling
1 bell pepper or 1 jarred roasted pepper
2 tablespoons olive oil
6 ounces portobello mushrooms, sliced ⅛ inch thick
Salt and freshly ground black pepper to taste
4 artichoke hearts, canned or jarred marinated, thinly sliced
6 ounces of *chèvre* (goat) cheese

1. **Preparing the vegetables**: If grilling your own pepper, cut the pepper into quarters and then flatten the pieces, making additional cuts as needed to flatten. Grill the pepper on a gas or charcoal grill, with the skin side closest to the heat source, or place it under the broiler. Check often and remove it when the skin is blackened, about 10 minutes or more, depending on the heat source.

2. Drop the roasted pieces into a bowl or pot and cover. The skin will loosen by steaming in its own heat and moisture for 10 minutes.

3. Gently hand-peel the pepper and discard the blackened skin; it's fine if some dark bits adhere to the pepper's flesh.

4. Heat the olive oil in a skillet over medium heat. Add the portobello mushrooms and sauté them until wilted. Add salt and pepper to taste. Set aside.

5. Lightly grease an 8½×4½-inch nonstick loaf pan. Dust the surface of the refrigerated dough with flour and cut off a 1-pound (grapefruit-size) piece. Dust the piece with more flour and quickly shape it into a ball by stretching the surface of the dough around to the bottom on all four sides, rotating the ball a quarter-turn as you go.

6. With a rolling pin, roll the dough out until it is a ¼-inch-thick rectangle. As you roll out the dough, use enough flour to prevent it from sticking to the work surface but not so much as to make the dough dry.

7. Spread the roasted pepper, sautéed mushroom mixture, artichoke hearts, and *chèvre* over the rolled-out dough. Leave a border all around the edge. Roll the dough into a log, starting at the short end. Using wet hands, crimp the ends shut and tuck them under. Place the log in the loaf pan and allow it to rest, loosely covered with plastic wrap, for 90 minutes (40 minutes if you're using fresh unrefrigerated dough).

8. **Thirty minutes before baking time, preheat the oven to 350°F,** with a baking stone placed on the middle rack. If you're not using a stone in the oven, a 5-minute preheat is adequate.

9. Just before baking, use a pastry brush to paint the top crust with water.

10. Slide the loaf directly onto the hot stone or on a rack near the middle of the oven. Bake for about 50 to 60 minutes, until deeply browned and firm. Smaller or larger loaves will require adjustments in resting and baking time.

11. Remove the bread from the pan (see page 50) and allow it to cool before slicing and eating.

VARIATIONS

Spinach, Feta, and Turkey Filling
2 cups fresh whole spinach leaves, loosely packed
4 ounces crumbled feta cheese
4 to 6 slices thinly sliced cooked turkey breast

Ham, Emmental Cheese, and Sautéed Cabbage Filling
2 tablespoons olive oil
2 cups cabbage, shredded
4 to 6 slices thinly sliced ham
6 ounces grated Emmental cheese
Salt and freshly ground black pepper to taste
2 tablespoons grainy Dijon mustard

To prepare the cabbage: Heat the olive oil in a skillet over medium heat. Add the cabbage and sauté it until wilted. Add salt and pepper to taste. Allow to cool slightly before rolling into the dough.

Turkish Pear Coffee Bread

This is a very unusual bread with some unlikely ingredients: pear puree and ground coffee (which turns out to have plenty of antioxidants, see the Chocolate Espresso Bread sidebar on page 301). We were dubious about ground coffee in a bread, but its slightly bitter and delicious flavor, combined with the juicy pears, sweet spices, and brown sugar add up to a bread even our kids love. There's not much caffeine in each slice—the entire four-loaf batch has the equivalent of two cups of coffee, but it can also be made with decaf.

Turkish Pear Coffee Bread has a tendency to spread sideways, so don't be surprised if your bread looks more flat than tall.

Makes enough dough for at least four 1-pound loaves. The recipe is easily doubled or halved. Any leftover dough can be made into buns (see page 180).

¼ cup whole wheat flour
6 cups unbleached all-purpose flour
4 teaspoons ground coffee beans (regular grind)
½ teaspoon ground cardamom
¼ cup brown sugar
1½ tablespoons granulated yeast, or 2 packets
1 tablespoon kosher salt (increase or decrease to taste, page 17)
¼ cup vital wheat gluten
3 ripe pears, cored and pureed with skin, or six canned pear halves, pureed
1 cup lukewarm water
2 large eggs, lightly beaten
¼ cup neutral-flavored oil
½ teaspoon pure vanilla extract
¼ cup plain nonfat (or whole milk) yogurt
Egg wash (1 egg beaten with 1 tablespoon water) for painting the top crust
Raw sugar for sprinkling on top crust

1. **Mixing and storing the dough:** Whisk together the flours, coffee, cardamom, brown sugar, yeast, salt, and vital wheat gluten in a 5-quart bowl, or a lidded (not airtight) food container.

2. Combine the pears with all the liquid ingredients and mix them with the dry ingredients without kneading, using a spoon, a 14-cup food processor (with dough attachment), or a heavy-duty stand mixer (with paddle). You might need to use wet hands to get the last bit of flour to incorporate if you're not using a machine.

3. Cover (not airtight), and allow the dough to rest at room temperature until it rises and collapses (or flattens on top), approximately 2 hours.

4. The dough can be used immediately after its initial rise, though it is easier to handle when cold. Refrigerate it in a lidded (not airtight) container and use over the next 5 days. The dough can be frozen in single-loaf portions and defrosted overnight in the refrigerator.

5. **On baking day,** dust the surface of the refrigerated dough with flour and cut off a 1-pound (grapefruit-size) piece. Dust the piece with more flour and quickly shape it into a ball by stretching the surface of the dough around to the bottom on all four sides, rotating the ball a quarter-turn as you go.

6. Elongate the ball into a narrow oval. Allow the dough to rest, loosely covered with plastic wrap, on a pizza peel prepared with cornmeal or lined with parchment paper for 90 minutes (40 minutes if you're using fresh, unrefrigerated dough). Alternatively, you can rest the loaf on a silicone mat or a greased cookie sheet without using a pizza peel.

7. **Thirty minutes before baking time, preheat the oven to 350°F,** with a baking stone placed on the middle rack.

8. Just before baking, use a pastry brush to paint the top crust with egg wash, then sprinkle it with raw sugar. Slash the loaf diagonally with ¼-inch-deep parallel cuts, using a serrated bread knife.

9. Slide the loaf directly onto the hot stone (or place the silicone mat or cookie sheet on the stone if you used one). Bake for about 35 to 40 minutes, until richly browned and firm. If you used parchment paper, a silicone mat, or a cookie sheet under the loaf, carefully remove it and bake the loaf directly on the stone or an oven rack two-thirds of the way through baking. Smaller or larger loaves will require adjustments in resting and baking time.

10. Allow the bread to cool on a rack before slicing and eating.

Brown Rice and Prune Bread (. . . Try It, You'll Like It)

We know, we know, these two ingredients don't sound like the most obvious pairing. But you simply have to try it; they are fantastic together. The sweet prune juice caramelizes the crust and helps it to crisp, countering the tendency of whole grain doughs to produce a soft crust. You'll need to turn down the heat a bit to prevent the crust from burning—to 425°F. Pomegranate juice and açai are much more fashionable than prune juice these days, so try the variations below if they strike your fancy.

Makes enough dough for at least five 1-pound loaves. The recipe is easily doubled or halved.

5 cups whole wheat flour

3 cups unbleached all-purpose flour

1½ tablespoons granulated yeast, or 2 packets (decrease to taste, page 15)

1 tablespoon kosher salt (increase or decrease to taste, page 17)

¼ cup vital wheat gluten

1 cup lukewarm water

3 cups lukewarm prune juice

1 cup cooked brown rice

¾ cup finely chopped prunes

1. **Mixing and storing the dough:** Whisk together the flours, yeast, salt, and vital wheat gluten in a 5-quart bowl, or a lidded (not airtight) food container.

2. Add the liquid ingredients, brown rice, and prunes, and mix without kneading, using a spoon, a 14-cup food processor (with dough attachment), or a heavy-duty stand mixer (with paddle). You might need to use wet hands to get the last bit of flour to incorporate if you're not using a machine.

3. Cover (not airtight), and allow the dough to rest at room temperature until it rises and collapses (or flattens on top), approximately 2 hours.

4. The dough can be used immediately after its initial rise, though it is easier to handle when cold. Refrigerate it in a lidded (not airtight) container and use over the next 10 days. The flavor will be best if you wait for at least 24 hours of refrigeration.

5. **On baking day,** dust the surface of the refrigerated dough with flour and cut off a 1-pound (grapefruit-size) piece. Dust the piece with more flour and quickly shape it into a ball by stretching the surface of the dough around to the bottom on all four sides, rotating the ball a quarter-turn as you go.

6. Elongate the ball into a narrow oval. Allow the loaf to rest, loosely covered with plastic wrap, on a pizza peel prepared with cornmeal or lined with parchment for 90 minutes (40 minutes if you're using fresh, un-refrigerated dough). Alternatively, you can rest the loaf on a silicone mat or a greased cookie sheet without using a pizza peel.

7. **Thirty minutes before baking time, preheat the oven to 425°F,** with a baking stone placed on the middle rack. Place an empty metal broiler tray on any other rack that won't interfere with the rising bread.

POMEGRANATE JUICE appears to have a variety of terrific health benefits. It's chock full of vitamin C, calcium, potassium, and iron, plus three kinds of antioxidants. If you find the juice too sour to drink by itself, you'll find this bread is a great way to get the health benefits in a delicious and mellower form. Açai juice is another fruit juice that has been touted as a super-food, even more loaded with antioxidants than pomegranate. The juice comes from a Brazilian berry that's just starting to be imported to the U.S. Most of the açai products available to us are made from a blend of fruits, with only modest contributions from açai. 100% açai juice is available through the Web or mail order, but it's prohibitively expensive.

8. Just before baking, use a pastry brush to paint the top crust with water. Slash the loaf diagonally with ¼-inch-deep parallel cuts, using a serrated bread knife.

9. Slide the loaf directly onto the hot stone (or place the silicone mat or cookie sheet on the stone if you used one). Pour 1 cup of hot tap water into the broiler tray, and quickly close the oven door (see pages 27 and 28 for steam alternatives). Bake for about 30 minutes, until richly browned and firm. If you used parchment paper, a silicone mat, or a cookie sheet under the loaf, carefully remove it and bake the loaf directly on the stone or an oven rack two-thirds of the way through baking. Smaller or larger loaves will require adjustments in resting and baking time.

10. Allow the bread to cool on a rack before slicing and eating.

VARIATION: Brown Rice and Pomegranate (or Açai) Bread
Simply substitute an equal volume of pomegranate or açai juice in place of the prune juice in the recipe above. You'll get the same caramelization but a more tart flavor. If prunes border on the cloyingly sweet, then pomegranate juice borders on the bracingly sour. A 50/50 blend of prune juice with pomegranate or açai juice also works nicely and plays the opposing sweet and tart off each other. Try varying the fruit as well—raisins or dried cranberries work beautifully instead of prunes.

Oatmeal Date Bread

You'll make this loaf over and over, not for the high fiber and nutrition of the steel-cut oats (often sold as "Scottish" or "Irish" oats) and dates, but because it is absolutely delicious. Ignore our rule of waiting until the bread is perfectly cool—slice into this one when it is still a touch warm.

Makes enough dough for at least two 2-pound loaves. The recipe is easily doubled or halved.

3 cups whole wheat flour
2 cups unbleached all purpose flour
2 cups steel-cut oats (can substitute old-fashioned rolled oats)
1½ tablespoons granulated yeast, or 2 packets (decrease to taste, page 15)
1 tablespoon kosher salt (increase or decrease to taste, page 17)
¼ cup vital wheat gluten
3 cups lukewarm water
⅓ cup maple syrup
¼ cup neutral-flavored oil
1½ cups dates, finely chopped (about 15 large dates)
1½ cups walnuts, finely chopped (optional, for walnut variation)
Egg wash (1 egg beaten with 1 tablespoon water) for brushing on the top crust
Raw sugar for sprinkling on top

1. **Mixing and storing the dough:** Whisk together the flours, oats, yeast, salt, and vital wheat gluten in a 5-quart bowl, or a lidded (not airtight) food container.

2. Combine the liquid ingredients and dates and mix them with the dry ingredients without kneading, using a spoon, a 14-cup food processor (with dough attachment), or a heavy-duty stand mixer (with paddle). You might need to use wet hands to get the last bit of flour to incorporate if you're not using a machine.

3. Cover (not airtight), and allow the dough to rest at room temperature until it rises and collapses (or flattens on top), approximately 2 hours.

4. The dough can be used immediately after its initial rise, though it is easier to handle when cold. Refrigerate it in a lidded (not airtight) container and use over the next 7 days.

5. **On baking day,** lightly grease an 8 1/2 × 4 1/2-inch nonstick loaf pan. Dust the surface of the refrigerated dough with flour and cut off a 2-pound (cantaloupe-size) piece. Dust the piece with more flour and quickly shape it into a ball by stretching the surface of the dough around to the bottom on all four sides, rotating the ball a quarter-turn as you go.

6. Elongate the ball into an oval and place it into the loaf pan; your goal is to fill the pan about three-quarters full. Cover loosely with plastic wrap. Allow the loaf to rest and rise for 1 hour 45 minutes (60 minutes if you're using fresh, unrefrigerated dough).

7. **Thirty minutes before baking time, preheat the oven to 375°F,** with a baking stone placed on the middle rack. The baking stone is not essential for loaf-pan breads; if you omit it, the preheat can be as short as 5 minutes.

8. Just before baking, use a pastry brush to paint the top crust with egg wash, then sprinkle it with raw sugar.

9. Place the loaf on the stone or on a rack near the center of the oven. Bake for about 45 to 50 minutes, until richly browned and firm.

10. Remove the bread from the pan (see page 50) and allow it to cool slightly on a rack before slicing and eating.

VARIATION: Oatmeal Date-Walnut Bread

After shaping the ball in step 5, flatten the dough with wet hands to a thickness of ½ inch and sprinkle with the walnuts. Roll up the dough from the short end, like a jelly roll, to form a log. Using wet hands, crimp the ends shut and tuck them under to form an oval loaf. Place it into the loaf pan, as in step 6, and follow the baking instructions starting at step 7.

Apple-Barley Bread

This bread is all about fall, when apples are at their peak. Combined with the warm, comforting taste of barley flour they make a great marriage. Barley is a much underused flour for baking; it not only has great flavor but is also incredibly high in fiber. This bread is sweetened with barley malt, normally associated with the taste of beer. It jump-starts the development of yeasty flavors, giving the dough more character quickly. They say an apple a day keeps the doctor away, and it's true that apples contain plenty of fiber and antioxidants, but what's more important is that they're irresistible. Use a combination of tart, sweet, soft, and firm apples for the best flavor, like the McIntosh and Granny Smith. We've combined the fresh grated fruit with dried apples and cider to give a nice chew and an even more intense flavor.

Makes enough dough for at least two 2-pound loaves. The recipe is easily doubled or halved. Use leftover dough for muffins (see page 199).

2¾ cups barley flour
3½ cups unbleached all-purpose flour
½ cup rye flour
1½ tablespoons granulated yeast, or 2 packets (decrease to taste, page 15)
1 tablespoon kosher salt (increase or decrease to taste, page 17)
¼ cup vital wheat gluten
2½ cups lukewarm apple cider
¼ cup honey
½ cup barley malt syrup
¼ cup neutral-flavored oil
2 medium apples, grated (include the skin)
4 ounces dried apples, chopped
Egg wash (1 egg beaten with 1 tablespoon water) for painting the top crust
Raw sugar for sprinkling on top

1. **Mixing and storing the dough:** Whisk together the flours, yeast, salt, and vital wheat gluten in a 5-quart bowl, or a lidded (not airtight) food container.

2. Add the liquid ingredients and the apples and mix them with the dry ingredients without kneading, using a spoon, a 14-cup food processor (with dough attachment), or a heavy-duty stand mixer (with paddle). You might need to use wet hands to get the last bit of flour to incorporate if you're not using a machine.

3. Cover (not airtight), and allow the dough to rest at room temperature until it rises and collapses (or flattens on top), approximately 2 hours.

4. The dough can be used immediately after its initial rise, though it is easier to handle when cold. Refrigerate it in a lidded (not airtight) container and use over the next 7 days.

5. **On baking day,** lightly grease an 8 ½ × 4½-inch nonstick loaf pan. Dust the surface of the refrigerated dough with flour and cut off a 2-pound (cantaloupe-size) piece. Dust the piece with more flour and quickly shape it into a ball by stretching the surface of the dough around to the bottom on all four sides, rotating the ball a quarter-turn as you go.

6. Elongate the ball into an oval and place it into the loaf pan; your goal is to fill the pan about three-quarters full. Allow the loaf to rest and rise for 1 hour 45 minutes (60 minutes if you're using fresh, unrefrigerated dough).

7. **Thirty minutes before baking time, preheat the oven to 375°F,** with a baking stone placed on the middle rack. The baking stone is not essential for loaf-pan breads; if you omit it, the preheat can be as short as 5 minutes.

8. Just before baking, use a pastry brush to paint the top crust with egg wash, then sprinkle it with raw sugar.

9. Place the loaf on the stone or on a rack near the center of the oven. Bake for about 45 to 50 minutes, until richly browned and firm.

10. Remove the bread from the pan (see page 50) and allow it to cool on a rack before slicing and eating.

Whole Wheat Mixed Berry Bread (or Muffins)

Inspired by a muffin, but even better! We bake them as a loaf, but they make fantastic buns baked in muffin tins as well (see the variation below). The key is lots of berries—frozen are preferred for the juice they give off and they're available all year. The result is a purple-tinted bread with the incredible taste of summer berries. Here's another loaf that's okay to eat just slightly warm, with honey butter.

Makes enough dough for at least two 2-pound loaves. The recipe is easily doubled or halved. Use leftover dough for muffins (see page 199).

4 cups white whole wheat flour

4 cups unbleached all-purpose flour

1½ tablespoons granulated yeast, or 2 packets (decrease to taste, page 15)

1 tablespoon kosher salt (increase or decrease to taste, page 17)

¼ cup vital wheat gluten

2¼ cups lukewarm water

¼ cup honey

3 cups mixed frozen berries and their juices, defrosted

Egg wash (1 egg beaten with 1 tablespoon water) for brushing on top crust

Raw sugar for sprinkling on top

The Honey Butter (optional)

4 tablespoons (½ stick) unsalted butter, at room temperature, or zero trans fat, zero hydrogenated oil margarine, at room temperature

2 tablespoons honey

¼ teaspoon pure vanilla extract

~

BERRIES ARE CHOCK-FULL OF ANTIOXIDANTS: Berries, and in particular blueberries, are rich in antioxidants. Blueberry skin contains the pigment anthocyanin, accounting for the vibrant color and also awarding the happy eater with an anti-inflammatory effect in the blood vessels, which may prevent heart attack and stroke.

1. **Mixing and storing the dough:** Whisk together the flours, yeast, salt, and vital wheat gluten in a 5-quart bowl, or a lidded (not airtight) food container.

2. Combine the water, honey, and berries and mix with the dry ingredients without kneading, using a spoon, a 14-cup food processor (with dough attachment), or a heavy-duty stand mixer (with paddle). You might need to use wet hands to get the last bit of flour to incorporate if you're not using a machine.

3. Cover (not airtight), and allow the dough to rest at room temperature until it rises and collapses (or flattens on top), approximately 2 hours.

4. The dough can be used immediately after its initial rise, though it is easier to handle when cold. Refrigerate it in a lidded (not airtight) container and use over the next 5 days.

5. **On baking day,** grease an 8½×4½-inch nonstick loaf pan. Dust the surface of the refrigerated dough with flour and cut off a 2-pound (cantaloupe-size) piece. Dust the piece with more flour and quickly shape it into a ball by stretching the surface of the dough around to the bottom on all four sides, rotating the ball a quarter-turn as you go.

6. Elongate the ball into an oval and place it into the loaf pan; your goal is to fill the pan about three-quarters full. Allow the loaf to rest, loosely covered with plastic wrap, for 1 hour 45 minutes (60 minutes if you're using fresh, unrefrigerated dough).

7. **Thirty minutes before baking time, preheat the oven to 375°F,** with a baking stone placed on the middle rack. The baking stone is not essential for loaf-pan breads; if you omit it, the preheat can be as short as 5 minutes.

8. Just before baking, use a pastry brush to paint the top crust with egg wash, then sprinkle the top with raw sugar.

9. Place the pan on the stone or on a rack near the center of the oven. Bake for about 45 to 50 minutes, until richly browned and firm.

10. Remove the bread from the pan (see page 50), allow it to cool slightly on a rack before slicing and eating. Slice and serve with honey butter.

11. **To make honey butter, if desired:** Cream together the butter, honey, and vanilla in a small bowl.

VARIATION: Muffins—a great way to use up any extra dough.

1. **On baking day,** grease a muffin pan. Dust the surface of the refrigerated dough with flour and cut off a 1½-pound (small cantaloupe-size) piece. Dust the piece with more flour and quickly shape it into a loose ball by stretching the surface of the dough around to the bottom on all four sides, rotating the ball a quarter-turn as you go.

2. **To form the muffins:** Divide the ball into 12 roughly equal portions (each about the size of a golf ball). Shape each one into a smooth ball as in the recipe above. Place the balls in the prepared muffin tin. Allow them to rest, loosely covered with plastic wrap, for 40 minutes (20 minutes if you're using fresh, unrefrigerated dough).

3. **Thirty minutes before baking time, preheat the oven to 375°F,** with a baking stone placed on the middle rack. The baking stone is not essential; if you omit it, the preheat can be as short as 5 minutes.

4. Just before baking, use a pastry brush to paint the tops with egg wash, then sprinkle with raw sugar. Slide the muffin tin directly on the stone or on a rack near the middle of the oven. Bake for about 20 minutes, until richly browned and firm.

5. Remove the muffins from the tin and allow them to cool slightly on a rack before eating.

Whole Wheat Banana Bread

Banana bread without the guilt! Let's face it: Despite the healthy attributes of this wonderful fruit, traditional banana bread is packed with sugar and fat. We love it, but it doesn't exactly deserve its healthy reputation. This version has the fabulous taste with a fraction of the oil and just a touch of honey. Kids will devour it toasted with chunky peanut butter in the morning and it also makes a killer French toast. This is a great way to use up all of those over-ripe bananas on your counter and get some extra potassium in your diet—bananas are one of the best sources of this essential mineral.

Makes enough dough for at least two 2-pound loaves. The recipe is easily doubled or halved. Use leftover dough to make muffins (see page 199).

4 cups white whole wheat flour
2½ cups unbleached all-purpose flour
1 teaspoon ground cinnamon
1½ tablespoons granulated yeast, or 2 packets (decrease to taste, page 15)
1 tablespoon kosher salt (increase or decrease to taste, page 17)
¼ cup vital wheat gluten
1½ cups lukewarm water
½ cup neutral-flavored oil
½ cup honey
2 teaspoons pure vanilla extract
2 cups very ripe banana puree
2 cups walnut pieces (optional)
Egg wash (1 egg beaten with 1 tablespoon water) for brushing on top crust
Raw sugar for sprinkling on the top of the loaf

1. **Mixing and storing the dough:** Whisk together the flours, cinnamon, yeast, salt, and vital wheat gluten in a 5-quart bowl, or a lidded (not airtight) food container.

2. Combine the liquid ingredients with the banana and optional walnuts and mix with the dry ingredients without kneading, using a spoon, a 14-cup food processor (with dough attachment), or a heavy-duty stand mixer (with paddle). You might need to use wet hands to get the last bit of flour to incorporate if you're not using a machine.

3. Cover (not airtight), and allow the dough to rest at room temperature until it rises and collapses (or flattens on top), approximately 2 hours.

4. The dough can be used immediately after its initial rise, though it is easier to handle when cold. Refrigerate it in a lidded (not airtight) container and use over the next 7 days.

5. **On baking day,** lightly grease an 8 ½ × 4½-inch nonstick loaf pan. Dust the surface of the refrigerated dough with flour and cut off a 2-pound (cantaloupe-size) piece. Dust the piece with more flour and quickly shape it into a ball by stretching the surface of the dough around to the bottom on all four sides, rotating the ball a quarter-turn as you go.

6. Elongate the ball into an oval and place the loaf into the loaf pan; your goal is to fill the pan about three-quarters full. Allow the loaf to rest, loosely covered with plastic wrap, for 1 hour 45 minutes (60 minutes if you're using fresh, unrefrigerated dough).

7. **Thirty minutes before baking time, preheat the oven to 350°F**, with a baking stone placed on the middle rack. The baking stone is not essential for loaf pan breads; if you omit it, the preheat can be as short as 5 minutes.

8. Just before baking, use a pastry brush to paint the top crust with egg wash, then sprinkle it with raw sugar. Place the pan on the stone or on a rack in the center of the oven. Bake for about 45 to 50 minutes, until richly browned and firm.

9. Remove the bread from the pan (see page 50) and allow it to cool on a rack before slicing and eating.

8

FLATBREADS AND PIZZA

⟡

When we teach bread classes, busy people tell us that our flatbreads and pizza recipes are the ones they come back to the most often. That's because dough turns into flatbread in record time. Whether whole grain or not, thin breads need little or no resting time, and take short baking times. And people keep telling us that speed is the name of the game. But it's not the only game—it turns out that **pizza is the easiest hiding place for whole grains.** Because of the toppings, even the most finicky kids don't seem to notice whole grains in pizza dough. The stronger the topping flavors, the easier it will be to pass off super-healthy pizza as the same old stuff. Eventually they'll think this pizza is superior to any chain restaurant's.

We bake pizza three ways:

- **Old-fashioned high-temperature oven baking:** This will be the most familiar to you. No steam is needed; just bake it without steam in the bottom third of the oven.
- **Directly over the grates on an outdoor gas grill:** This gives the crunchiest, most rustic result, adding some smoky notes to the pizza.
- **On top of a baking stone on the outdoor gas grill:** The pizza will be pretty close to what you get inside an oven. You can even bake loaf breads outside using this technique if you cover them with a roomy aluminum foil roasting pan to trap steam and heat. No added steam is needed.

With any pizza method, have all your toppings prepared and measured in advance so that the dough doesn't sit on the board waiting once it's rolled out (that would give it time to stick). And you can bake any of these pizzas with any of the methods you choose. The same three techniques work with any other flatbread you like. Seed-Encrusted Pita Bread (page 223), Turkish-Style Pita Bread with Black Sesame Seeds (page 66), Southwestern Focaccia with Roasted Corn and Goat Cheese (page 220), Cherry Black Pepper Focaccia (page 218) . . . our outdoor methods are a great way to keep you baking all summer long.

And of course, vary the toppings however you like. You can't go wrong once you learn the methods.

〜

In 2007, University of Maryland researchers showed that **pizza has more antioxidants when the crust is whole grain baked at high temperature.** How do we get on that research team? Pizza's antioxidant activity was highest when the crust was whole grain, and the baking temperature was high, resulting in rich browning. Works for us—we've always favored high-heat pizza, in the Neapolitan style. The research fits well with other studies that showed that there are more antioxidants in the browned crust of white bread than in the white crumb. Maybe that's why Mom always told us to finish our crusts.

Oven-Baked Whole Grain Pizza with Roasted Red Peppers and Fontina

This is the traditional indoor method for baking pizza; you can do any of our other pizzas inside as well. For this recipe, we decided to pair traditional baking with somewhat nontraditional toppings. Of course, you can put whatever you like on this pizza. Leaving out tomatoes really lets you savor the unique smoky flavor of roasted red peppers. Chop them into a coarse dice and make sure to use the juices that run out of the peppers to infuse the whole pie with the flavor of the roasted pepper. It's a perfect blend with lovely fontina cheese.

Makes one medium-size pizza (12 to 14 inches) to serve 2 to 4

Use any of these refrigerated pre-mixed doughs: Master Recipe (page 53), Soft Whole Wheat Sandwich Bread (page 92), 100% Whole Wheat Bread with Olive Oil (page 81), or other non-enriched dough

1 pound (grapefruit-size portion) of any pre-mixed dough listed above

1 red bell pepper

¼ pound coarsely grated fontina cheese

Olive oil for drizzling

Extra flour for dusting the pizza peel

1. **Roasting the pepper:** Grill the pepper on a gas or charcoal grill, with the skin side closest to the heat source, or place it under the broiler. Check often and remove the pepper when the skin is blackened, about 10 minutes or more, depending on the heat source.

2. Drop the roasted pepper into a bowl or pot and cover. The skin will loosen by steaming in its own heat and moisture for 10 minutes.

3. Gently hand-peel the pepper and discard the blackened skin. Some dark bits will adhere to the pepper's flesh—this is fine.

4. Cut the pepper into a coarse dice, reserving any liquid.

5. **Thirty minutes before baking time, preheat the oven to 550°F (or 500°F if that's your oven's maximum)** with a baking stone placed near the bottom third of the oven. You won't be using steam, so you can omit the broiler tray.

6. Prepare and measure all the toppings in advance. The key to a pizza that slides right off the peel is to work quickly—don't let the dough sit on the peel any longer than necessary.

> ∽
>
> **TURN ON YOUR EXHAUST FAN IF YOU HAVE ONE:** This recipe calls for an exhaust fan because there'll be a lot of smoke from stray flour on such a hot stone. Make sure the stone is scraped clean before preheating. If you don't have an exhaust fan, choose a lower oven temperature (450°F), and bake about 15 to 20 percent longer.

7. Dust the surface of the refrigerated dough with flour and cut off a 1-pound (grapefruit-size) piece. Dust the piece with more flour and quickly shape it into a ball by stretching the surface of the dough around to the bottom on all four sides, rotating the ball a quarter-turn as you go. You don't need to be careful about shaping a perfect ball because it won't be your final shape anyway.

8. Directly on a wooden pizza peel, flatten the dough with your hands and a rolling pin to produce a 1/8-inch-thick round. Dust with flour to keep the dough from adhering to the board. A little sticking to the board can be helpful in overcoming the dough's resistance to stretch. Use a dough scraper to unstick the dough as needed. When you're done, the dough round should have enough flour under it to move easily when you shake the peel.

9. Scatter the fontina cheese over the surface of the dough, then distribute the diced peppers and their liquid. No further resting is needed prior to baking. Drizzle with olive oil.

10. If you have an exhaust fan, turn it on now, because some of the flour on the pizza peel will smoke at this temperature (see sidebar). Slide the pizza directly onto the stone (it may take a number of back-and-forth shakes to dislodge). Check for doneness in 8 to 10 minutes; at this time, turn the pizza around in the oven if one side is browning faster than the other. It may take up to 5 minutes more in the oven.

11. Allow the pizza to cool slightly on a cooling rack before serving, to allow the cheese to set.

Zucchini Flatbread

Seems that everyone who *doesn't* have a green thumb grows zucchini—they grow like weeds. The problem is that you end up with bushels of zucchini and no one could possibly eat it all. If you have stored dough, some Parmigiano-Reggiano or other grating cheese, and parsley, you can create this very fast zucchini flatbread— it's absolutely scrumptious (see photo, color insert).

Makes one medium-size flatbread (12 to 14 inches) to serve 2 to 4

Use any of these refrigerated pre-mixed doughs: Master Recipe (page 53), 100% Whole Wheat Bread (page 79), 100% Whole Wheat Bread with Olive Oil (page 81), other non-enriched dough, or Gluten-Free Olive Oil Bread (page 238)

1 pound (grapefruit-size portion) of any pre-mixed dough listed above

¼ cup olive oil

2 scallions, sliced thinly into rounds

½ bunch parsley, tough stems removed, chopped (about ¾ loosely packed cup)

2 small or 1 large zucchini, coarsely grated

½ cup grated Parmigiano-Reggiano cheese

½ teaspoon kosher salt, plus additional for sprinkling

Freshly ground black pepper to taste

2–4 tablespoons raw pine nuts

Extra flour for dusting the pizza peel

1. **Thirty minutes before baking time, preheat the oven to 450°F,** with a baking stone placed in the bottom third of the oven. You won't be using steam, so you can omit the broiler tray.

2. **Prepare the topping:** Heat the olive oil over medium heat in a skillet. Add the scallions and sauté until softened and fragrant, then add the parsley, zucchini, salt, and pepper, continuing to sauté until the vegetables are wilted and the liquid has mostly evaporated, about 10 minutes. Remove from heat for 10 minutes, and then stir in the grated cheese.

3. Dust the surface of the refrigerated dough with flour and cut off a 1-pound (grapefruit-size) piece. Dust the piece with more flour and quickly shape it into a rough ball by stretching the surface of the dough around to the bottom on all four sides, rotating the ball a quarter-turn as you go. You don't need to be as careful about shaping a perfect ball because it won't be your final shape anyway.

4. Flatten the dough with your hands and a rolling pin directly onto a wooden pizza peel to produce a $1/8$-inch-thick round, dusting with flour to keep the dough from sticking to the board. A little sticking to the board can be helpful in overcoming the dough's resistance. Use a dough scraper to unstick the dough when it sticks to the board. When you're done, the dough should have enough flour under it to move easily when you shake the peel.

5. Working quickly, cover the surface of the dough with about a quarter-inch coating of the sautéed vegetables (you may have more than you need). Sprinkle with the pine nuts.

6. Slide the pizza directly onto the stone (it may take a number of back-and-forth shakes to dislodge the pizza). Check for doneness in 12 to 15 minutes; at this time, turn the pizza around in the oven if one side is browning faster than the other. Continue baking until nicely browned. Finish with a grinding of fresh pepper and additional kosher salt if desired.

7. Allow the pizza to cool slightly on a rack before serving.

Whole Grain Pizza on the Gas Grill (Right on the Grates)

Baking pizza outside on the gas grill answers one of the age-old problems that face home bakers: Who'd want to bake inside in the summer? We sure don't. We wondered whether dough this wet would stick to the grates, fall into the flames, or otherwise cause mayhem. It didn't. As long as your grates are in good shape and you keep the dough well dusted before sliding it onto the grill, it's no problem at all. Just remember to first bake the crust "blind" (without toppings), flipping when the bottom browns. Otherwise it's hard to get pizza to bake through without burning unless you use a stone (see page 213).

"This pizza has been the source of many happy summer lawn parties in my backyard, where it is served with lots of cold semi-sparkling Italian wine. Have your guests make their own pizza by having a variety of toppings all ready to go—see who can throw their dough into the air the highest."—Jeff

Makes one medium-size pizza (12 to 14 inches) to serve 2 to 4

Use any of these refrigerated pre-mixed doughs: Master Recipe (page 53), 100% Whole Wheat Bread (page 79), 100% Whole Wheat Bread with Olive Oil (page 81), or other non-enriched dough
1 pound (grapefruit-size portion) of any pre-mixed dough listed above
½ cup canned Italian-style chopped tomatoes, strained and pressed of liquid (or substitute canned tomato sauce)
¼ pound sliced fresh mozzarella cheese
10 fresh basil leaves, cut into thin strips
2 to 4 anchovy fillets, chopped optional (see sidebar)

YOU SAY YOU DON'T LIKE ANCHOVIES? We made anchovies optional in this pizza because, well, they're not for everyone. Kids in particular can be a little closed-minded about these salty, oily little guys. But if you don't like anchovies, maybe you should reconsider. They're extraordinarily rich in omega-3 fatty acids, pretty much the healthiest fat you can eat. If your kids simply won't eat them . . . send them off to sleepovers, chop up some anchovies, throw them on your pizza, and serve with a big glass of red wine.

Olive oil for drizzling

Additional olive oil for oiling the grates (may not be needed if grates are clean and in good condition)

Extra flour for dusting the pizza peel

1. **Preheat your gas grill with medium flame on all burners.** Prepare and measure all toppings in advance.

2. Dust the surface of the refrigerated dough with flour and cut off a 1-pound (grapefruit-size) piece. Dust the piece with more flour and quickly shape it into a rough ball by stretching the surface of the dough around to the bottom on all four sides, rotating the ball a quarter-turn as you go. You don't need to be as careful about shaping a perfect ball because it won't be your final shape anyway.

3. Directly on a wooden pizza peel, flatten the dough with your hands and a rolling pin to produce a $\frac{1}{8}$-inch-thick round, dusting with flour to keep the dough from adhering to the board. A little sticking to the board can be helpful in overcoming the dough's resistance to stretch. Use a dough scraper to unstick the dough as needed. When you're done, the dough round should have enough flour under it to move easily when you shake the peel. Dock (puncture) the dough all over with a fork.

4. **Baking the crust "blind":** Bring the dough round and all ingredients to the outdoor gas grill. Slide the dough onto the grates, directly over the lit burners, and close the lid. Keep the lid closed except for the occasional peek or it's going to be difficult to get the dough to bake through. You may have to rotate the dough, or adjust the heat, in order to get an even doneness. If the dough puffs too much, poke it with a fork. Flip the dough with a spatula when the top surface looks puffy and the bottom surface is nicely browned (it may char a bit in places), about 2 to 3 minutes.

5. Distribute the tomato, cheese and other toppings; be relatively sparing with them. Drizzle with olive oil and close the grill lid. It's difficult to get the

cheese to brown, but the crust will caramelize so beautifully that you won't be disappointed. It will take another 3 to 5 minutes, depending on how much heat your grill delivers. Watch carefully and remove before the bottom burns. Keep the lid closed as much as possible to trap the heat, which will help to bake the toppings. Use your nose to detect when the bottom crust is just beginning to char.

6. Allow to cool slightly on a rack before eating.

Boule, Master Recipe, page 53

Wreath Bread, Master Recipe, page 73

Cinnamon-Raisin Whole Wheat Bagels, page 74

Black-and-White Braided Pumpernickel and Rye Loaf, page 118

Cherry Tomato Baguette, page 155

Pain au Potiron (Peppery Pumpkin and Olive Oil Loaf), page 162

Red Beet Buns, page 180

Zucchini Flatbread, page 208

Aloo Paratha (Indian stuffed flatbread with potato and peas), page 225

Msemmen (Algerian Flatbread), page 228

Grissini (Olive Oil Bread Sticks), page 231

100% Whole Wheat Christmas Stollen, page 279

Indian Spiced Whole Grain Doughnuts, page 287

Pear Tarte Tatín, page 290

Cinnamon Crescent Rolls, page 294

Chocolate Espresso Cupcakes, page 303

Pesto Pizza with Grilled Chicken on the Gas Grill (with a Stone)

Many recipes specify boneless skinless chicken breasts, but we use boneless skinless chicken thighs in this kind of preparation; they're much less likely to become dry and overcooked. When you use a stone on the grill, you don't have to bake the crust "blind" (see page 211) because the stone will allow longer baking time without burning.

Makes one medium-size pizza (12 to 14 inches) to serve 2 to 4

Use any of these refrigerated pre-mixed doughs: Master Recipe (page 53), 100% Whole Wheat Bread (page 79), 100% Whole Wheat Bread with Olive Oil (page 81), other non-enriched dough or Gluten-Free Olive Oil Bread (page 238)

1 pound (grapefruit-size portion) of any pre-mixed dough listed above

4 garlic cloves

2 cups fresh basil leaves, loosely packed

½ cup pine nuts

2 ounces grated Parmigiano-Reggiano cheese

1 cup olive oil

½ teaspoon kosher salt

¼ teaspoon freshly ground black pepper

3 or 4 boneless skinless chicken thighs, brushed with olive oil and seasoned with salt and freshly ground black pepper

Extra flour for dusting the pizza peel

THERE'S PLENTY OF BASIL IN THIS PIZZA, one of the vegetable world's richest sources of vitamin K (essential for normal blood clotting).

1. Process the garlic, basil, pine nuts, cheese, olive oil, salt, and pepper in a food processor until smooth.

2. Grill the chicken over medium heat on an outdoor grill, until just cooked through. Cool briefly, then chop coarsely.

3. **Thirty minutes before grilling time, preheat a baking stone on an outdoor gas grill over medium flame on all burners;** try to achieve a constant temperature of about 500°F.

4. Dust the surface of the refrigerated dough with flour and cut off a 1-pound (grapefruit-size) piece. Dust the piece with more flour and quickly shape it into a rough ball by stretching the surface of the dough around to the bottom on all four sides, rotating the ball a quarter-turn as you go. You don't need to be as careful about shaping a perfect ball because it won't be your final shape anyway.

5. Directly on a wooden pizza peel, flatten the dough with your hands and a rolling pin to produce a ⅛-inch-thick round, dusting with flour to keep the dough from adhering to the board. A little sticking to the board can be helpful in overcoming the dough's resistance to stretch. Use a dough scraper to unstick the dough as needed. When you're done, the dough round should have enough flour under it to move easily when you shake the peel.

6. Thinly coat the dough with pesto and top with the chicken (you might have enough pesto left over for using as pasta sauce or on another small pizza).

7. Slide the pizza directly onto the stone (it may take a number of back-and-forth shakes to dislodge the pizza) and close the grill lid.

~

THE GAS GRILL MAKES GREAT LOAF BREADS, TOO! The gas grill with a baking stone can also be used to bake loaf breads (free-form or pan). Preheat the stone to the desired temperature for 30 minutes and place the loaf (or pan) onto it. Then cover it with a roomy aluminum roasting pan and bake for the usual time (with the grill's lid closed). You can also use any of the steam alternatives (see pages 27 and 28).

Check for doneness in 8 to 10 minutes; at this time, turn the pizza around if one side is browning faster than the other.

8. Bake for another 3 to 5 minutes, depending on the heat your grill delivers. Watch carefully and remove from heat before the bottom burns. Keep the lid closed as much as possible, and use your nose to detect when the bottom crust is just beginning to char in places.

9. Allow to cool slightly on a rack before eating.

Focaccia with Garlic Shards, Artichokes, and Rosemary

"My friend Theresa is not allergic to onions, but she can't abide them. It's just their smell, taste, and basically, their presence in the world that offends her. So when we showed up at the cabin that she and her husband Jim built in the North Woods, bearing a gift of pre-risen bread dough (mix just before you get in the car and let it rise during the car ride), we needed to think fast because the classic onion-rosemary focaccia *wasn't going to work as our pre-dinner appetizer (not if we expected to be invited back). There were jarred marinated artichokes in the pantry, and Jim and Theresa always have plenty of garlic and herbs. Voilà! A rustic Mediterranean hors d'oeuvre bearing the goodness of artichokes, but no onion."*—Jeff

Makes six appetizer portions

Use any of these refrigerated pre-mixed doughs: 100% Whole Wheat Bread with Olive Oil is our first choice (page 81), but you can also use the Master Recipe (page 53), any other non-enriched dough, or Gluten-Free Olive Oil Bread (page 238)
1 pound (grapefruit-size portion) of any pre-mixed dough listed above
2 large garlic cloves, sliced as thinly as possible with a very sharp knife
2 tablespoons extra-virgin olive oil, plus additional for drizzling
¼ to ½ cup canned or jarred marinated artichokes, drained well and sliced thinly (you can use both the "hearts" and the leafy layers)
¾ teaspoon dried rosemary leaves (or 1½ teaspoons fresh)
Coarse salt and freshly ground black pepper for sprinkling on the top crust

1. **Thirty minutes before baking time, preheat the oven to 425°F,** with an empty metal broiler tray placed on any rack that won't interfere with the *focaccia.* The baking stone is not essential when using a cookie sheet; if you omit the stone the preheat can be as short as 5 minutes.

2. Sauté the garlic slices in the 2 tablespoons of olive oil until softened but not browned; if you brown them they'll burn in the oven. Set aside while preparing the dough.

3. Grease a cookie sheet with olive oil or line it with parchment paper or a silicone mat. Dust the surface of the refrigerated dough with flour and cut off a 1-pound (grapefruit-size) piece. Dust the piece with more flour and quickly shape it into a ball by stretching the surface of the dough around to the bottom on all four sides, rotating the ball a quarter-turn as you go.

4. Flatten it into a ½- to ¾-inch-thick round, using your hands and/or a rolling pin and a minimal amount of flour. Place the round on the prepared cookie sheet. Using your fingertips, deeply "dimple" the surface of the dough to hold olive oil.

5. Scatter the garlic sparingly over the surface of the dough, leaving a ½-inch border at the edge, then do the same with the artichoke slices. Allow some of the dough surface to show through as bare dough. You may have leftover garlic and artichoke at the end. Sprinkle the loaf with rosemary, coarse salt, and freshly ground pepper. Finish with a drizzle of olive oil from the sauté pan. You can drizzle with additional olive oil, but not so much that it starts dripping off the sides.

6. Allow the *focaccia* to rest for 20 minutes.

7. Place the cookie sheet on the stone or on a rack near the center of the oven. Pour 1 cup of hot tap water into the broiler tray, and quickly close the oven door (see pages 27 and 28 for steam alternatives). Bake for about 20 to 25 minutes, until the crust is medium brown. Be careful not to burn the garlic. The baking time will vary according to the *focaccia's* thickness. *Focaccia* will not develop a crackling crust, because of the olive oil.

8. Cut into wedges and serve warm.

Cherry Black Pepper Focaccia

This is a great balance between sweet and savory. The sweet dried cherries are soaked in wine, black pepper, and shallot as the dough rises. When the dough is ready to go into the oven, it is sprinkled with the plumped cherries and drizzled with olive oil. Soaking the cherries first prevents them from drying out and burning in the hot oven. This delightful bread can be paired with pastas, cheeses, or just the red wine you used to poach the cherries.

CHERRIES are a healthy winner because they contain three fantastic phytochemicals (beneficial plant chemicals): the antioxidant quercetin, in addition to anthocyanins and cyanidin. They're also rich in vitamins C and E (which work together as a dynamic duo of antioxidant effect; see page 4), and the essential mineral potassium, which can lower blood pressure, especially in people eating lots of sodium.

"There's some evidence that cherries may also help prevent jet lag, though it's too early to tell if that's going to hold up. But they were a much healthier snack than the weird box the airline was selling on my family's recent transatlantic flight."—Jeff

Makes six appetizer portions

Use any of these refrigerated pre-mixed doughs: Master Recipe (page 53), 100% Whole Wheat Bread (page 79), 100% Whole Wheat Bread with Olive Oil (page 81), any other non-enriched dough, or Gluten-Free Olive Oil Bread (page 238)

1 pound (grapefruit-size portion) of any pre-mixed dough listed above)
½ cup dried cherries
¼ cup red wine
¼ cup water
½ teaspoon freshly ground black pepper
Pinch salt
¼ cup finely minced shallots
2 tablespoons olive oil for drizzling
Coarse sea salt and freshly ground black pepper for sprinkling on top crust

1. **Thirty minutes before baking time, preheat the oven to 425°F,** with an empty metal broiler tray placed on any rack

that won't interfere with the *focaccia*. The baking stone is not essential when using a cookie sheet; if you omit the stone the preheat can be as short as 5 minutes.

2. In a small bowl combine the cherries, wine, water, pepper, salt, and shallots. Allow to sit while your dough is resting.

3. Grease a cookie sheet with olive oil or line it with parchment paper or a silicone mat. Dust the surface of the refrigerated dough with flour and cut off a 1-pound (grapefruit-size) piece. Dust with more flour and quickly shape it into a ball by stretching the surface of the dough around to the bottom on all four sides, rotating the ball a quarter-turn as you go.

4. Flatten it into a ½- to ¾-inch-thick round, using your hands and/or a rolling pin and a minimal amount of flour. Place the round on the prepared cookie sheet. Using your fingertips, deeply "dimple" the surface of the dough to hold olive oil. Allow the *focaccia* to rest for 20 minutes.

5. After the *focaccia* has rested, strain the cherries and spread them over the surface of the dough. Press them into the dough so that they won't pop off while baking. Drizzle with olive oil and sprinkle with coarse sea salt and freshly ground black pepper.

6. Place the cookie sheet on the stone or on a rack near the center of the oven. Pour 1 cup of hot top water into the broiler tray, and quickly close the oven door (see pages 27 and 28 for steam alternatives). Bake for approximately 25 minutes, but check for browning at 20 minutes. Continue baking until medium brown without burning the cherries; baking time will be dependent on the *focaccia*'s thickness. *Focaccia* does not develop a crackling crust because of the olive oil.

7. Cut into wedges and serve warm.

Southwestern Focaccia with Roasted Corn and Goat Cheese

When Minnesotans spend time in Arizona during March, they come back and want to cook every Southwestern specialty there is; every roasted pepper and roasted corn tidbit. Maybe it brings on spring a little faster. So after returning from Phoenix one winter, we wanted to find other ways to enjoy our mesquite dough (page 171).

The poblano peppers in this recipe are becoming more and more available in U.S. supermarkets, but if yours doesn't have them you can find them in your local Mexican market. They're milder than jalapeños, but hotter than American green peppers, so they add some heat to this *focaccia*. If you don't like hot peppers at all, substitute sweet green or red ones. This recipe is designed to be vegetarian, but it works quite nicely with the same grilled chicken we used in the Pesto Pizza with Grilled Chicken (see page 213).

We like to roast the corn on a gas grill with the silks mostly removed but just a thin layer of husk left on the ear; that allows for a little charring. Wrapping husked corn in aluminum foil works, too, but it tends to eliminate the charring.

Makes one medium-size focaccia *(about 10 to 12 inches) for six appetizer portions*

Use any of these refrigerated pre-mixed doughs: Mesquite (page 171), Master Recipe (page 53), 100% Whole Wheat Bread (page 79), 100% Whole Wheat Bread with Olive Oil (page 81), or other non-enriched dough

1 pound (grapefruit-size portion) of any pre-mixed dough listed above

1 ear fresh corn (can substitute ¼ cup frozen corn niblets, especially the roasted variety)

1 dried chili pepper (New Mexico red, *guajillo*, or *ancho* variety), or substitute 1½ teaspoons of your favorite chili powder

1 tablespoon olive oil for the sauté pan

1 medium onion, chopped

1 fresh poblano pepper, seeded, stemmed, and diced

1 teaspoon ground cumin

One 14-ounce can pureed or diced tomatoes

1 teaspoon kosher salt

2 ounces semisoft goat cheese

1 or 2 grilled chicken thighs (optional) (see page 213)

1 tablespoon chopped fresh cilantro leaves

Additional kosher salt to sprinkle on the finished *focaccia*

Corn masa or cornmeal for dusting the pizza peel

1. **Roasting the corn:** Peel off most of the corn husk layers but leave some of the inner layers in place; try to pull out the silks without disrupting the inner layers of corn husk. This allows for a little charring of the kernels but protects against burning. If you prefer, you can peel the ear of corn completely and wrap it in aluminum foil. Preheat a gas grill with burners set to medium for 5 minutes. Roast the corn over direct heat for about 15 minutes, turning every 5 minutes but otherwise keeping the cover closed. Check frequently to be sure that the corn isn't burning. When done, cool slightly, remove the husk if needed, and then use a sharp knife to slice the kernels from the cob.

2. **If you're grinding your own chili powder,** briefly toast the dried pepper in a 400°F oven until fragrant but not burned, 1 to 2 minutes (it will remain flexible but will firm up when cool). Break up the cooled pepper and discard the stems and seeds. Grind the pepper in a spice grinder (or a coffee grinder used just for spices).

3. **Sauté the onions and pepper:** Heat the olive oil over medium heat in a skillet. Add the onion and sauté until beginning to brown, then add the poblano pepper and continue cooking until softened. Add the cumin and chili powder to the skillet and sauté until fragrant, about 2 minutes.

4. Add the tomato and salt, bring to a simmer for 2 minutes, then remove from heat.

5. **Thirty minutes before baking time, preheat the oven to 425°F,** with a baking stone placed on the middle rack. Place an empty metal broiler tray on any other rack that won't interfere with the *focaccia*.

6. Dust the surface of the refrigerated dough with flour and cut off a 1-pound (grapefruit-size) piece. Dust the piece with more flour and quickly shape it into a rough ball by stretching the surface of the dough around to the bottom on all four sides, rotating the ball a quarter-turn as you go.

7. Flatten it into a ½- to ¾-inch-thick round, using your hands and/or a rolling pin and a minimal amount of flour. Place the round on a pizza peel prepared with corn masa, cornmeal, parchment paper, or a silicone mat, and allow it to rest, loosely covered with plastic wrap, for 20 minutes.

8. Cover the surface of the dough with the sauce, leaving a narrow border at the edge—don't layer it too thickly; you might have some left over for next time. Make sure you use the pepper and onion chunks in the sauce. Dot the surface with pieces of goat cheese and finish with the roasted corn kernels. If you're using the chicken, roughly chop it and add to the dough round.

9. Slide the *focaccia* onto the stone. Pour 1 cup of hot tap water into the broiler tray, and quickly close the oven door (see pages 27 and 28 for steam alternatives). Bake for about 25 minutes, or until the crust has browned. The baking time will vary according to the *focaccia*'s thickness.

10. Remove the *focaccia* from the oven and sprinkle it with chopped cilantro and salt to taste. Cut into wedges and serve warm.

Seed-Encrusted Pita Bread

Traditional Middle Eastern puffed pita works just as beautifully with our whole grain dough as it does with the traditional white flour dough. One way to boost the fiber and vitamins in pita (or any bread) is to top the loaf with a generous mixture of seeds and cracked grain. It's not a traditional pita, but it's delicious.

"*In my house, we use little round or rectangular pita breads as a lazy-man's hamburger or hot dog bun. Just cut rolled-out pita dough into the shapes and sizes that you need and bake while you're grilling the meat. The burgers and hot dogs go into the pocket. For more authentic American-style hamburger and hot dog buns, see page 94.*"—Jeff

Makes 1 pita

Use any of these refrigerated pre-mixed doughs: Master Recipe (page 53), 100% Whole Wheat Bread (page 79), 100% Whole Wheat Bread with Olive Oil (page 81), or other non-enriched dough
1 pound (grapefruit-size portion) of any pre-mixed dough listed above
Seed and grain mixture for sprinkling to your taste, about 1 to 2 tablespoons: sesame, flaxseed, caraway, raw sunflower, poppy, and/or anise seeds

1. **Thirty minutes before baking time, preheat the oven to 500°F**, with a baking stone. You don't need a broiler tray, and rack placement of the stone is not critical.

2. Just before baking, dust the surface of the refrigerated dough with flour and cut off a 1-pound (grapefruit-size) piece. Dust the piece with more flour and quickly shape it into a ball by stretching the surface of the dough around to the bottom on all four sides, rotating the ball a quarter-turn as you go. Place the dough on a flour-dusted pizza peel.

3. Using your hands and a rolling pin, roll the dough out into a round (or several rounds) with a uniform thickness of ⅛ inch throughout. This is crucial,

❧

**DON'T GET SMOKED OUT OF HOUSE AND
HOME:** This recipe calls for an exhaust fan
because there'll be a lot of smoke from
stray flour on such a hot stone. Make sure
the stone is scraped clean before preheating. If you don't have an exhaust fan,
choose a lower oven temperature (450°F),
and bake about 15 to 20 percent longer.

Once you gain experience, you can
minimize this problem by using only as
much flour on the peel as is absolutely
needed to prevent sticking.

because if it's too thick, it may not puff. You'll need to sprinkle the peel lightly with flour as you work, occasionally flipping to prevent sticking to the rolling pin or to the board. Use a dough scraper to remove the round of dough from the peel if it sticks. Do not slash the pita or it will not puff. No rest/rise time is needed. If you are making smaller individual-size pitas, form, roll, and shape the rest. Before trying to slide the pita onto the baking stone, be sure it's moving well on the board and not sticking anywhere.

4. Brush the top of the dough with water and sprinkle seeds over the surface.

5. Slide the pita directly onto the hot stone (it may take a number of back-and-forth shakes to dislodge the pita). Bake for about 5 to 7 minutes, until very lightly browned and puffed. Don't overbake whole-grain pitas.

6. For the most authentic, soft-crusted result, wrap the pita in a clean cotton dish towel and set on a cooling rack when baking is complete. The pita will deflate slightly as it cools. The space between the crusts will still be there, but may have to be nudged apart with a fork. Pitas made from 100% whole grain dough may puff only a little.

7. Once the pita is cool, store it in a plastic bag. Unlike hard-crusted breads, pita is not harmed by airtight storage.

Aloo Paratha (Potato and Pea–Stuffed Flatbread)

In our first book, we included a recipe for *naan*, an Indian flatbread that we pan-fried in *ghee* (Indian-style clarified butter). In truth, *naan* isn't intended for pan-frying; it traditionally gets its enrichment from *ghee* that's brushed on after baking in an enormous *tandoor* (traditional stone oven). It's really *paratha* that's fried in India, but for our healthy-ingredients book, we decided to include a stuffed (*aloo*) *paratha* as an oven-baked bread. We're filling it with a mixture of potato, peas, and curry, and it works beautifully as an appetizer before just about anything, or as the first course of an Indian or vegetarian dinner. Use a thin-skinned potato and leave the skin on for more fiber; with the protein and vegetable benefits of peas in the mix, you can consider this a full and balanced vegetarian meal (see photo, color insert).

Makes one aloo paratha to serve six as an appetizer

Use any of these refrigerated pre-mixed doughs: Master Recipe (page 53), 100% Whole Wheat Bread (page 79), 100% Whole Wheat Bread with Olive Oil (page 81), or other non-enriched dough

1 pound (grapefruit-size portion) of any pre-mixed dough listed above

2 medium thin-skinned potatoes, such as Yukon Gold

1½ tablespoons *ghee* gently melted in the microwave or on the stovetop, plus

PARTAKE OF PEAS AS THE PERFECT FOOD?
Peas are readily available as a high-quality frozen product, and we really should be eating lots of them. Interestingly, we find that frozen peas generally are sweeter and fresher tasting than some fresh green peas. The explanation is that fresh peas become stale and starchy tasting within 24 hours of being picked; their nutrient content also declines. Frozen peas are usually frozen immediately after harvest, and that preserves their flavor and nutrition.

Like all legumes, peas are great sources of B vitamins, zinc, potassium, magnesium, calcium, and iron.

additional for brushing on top of the assembled *aloo paratha* (see page 18 to make your own)

1½ tablespoons neutral-flavored oil

1 teaspoon curry powder, plus additional for sprinkling on top

½ teaspoon kosher salt

½ cup frozen or fresh peas (no need to defrost or pre-cook)

1. **Thirty minutes before baking time, preheat the oven to 450°F,** with a baking stone placed on the middle rack. Place an empty metal broiler tray on any other rack that won't interfere with the *aloo paratha* as it rises (rise will be modest).

2. Boil the unpeeled potatoes whole in water for 30 minutes, or until tender. Drain and mash with a fork or potato-masher; use everything, including the skin.

3. Add the *ghee*, oil, curry powder, and salt to the potatoes and vigorously blend with a fork to distribute evenly. Gently fold in the peas so as not to mash them.

4. Dust the surface of the refrigerated dough with flour and cut off a 1-pound (grapefruit-size) piece. Dust the piece with more flour and quickly shape it into a ball by stretching the surface of the dough around to the bottom on all four sides, rotating the ball a quarter-turn as you go.

5. Flatten the dough with your hands and a rolling pin directly onto a wooden pizza peel to produce a ⅛-inch-thick round, dusting with flour to keep the dough from adhering to the board. A little sticking to the board can be helpful in overcoming the dough's resistance. Use a dough scraper to unstick the dough as needed. When you're done, the dough round should have enough flour under it to move easily when you shake the peel.

6. Cover half the dough round with the potato mixture, leaving a ½-inch border at the edge. Using a pastry brush, wet the border with water. Fold the

bare side of the dough over the potato mixture and seal the border by pinching it closed with your fingers.

7. Brush the top surface with some additional *ghee* mixture, and dust with additional curry powder. Cut three slits in the top crust, all the way through the top layer of dough, using a serrated knife. No resting time is needed.

8. Slide the *aloo paratha* directly onto the hot stone. Pour 1 cup of hot tap water into the broiler tray, and quickly close the oven door (see pages 27 and 28 for steam alternatives). Bake for about 25 minutes, or until golden brown.

9. Allow the *aloo paratha* to cool slightly before serving.

TURMERIC: A MODERN-DAY FOUNTAIN OF
YOUTH? The filling for our *msemmen* is flavored with turmeric, among other delicious spices. Turmeric's health effects (as
an anticancer agent) hit the news in 2000,
when it was touted as a marinade ingredient to counter the effects of carcinogens
(cancer-causing chemicals) that form in
grilled meat. Researchers cite the low rate
of cancer in India (where turmeric consumption is high), and even lower rates of
cancer in southern India, where more
turmeric is consumed than in the north.
The active ingredient is curcumin, which
makes up 2 to 3 percent of the weight of
turmeric. Curcumin appears to be a cancer
preventer, and may someday have a role in
cancer treatment.

In addition to finding anticancer properties, some researchers have suggested
that turmeric may have anti-inflammatory
properties in general, which means it may
be useful in countering arthritis, heart disease, and other degenerative conditions.
The jury's out on definitive health effects,
but the flavor's definitively delicious.

Msemmen (Algerian Flatbread)

This is one of the most fascinating breads we've ever made. The flavor is haunting: an otherworldly combination of richness, salt, and spice. Its color and spiral make it one of our most visually intriguing breads as well. Serve it with North African lamb dishes and other hearty fare (see photo, color insert).

Makes one 12-inch flatbread

Use any of these refrigerated pre-mixed doughs: 100% Whole Wheat Bread with Olive Oil (page 81), Master Recipe (page 53), 100% Whole Wheat Bread (page 79), or other non-enriched dough

¼ pound (peach-size portion) of any pre-mixed dough listed above
3 tablespoons olive oil
1 teaspoon ground cumin
1 teaspoon paprika
1 teaspoon turmeric
½ teaspoon cayenne pepper
¼ teaspoon kosher salt, plus additional for sprinkling on the top crust
2 tablespoons olive oil for the skillet

1. Mix the 3 tablespoons olive oil with the spices and ¼ teaspoon salt.

2. Dust the surface of the refrigerated dough with flour and cut off a ¼-pound (peach-size) piece. Dust the piece with more flour and quickly shape it into a ball by stretching the surface of the dough around to the bottom on all four sides, rotating the ball a quarter-turn as you go. Flatten the ball with your fingers and then with a rolling pin to about ⅛ inch thick.

3. Evenly spread the spice-oil mixture over the surface of the dough, leaving a ½-inch border, and roll it up into a log. Coil the rope tightly around itself. Place it on a work surface lightly greased with olive oil and allow it to rest, loosely covered with plastic wrap, for 20 minutes.

4. Once the dough has rested, roll the coil out until you have a ⅛-inch-thick circle.

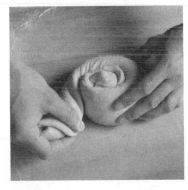

5. Heat a heavy 12-inch skillet over medium-high heat on the stovetop, until water droplets flicked into the pan skitter across the surface and evaporate quickly. Add 2 tablespoons olive oil, and allow to heat until hot *but not smoking.*

6. Drop the rolled-out dough into the skillet, decrease the heat to medium, and cover the skillet to trap steam and heat.

7. Check for doneness with a spatula at about 2 to 5 minutes, or sooner if you're smelling overly quick browning. Adjust the heat as needed. Flip the *msemmen* when the underside is richly browned.

8. Continue cooking another 2 to 5 minutes, until the *msemmen* feels firm, even at the edges, and the second side is browned. You'll need more pan time if you've rolled a thicker *msemmen*.

9. Allow to cool slightly on a rack before breaking apart and eating.

Grissini (Olive Oil Bread Sticks)

Grissini are Italian bread sticks infused with olive oil. Since the oil infuses just as nicely when drizzled over the unbaked sticks as when mixed into the dough, you have a variety of choices of which premixed dough to use—you don't have to use an olive oil dough (even our olive oil dough benefits from additional oil).

Immediately after being photographed (see photo, color insert), the *grissini* consented to being wrapped with strips of prosciutto and consumed with Italian white wine.

Makes twenty-four 12-inch grissini

Use any of these pre-mixed doughs: Master Recipe (page 53), 100% Whole Wheat Bread (page 79), 100% Whole Wheat Bread with Olive Oil (page 81), any other non-enriched dough, or any gluten-free dough

½ pound (orange-size portion) of any pre-mixed dough listed above

Olive oil for brushing on top, preferably extra virgin

Kosher salt for sprinkling

Rosemary for sprinkling (fresh or dried—some chopped, some whole leaves)

Prosciutto, cut into 1-inch strips (optional for serving)

1. **Preheat the oven to 400°F,** with a rack placed in the middle of the oven. A baking stone is optional, but if you're using one, allow for a 30-minute preheat, otherwise 5 minutes is adequate.

2. Line a cookie sheet with parchment paper or a silicone mat, or simply grease it well with olive oil.

3. Roll the dough into an 8 by 12-inch rectangle, ⅛ inch thick. Then cut ⅛-inch-wide strips with a pizza cutter or sharp knife.

4. Lay the strips out on the prepared cookie sheet with ½ inch or so between each strip. Generously

daub olive oil over each strip with a pastry brush. Sprinkle with salt and rosemary.

5. Bake near the center of the oven for approximately 10 to 16 minutes, depending on thickness and width. The *grissini* are done when they are nicely browned and beginning to crisp (they will firm up when they cool). Serve plain as an hors d'oeuvre or with one half wrapped in a prosciutto strip.

Spicy Chili Whole Grain Snack Crackers

Crackers were developed long ago as a baked product that could be stored for a long time, yet wouldn't go stale—they were hard and dry in the first place. If you make your own crackers, you won't need to store them long because they won't last—they taste too good. These colorful little squares are bursting with the flavors of grain and chili. Just make small quantities and use healthy oils like canola or olive, and salt them to your taste. Top them with a bit of cheese and you're ready to watch the game.

Makes about 50 small crackers

Use any of these refrigerated pre-mixed doughs: Master Recipe (page 53), 100% Whole Wheat Bread (page 79), 100% Whole Wheat Bread with Olive Oil (page 81), or any gluten-free dough

½ pound (orange-size portion) of any pre-mixed dough listed above

3 teaspoons chili powder (or make your own, see Southwestern Focaccia with Roasted Corn and Goat cheese, page 221)

½ teaspoon kosher salt

Olive or canola oil for brushing the crackers

Coarse salt for sprinkling on the top

1. Mix the chili powder and salt in a small bowl until uniform.

2. **Thirty minutes before baking time, preheat the oven to 400°F,** with a baking stone placed on the middle rack. Place an empty metal broiler tray on any other rack. The baking stone is optional and if you omit it, the preheat can be as short as 5 minutes.

3. Dust the surface of the refrigerated dough with flour and cut off a ½-pound (orange-size) piece. Dust the piece with more flour and quickly shape it into a ball by stretching the surface of the dough around to the bottom on all four sides, rotating the ball a quarter-turn as you go.

4.   Dust the dough with flour and flatten the dough with your hands and a rolling pin to get it as thin as possible without tearing. Paper-thin's the goal—no thicker than $1/16$ inch or it won't be like a cracker. Use as much flour as is needed to prevent sticking. It's easiest to get it super-thin by cutting the dough into smaller balls first.

5.   Use a pastry brush to paint the rolled-out dough generously with oil, then sprinkle it with spice mixture (you may have some of the spice mixture left over; it can be stored for the next batch). Dock (puncture) the dough all over with a fork to prevent the crackers from puffing.

6.   Cut the dough into $1\frac{1}{2}$-inch squares with a pizza wheel. Using a spatula, transfer them to a greased cookie sheet or one prepared with parchment paper or a silicone mat. Don't let the crackers touch or overlap.

7.   Place the cookie sheet in the preheated oven and pour 1 cup of hot tap water into the broiler tray, and quickly close the oven door (see pages 27 and 28 for steam alternatives). Bake for about 15 minutes, until browned and beginning to firm up. Don't overbake or you'll get a scorched flavor. You'll need less time if you successfully rolled them very thin. They will be a bit soft when they first come out of the oven but they will become crisper when they cool completely.

8.   Serve with robust cheeses, with beer, or all by themselves.

9

GLUTEN-FREE BREADS AND PASTRIES

On our Web site, many people asked us for gluten-free versions of our stored doughs, but only a few of them can't eat gluten themselves. The rest were people entertaining guests with celiac disease who can't tolerate this particular wheat protein. It quickly became obvious to us that many of our readers might want to have some delicious gluten free recipes, even if gluten wasn't a problem for them. If you're ever unsure whether an ingredient is a problem for people who can't eat gluten, a great resource is the University of Chicago's Celiac Disease Center. Their Web site, at www .celiacdisease.net/gluten-free-diet, has a terrific list of ingredients that do (and do not) contain gluten. Some foods containing gluten will surprise you (blue cheese?). The University of Chicago Web site is aimed at people with celiac disease, an allergic digestive condition. People with celiac absolutely cannot eat gluten at all.

We really wanted to create recipes that emulate both the taste and texture of traditional breads. Many of the existing gluten-free recipes tasted odd to us, or were overly sweetened—often they didn't taste much like bread to us at all. Creating recipes that met our standards and were able to be stored posed a challenge, but we are quite pleased with the results. Check out the flatbreads and pizza chapter; many of those recipes work beautifully with gluten-free doughs.

There are a few ingredients in gluten-free breads that you may not be familiar with (xanthan gum, tapioca starch, and others), so we covered them in some detail in Ingredients (chapter 2, pages 13 and 14).

Gluten-Free Crusty Boule

Shauna and Danny of the Gluten-Free Girl Web site generously shared their wealth of knowledge with us to develop this fabulous crusty loaf. The dough is incredibly versatile; we bake it as a classic boule or in a loaf pan for sandwiches (follow baking instructions on page 245). It also makes a wonderful pizza crust with your favorite toppings or great crackers if it is rolled thin.

Makes enough dough for at least four 1-pound loaves. The recipe is easily doubled or halved.

2 cups brown rice flour
1½ cups sorghum flour
3 cups tapioca starch (tapioca flour)
2 tablespoons granulated yeast
1 tablespoon kosher salt (increase or decrease to taste, page 17)
2 tablespoons xanthan gum
2⅔ cups lukewarm water
4 large eggs
⅓ cup neutral-flavored oil
2 tablespoons honey

1. **Mixing and storing the dough:** Whisk together the flours, tapioca starch, yeast, salt, and xanthan gum in a 5-quart bowl, or a lidded (not airtight) food container.

2. Combine the liquid ingredients and gradually mix them with the dry ingredients, using a spoon, a 14-cup food processor (with dough attachment), or a heavy-duty stand mixer (with paddle), until all of the dry ingredients are well incorporated. You might have to use wet hands to get the last bit of flour to incorporate if you're not using a machine.

3. Cover (not airtight), and allow the dough to rest at room temperature until it rises, approximately 2 hours.

4. The dough can be used immediately after the initial rise. Refrigerate in a lidded (not airtight) container and use over the next 7 days. The flavor will be best if you wait for at least 24 hours of refrigeration.

5. **On baking day,** use wet hands to take out a 1-pound (grapefruit-size) piece of the refrigerated dough. Quickly shape it into a ball; this dough isn't stretched because there is no gluten in it—just gently press it into the shape. You might need to wet your hands a little to prevent the dough from sticking and to create a smooth surface, but don't use so much water as to make the dough soggy.

6. Allow the dough to rest, loosely covered with plastic wrap, on a pizza peel prepared with cornmeal or lined with parchment for 90 minutes (40 minutes if you're using fresh, unrefrigerated dough). Alternatively, you can rest the loaf on a silicone mat or a greased cookie sheet.

7. **Thirty minutes before baking time, preheat the oven to 450°F, with a baking stone placed on the middle rack.** Place an empty metal broiler tray on any other rack that won't interfere with the rising bread.

8. Just before baking, slash the loaf with ¼-inch-deep parallel cuts, using a serrated bread knife.

9. Slide the loaf directly onto the hot stone (or place the silicone mat or cookie sheet on the stone if you used one). Pour 1 cup of hot tap water into the broiler tray, and quickly close the oven door (see pages 27 and 28 for steam alternatives). Bake for about 35 minutes, until lightly browned and firm. If you used parchment paper, a silicone mat, or a cookie sheet under the loaf, carefully remove it two-thirds of the way through baking and bake the loaf directly on the stone or an oven rack. Smaller or larger loaves will require adjustments in resting and baking time.

10. Allow to cool on a rack before slicing or eating.

Gluten-Free Olive Oil Bread

Our friends Debora and Ralph inspired this recipe—they've been experimenting with gluten-free ingredients for years. This dough is enriched with delicious olive oil, and is a great fit for pizza and other Mediterranean-style specialties. It is also lovely as a free-form loaf with a crispy crust.

Makes enough dough for at least four 1-pound loaves. The recipe is easily doubled or halved.

1 cup brown rice flour
½ cup soy flour
1 cup tapioca starch (tapioca flour)
3½ cups cornstarch
2 tablespoons granulated yeast
1 tablespoon kosher salt (increase or decrease to taste, page 17)
2 tablespoons xanthan gum
2½ cups lukewarm water
4 large eggs
⅔ cup olive oil
2 teaspoons white or cider vinegar

1. **Mixing and storing the dough:** Whisk together the flours, tapioca starch, cornstarch, yeast, salt, and xanthan gum in a 5-quart bowl, or a lidded (not airtight) food container.

2. Combine the liquid ingredients and gradually mix them into the dry ingredients without kneading, using a spoon, a 14-cup food processor (with dough attachment), or a heavy-duty stand mixer (with paddle).

3. Cover (not airtight), and allow the dough to rest at room temperature for approximately 2 hours.

4. The dough can be used immediately after its initial rise, or you can refrigerate it in a lidded (not airtight) container and use it over the next 7 days. The flavor will be best if you wait for at least 24 hours of refrigeration.

5. **On baking day**, use wet hands to take out a 1-pound (grapefruit-size) piece of the refrigerated dough. Quickly shape it into a ball; this dough isn't stretched because there is no gluten in it—just gently press it into the shape. You might need to wet your hands a little to prevent the dough from sticking and to create a smooth surface, but don't use so much water as to make the dough soggy.

6. Elongate the ball into a narrow oval. Allow the loaf to rest and rise, loosely covered with plastic wrap, on a pizza peel prepared with cornmeal or lined with parchment paper, for 90 minutes (40 minutes if you're using fresh, unrefrigerated dough). Alternatively, you can rest the loaf on a silicone mat or a greased cookie sheet without using a pizza peel.

7. **Thirty minutes before baking time, preheat the oven to 450°F,** with a baking stone placed on the middle rack. Place an empty metal broiler tray on any other rack that won't interfere with the rising bread.

8. Slide the loaf directly onto the hot stone (or place the silicone mat or cookie sheet on the stone if you used one). Pour 1 cup of hot tap water into the broiler tray, and quickly close the oven door (see pages 27 and 28 for steam alternatives). Bake for about 30 minutes, until lightly browned and firm. If you used parchment paper, a silicone mat, or a cookie sheet under the loaf, carefully remove it and bake the loaf directly on the stone or an oven rack two-thirds of the way through baking. Smaller or larger loaves will require adjustments in resting and baking time.

9. Allow the bread to cool on a rack before slicing and eating.

Gluten-Free Pizza with Fresh Mozzarella, Olives, Basil, and Anaheim Peppers

The secret to making really good gluten-free pizza is a thin crust. The Gluten-Free Olive Oil Bread dough (page 238) is our favorite and makes the toppings shine. Our testers thought they were eating traditional pizza crust.

Makes 1 pizza, 12 to 16 inches across

½ pound (orange-size portion) Gluten-Free Olive Oil Bread dough (page 238), or
     Gluten-Free Crusty Boule (page 236)
½ cup canned Italian-style chopped tomatoes, well drained by draining through a
     strainer, or use any prepared tomato sauce you like
¼ pound sliced mozzarella cheese, fresh buffalo-milk variety if available
6 basil leaves, roughly torn
⅛ cup sliced Mediterranean-style black or green olives
½ Anaheim pepper, thinly sliced crosswise
1 tablespoon grated Parmigiano-Reggiano cheese (optional)
Olive oil for drizzling on top of the pizza
White or brown rice flour for dusting

1. **Thirty minutes before baking time, preheat the oven to 500°F,** with a baking stone placed on the middle rack. You won't be using steam, so you can omit the broiler tray.

2. Prepare and measure all toppings in advance. The key to a pizza that slides right off the peel is to work quickly—don't let the dough sit on the peel any longer than necessary.

3. Dust the surface of the refrigerated dough with rice flour and cut off a ½-pound (orange-size) piece. Dust the piece with more rice flour and quickly shape it into a ball; this dough isn't stretched because there is no

gluten in it—just press it into the shape of a ball. You will need to use lots of rice flour to prevent the dough from sticking to your hands or the work surface, but avoid working lumps of flour into the dough.

4.　Flatten the dough with your hands and a rolling pin directly on a wooden pizza peel to produce a $1/16$ to $1/8$-inch-thick round, dusting with lots of rice flour to keep the dough from sticking to the rolling pin and board. A metal dough scraper is very helpful here; use it to scrape the expanding dough round off the work surface when it sticks. Be sure that the dough is still movable before adding the toppings; if it isn't, sprinkle more rice flour under the dough.

5.　Distribute a thin layer of tomatoes over the surface of the dough.

6.　Scatter the mozzarella over the surface of the dough, then the basil, olives, peppers, and Parmigiano-Reggiano, if desired. Drizzle the pizza with about a teaspoon of olive oil. No further resting is needed prior to baking.

7.　Slide the pizza directly onto the stone (it may take a number of back-and-forth shakes to dislodge the pizza—use the dough scraper to help). Check for doneness in 10 to 12 minutes; turn the pizza around in the oven if one side is browning faster than the other. It may need up to 5 more minutes in the oven, or until the cheese and crust are nicely browned.

8.　Allow the pizza to cool slightly on a rack before serving, to allow the cheese to set.

Gluten-Free Sesame Baguette

It's not traditionally French to put sesame seeds on top of a baguette, but who cares? It's delicious and really adds another dimension to this bread. These loaves look beautiful, too, with the slashes alternating with curving rows of sesame seeds.

Makes 1 large or 2 small baguettes

1 pound (grapefruit-size portion) Gluten-Free Olive Oil Bread dough (page 238), Gluten-Free Crusty Boule (page 236), or Gluten-Free Cheddar and Sesame Bread (page 244)
Sesame seeds for sprinkling on top crust

1. **On baking day**, use wet hands to break off a 1-pound (grapefruit-size) piece of the refrigerated dough. Quickly shape it into a cylinder; this dough isn't stretched because there is no gluten in it—just gently press it into the shape. You might need to wet your hands a little to prevent the dough from sticking and to create a smooth surface, but don't use so much water as to make the dough soggy.

2. Allow the loaf to rest, loosely covered with plastic wrap, on a pizza peel prepared with rice flour or lined with parchment paper for 60 minutes (40 minutes if you're using fresh, unrefrigerated dough). Alternatively, you can rest the loaf on a silicone mat or a greased cookie sheet without using a pizza peel.

3. **Thirty minutes before baking time, preheat the oven to 450°F,** with a baking stone placed on the middle rack. Place an empty metal broiler tray on any other rack that won't interfere with the rising bread.

4. Just before baking, use a pastry brush to paint the top crust with water, then sprinkle it with sesame seeds. Slash the loaf diagonally with longitudinal cuts, using a serrated bread knife.

5. Slide the loaf directly onto the hot stone (or place the silicone mat or cookie sheet on the stone if you used one). Pour 1 cup of hot tap water into the broiler tray, and quickly close the oven door (see pages 27 and 28 for steam alternatives). Bake for about 25 minutes, until richly browned and firm. If you used parchment, a silicone mat, or a cookie sheet under the loaf, carefully remove it and bake the loaf directly on the stone or an oven rack two-thirds of the way through baking. Smaller or larger loaves will require adjustments in resting and baking time.

6. Allow the bread to cool on a rack before cutting and eating.

Gluten-Free Cheddar and Sesame Bread

The sharpness of the cheddar and the nuttiness of the sesame make this a fantastic loaf to be served with sandwich meats or toasted and served with marmalade. The addition of soy flour, eggs, and cheese makes this loaf particularly high in protein. It is also excellent baked as crackers in the recipe that follows.

Makes enough dough for at least three 1½-pound loaves. The recipe is easily doubled or halved.

3 cups sorghum flour
½ cup soy flour
2 cups tapioca starch (tapioca flour)
½ cup cornstarch
½ cup sesame seeds, plus additional for sprinkling on top
2 tablespoons granulated yeast
1 tablespoon kosher salt (increase or decrease to taste, page 17)
2 tablespoons xanthan gum
3 cups lukewarm water
4 large eggs
½ cup olive oil
2 tablespoons honey
1½ cups cheddar cheese, shredded

1. **Mixing and storing the dough:** Mix the flours, tapioca starch, cornstarch, ½ cup sesame seeds, yeast, salt, and xanthan gum in a 5-quart bowl, or a lidded (not airtight) food container. Whisk the dry ingredients to be sure that the xanthan gum is thoroughly incorporated.

2. Combine the remaining ingredients and gradually mix them with the dry ingredients without kneading, using a spoon, a 14-cup food processor (with dough attachment), or a heavy-duty stand mixer (with paddle). You might need to use wet hands to get the last bit of flour to incorporate if you're not using a machine.

3. Cover (not airtight), and allow the dough to rest at room temperature for approximately 2 hours.

4. The dough can be used immediately after its initial rise, or you can refrigerate it in a lidded (not airtight) container and use it over the next 7 days.

5. **On baking day,** heavily grease an 8 ½ × 4 ½-inch nonstick loaf pan. Use wet hands to break off a 1½-pound (cantaloupe-size) piece of the refrigerated dough. Quickly shape it into a ball; this dough isn't stretched because there is no gluten in it—just gently press it into the shape. You might need to wet your hands a little more to prevent the dough from sticking and to create a smooth surface, but don't use so much water as to make the dough soggy.

6. Elongate the ball into a narrow oval and put it in the loaf pan. Allow the loaf to rest, loosely covered with plastic wrap, for 90 minutes (40 minutes if you're using fresh, unrefrigerated dough).

7. **Thirty minutes before baking time, preheat the oven to 425°F.** Place an empty metal broiler tray on any other rack that won't interfere with the rising bread.

8. Just before baking, use a pastry brush to paint the top with water, then sprinkle it with sesame seeds.

9. Place the pan on a rack near the center of the oven. Pour 1 cup of hot tap water into the broiler tray, and quickly close the oven door (see pages 27 and 28 for steam alternatives). Bake for about 40 minutes, until richly browned and firm. Smaller or larger loaves will require adjustments in resting and baking time.

10. Remove the bread from the pan (see page 50) and allow it to cool on a rack before slicing and eating.

Gluten-Free Cheddar and Sesame Crackers

These crackers are fantastic with just about everything from cheese to dips! You will need to use a silicone mat and plastic wrap to roll out this dough.

Makes enough dough for at least twelve 2-inch crackers

½ pound Gluten-Free Cheddar and Sesame Bread dough (page 244), Gluten-Free Crusty Boule (page 236), Gluten-Free Olive Oil Bread (page 238), or Not Rye (page 249)
2 tablespoons sesame seeds for sprinkling on top

1. **Thirty minutes before baking time, preheat the oven to 400°F,** with a baking stone placed on the middle rack.

2. Dust the surface of the refrigerated dough with rice flour and cut off a ½-pound (orange-size) piece of dough from the container. Place the dough on a silicone mat and cover the dough with a piece of plastic wrap. Using a rolling pin, roll the dough between the plastic wrap and the silicone mat until you have a ¹⁄₁₆-inch-thick rectangle. Peel off the plastic wrap, and transfer the silicone mat to a baking sheet.

3. Using a pizza cutter, very gently score the dough into crackers in the shape and size you desire. **Warning: It is important not to cut through the dough with too much pressure or you may damage your silicone mat.**

4. Just before baking, use a pastry brush to paint the surface with water, then sprinkle the surface of the dough with sesame seeds. Bake for 15 minutes, or until the crackers just start to turn golden brown. The crackers on the edges may turn brown first; use a spatula to take them off the baking sheet and continue baking the rest.

5. Allow the crackers to cool on a rack before eating.

Gluten-Free Parmesan Bread Sticks

If gluten-free doughs can make a crusty baguette (page 242), it should be a natural as a bread stick—it's just skinnier! A little olive oil, salt, and parmesan cheese perk up the flavor. Serve them plain or as an hors d'oeuvre with dips.

Makes a generous handful of bread sticks

Use any of these refrigerated, pre-mixed doughs: Gluten-Free Crusty Boule. (page 236), Gluten-Free Olive Oil Bread (page 238), Gluten-Free Cheddar and Sesame Bread (page 244), or Not Rye (page 249)
½ pound (orange-size portion) of any pre-mixed dough above
Olive oil for drizzling, preferably extra virgin
1 to 2 tablespoons finely grated Parmigiano-Reggiano cheese
Kosher salt for sprinkling, to taste

1. **Thirty minutes before baking time, preheat the oven to 425°F.** A baking stone is optional, but if you're using one, allow for a 30-minute preheat, otherwise 5 minutes is adequate.

2. Line a cookie sheet with parchment paper or a silicone mat, or simply grease it well with olive oil.

3. Dust the surface of the refrigerated dough with rice flour and cut off a ½-pound (orange-size) piece. Dust the piece with more rice flour and quickly shape it into a ball; this dough isn't stretched because there is no gluten in it—just press it into the shape of a ball. Roll it out with a rolling pin on a wooden board, using lots of rice flour, until you have an oval ⅛ inch thick. Then cut ⅛-inch-wide strips with a pizza cutter or sharp knife.

4. Carefully lay the strips out on the prepared cookie sheet with ½ inch or so between each strip. Drizzle olive oil over the strips, and sprinkle with Parmigiano-Reggiano and a light sprinkling of salt.

5. Bake for about 15 minutes. The bread sticks are done when they are nicely browned but not scorched. Smaller bread sticks might turn brown first; use a spatula to take them off the baking sheet and continue baking the rest. They may still feel soft when done but will firm up when they cool.

6. Cool the bread sticks on a rack before eating.

Not Rye (But So Very Close), and Gluten-Free

We both grew up eating rye bread; it was the bread that was the muse for our first book. When we decided to add a chapter on gluten-free breads, we made a list of all the essentials to be included, and rye was at the top of our lists. But rye has some gluten in it. So nothing doing.

In place of rye we have used teff flour, which is completely gluten-free. It has a sweet-sour molasses flavor, which lends itself perfectly to a mock rye bread. Add the caraway seeds and we're very close to childhood memories.

TEFF is high in protein, calcium, and iron, and its iron is particularly easily absorbed by humans (often a difficult trick for plant-based iron sources). It's a major source of nutrition in the world, and especially in northeast Africa, where it is made into Ethiopia's national flatbread, *injera*.

Makes enough dough for at least four 1-pound loaves. The recipe is easily doubled or halved.

2 cups brown rice flour
1½ cups teff flour
3 cups tapioca starch (tapioca flour)
2 tablespoons granulated yeast
1 tablespoon kosher salt (increase or decrease to taste, page 17)
2 tablespoons xanthan gum
¼ cup caraway seeds, plus extra for sprinkling
2⅔ cups lukewarm water
4 large eggs
⅓ cup oil
2 tablespoons honey
2 tablespoons molasses

1. **Mixing and storing the dough:** Whisk together the flours, tapioca starch, yeast, salt, xanthan gum, and caraway seeds in a 5-quart bowl, or a lidded (not airtight) food container.

2. Combine the liquid ingredients and gradually mix them with the dry ingredients without kneading, using a spoon, a 14-cup food processor (with dough attachment), or a heavy-duty stand mixer (with paddle), until all the dry ingredients are well incorporated.

3. Cover (not airtight), and allow the dough to rest at room temperature for approximately 2 hours.

4. The dough can be used immediately after its initial rise, or you can refrigerate it in a lidded (not airtight) container and use it over the next 7 days. The flavor will be best if you wait for at least 24 hours of refrigeration.

5. **On baking day,** use wet hands to take out a 1-pound (grapefruit-size) piece of the refrigerated dough. Quickly shape it into a ball; this dough isn't stretched because there is no gluten in it—just gently press it into the shape. You might need to wet your hands a little more to prevent the dough from sticking and to create a smooth surface, but don't use so much water as to make the dough soggy.

6. Elongate the ball into a narrow oval. Allow the loaf to rest, loosely covered with plastic wrap, on a pizza peel prepared with cornmeal or lined with parchment paper for 90 minutes (40 minutes if you're using fresh, unrefrigerated dough). Alternatively, you can rest the loaf on a silicone mat or a greased cookie sheet without using a pizza peel.

7. **Thirty minutes before baking time, preheat the oven to 450°F,** with a baking stone placed on the middle rack. Place an empty metal broiler tray on any other rack that won't interfere with the rising bread.

8. Just before baking, use a pastry brush to paint the loaf's top crust with water and sprinkle it with caraway seeds. Slash the dough with ¼-inch-deep parallel cuts, using a serrated bread knife.

9. Slide the loaf directly onto the hot stone (or place the silicone mat or cookie sheet on the stone if you used one). Pour 1 cup of hot tap water into the broiler tray, and quickly close the oven door (see pages 27 and 28 for steam alternatives). Bake for about 30 minutes, until richly browned and firm. If you used parchment paper, a silicone mat, or a cookie sheet under the loaf, carefully remove it and bake the loaf directly on the stone two-thirds of the way through baking. Smaller or larger loaves will require adjustments in resting and baking time.

10. Allow the bread to cool on a rack before slicing and eating.

Gluten-Free Brioche

This recipe is dynamite baked as a traditional shaped brioche or as a sandwich loaf for your kids' lunches, and is also perfect in the "Super Sam" Gluten-Free Cinnamon Buns on page 254. It has a soft texture with a light sweetness from the honey and vanilla that is pure comfort food. It can also be used in place of the brioche dough in chapter 10 for many of the pastries in that chapter.

Makes enough dough for at least three 1½-pound loaves. The recipe is easily doubled or halved.

1 cup brown rice flour
1 cup tapioca starch (tapioca flour)
3¾ cups cornstarch
2 tablespoons granulated yeast
1 tablespoon kosher salt (increase or decrease to taste, page 17)
2 tablespoons xanthan gum
2½ cups milk
1 cup honey
4 large eggs
1 cup neutral-flavored oil
1 tablespoon pure vanilla extract
Egg wash (1 egg beaten with 1 tablespoon water) for brushing on the loaf
Raw sugar for sprinkling on top crust

1. **Mixing and storing the dough:** Whisk together the flour, tapioca starch, cornstarch, yeast, salt, and xanthan gum in a 5-quart bowl, or a lidded (not airtight) food container.

2. Combine the liquid ingredients and gradually mix them into the dry ingredients, using a spoon, a 14-cup food processor (with dough attachment), or a heavy-duty stand mixer (with paddle), until there is no sign of dry bits of

flour. You might need to use wet hands to get the last bit of flour to incorporate if you're not using a machine.

3. Cover (not airtight), and allow the dough to rest at room temperature for approximately 2 hours.

4. The dough can be used immediately after its initial rise. Refrigerate it in a lidded (not airtight) container and use over the next 5 days.

5. **On baking day,** grease a brioche pan or an 8 ½ × 4½-inch nonstick loaf pan. Use wet hands to break off a 1½-pound (small cantaloupe-size) piece of the refrigerated dough. Quickly shape it into a ball; this dough isn't stretched because there is no gluten in it—just gently press it into the shape. You might need to wet your hands a little more to prevent the dough from sticking and to create a smooth surface, but don't use so much water as to make the dough soggy.

6. Elongate the ball into a narrow oval and put it in the brioche or loaf pan. Allow the loaf to rest, loosely covered with plastic wrap, for 90 minutes (40 minutes if you're using fresh, unrefrigerated dough).

7. **Preheat the oven to 350°F.** If you're not using a stone in the oven, a 5-minute preheat is adequate.

8. Just before baking, use a pastry brush to paint the loaf's top crust with egg wash and sprinkle it with raw sugar.

9. Bake near the center of the oven for approximately 40 to 45 minutes. The loaf is done when caramel brown and firm. Smaller or larger loaves will require adjustments in resting and baking time.

10. Remove the brioche from the pan (see page 50) and allow it to cool on a rack before slicing and eating.

"Super Sam" Gluten-Free Cinnamon Buns

"This recipe was inspired by my friend's young nephew, who has celiac disease. 'Super Sam,' as his family calls him, had been flipping through Artisan Bread in Five Minutes a Day *and said he really wished he could eat the pecan sticky buns. His aunt Jenny called me and asked what we could come up with. I created these buns and then tested the recipe on a group of 4- to 9-year-olds—they all ate them, came back for seconds, and had no idea that the buns were gluten-free. Now 'Super Sam' can have sticky buns, too!"—Zoë*

Makes twelve buns

1½ pounds (small cantaloupe-size portion) of Gluten-Free Brioche dough (page 252)

The Filling
⅔ cup brown sugar
1½ teaspoons ground cinnamon
⅔ cup chopped nuts (optional)

The Glaze
1 cup confectioners' sugar
1 teaspoon pure vanilla extract
2 tablespoons milk (add 1 tablespoon at a time)
1 tablespoon unsalted butter, at room temperature, or zero trans fat, zero hydrogenated
   oil margarine, at room temperature
½ teaspoon orange zest

1. **On baking day:** Grease an 8-inch cake pan. Using wet hands, take a 1½-pound (small cantaloupe-size) piece of dough from the bucket.

2. Sprinkle sugar on a silicone mat and place the dough on top of the sugar. Cover the dough with a piece of plastic wrap. Using a rolling pin, roll the

dough between the plastic and silicone mat until you have a ¼-inch-thick rectangle. Peel off the plastic wrap.

3. **Make the filling:** Combine the filling ingredients. Sprinkle the filling over the surface of the dough. Roll the dough, starting at the long end, into a log, lifting the silicone mat to help ease the dough from its surface.

4. Remove the dough from the silicone mat and, with a very sharp knife or kitchen shears, cut the log into 12 equal pieces and arrange them in the pan, with the "swirled" edge visible to you. Cover loosely with plastic wrap and allow to rest about 1 hour.

5. **Twenty minutes before baking time, preheat the oven to 350°F,** with a rack placed in the center of the oven.

6. Bake the buns for about 20 to 25 minutes, or until the tops are lightly brown and the dough feels set when touched.

7. Allow the buns to cool on a rack for 5 minutes, and then invert onto a serving plate.

8. **Make the glaze:** Mix together the glaze ingredients and spread the glaze over the tops of the warm buns. These are best eaten while slightly warm.

10

ENRICHED BREADS
AND PASTRIES FROM
HEALTHY INGREDIENTS

∽

Even when trying to maintain a healthy diet, we still need a bit of decadence in our lives. We've re-created some of our favorite enriched breads using the same fast method, but with a healthier philosophy. You can have challah, Christmas *stollen*, pumpkin brioche, and many more sweet breads and pastries without feeling as though you are breaking your commitment to eating well—just eat enriched breads and pastries in moderation.

In this chapter we have tried to give you alternatives to using white flours, white sugar, and butter. Not that they can't be used in small amounts in a healthy diet, but there are so many other wonderful flavors that lend themselves well to our breads. We used whole grains, natural sweeteners, and unsaturated oils as much as possible, and in all cases we've cut way back. If you eat these breads in moderation you will continue on a healthy path that is just a bit more enjoyable.

Braided Challah with Whole Wheat and Wheat Germ

Here's a delicious and nutritious braided loaf, with all the classic flavors of challah: eggs, poppy seeds, and honey. The eggy dough for this traditional Jewish bread is very similar to doughs used in some spectacular Scandinavian holiday treats, so don't forget to try the variations at the end of this recipe.

Makes enough dough for at least five 1-pound loaves. The recipe is easily doubled or halved.

5 cups whole wheat flour
3 cups unbleached all-purpose flour
¼ cup wheat germ
1½ tablespoons granulated yeast, or 2 packets
1 tablespoon kosher salt (increase or decrease to taste, page 17)
¼ cup vital wheat gluten
3 cups lukewarm water
¼ cup neutral-flavored oil, melted unsalted butter, or melted zero trans fat, zero hydrogenated oil margarine
½ cup honey
3 large eggs
1 teaspoon pure vanilla extract
Egg wash (1 egg beaten with 1 tablespoon water) for brushing on the loaf
Poppy seeds for sprinkling on top

1. **Mixing and storing the dough:** Whisk together the flours, wheat germ, yeast, salt, and vital wheat gluten in a 5-quart bowl, or a lidded (not airtight) food container.

2. Combine the liquid ingredients and mix them with the dry ingredients without kneading, using a spoon, a 14-cup food processor (with dough attachment), or a heavy-duty stand mixer (with paddle). You might need to use wet hands to get the last bit of flour to incorporate if you're not using a machine.

3. Cover (not airtight), and allow the dough to rest at room temperature until it rises and collapses (or flattens on top), approximately 2 hours.

4. The dough can be used immediately after its initial rise, though it is easier to handle when cold. Refrigerate it in a lidded (not airtight) container and use over the next 5 days. Or store the dough for up to 2 weeks in the freezer in 1-pound portions. When using frozen dough, thaw it in the refrigerator for 24 hours before use, then allow the usual rest/rise time.

5. **On baking day,** dust the surface of the refrigerated dough with flour and cut off a 1-pound (grapefruit-size) piece. Dust the piece with more flour and quickly shape it into a ball by stretching the surface of the dough around to the bottom on all four sides, rotating the ball a quarter-turn as you go.

6. Gently roll and stretch the dough, dusting with flour so your hands don't stick to it, until you have a long rope about ¾ inch thick. You may need to let the dough relax for 5 minutes so it won't resist your efforts. Using a dough scraper or knife, make angled cuts to divide the rope into three equal-length strands with tapering ends.

7. **Braiding the challah:** Starting from the middle of the loaf, pull the left strand over the center strand and lay it down; always pull the outer strands into the middle, never moving what becomes the center strand.

8. Now pull the right strand over the center strand. Continue, alternating outer strands but always pulling into the center. When you get to the end, pinch the strands together.

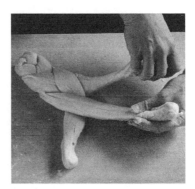

9. Flip the challah over so that the loose strands fan away from you. Start braiding again by pulling an outside strand to the middle, but this time *start with the right strand*. Braid to the end again, and pinch the strands together.

10. If the braid is oddly shaped, fix it by nudging and stretching. Place the braid on a greased cookie sheet or one prepared with parchment paper or a silicone mat, and allow it to rest, loosely covered with plastic wrap, for 90 minutes (or 40 minutes if you're using fresh, unrefrigerated dough).

11. **Thirty minutes before baking time, preheat the oven to 350°F,** with a rack placed in the center of the oven. If you're not using a stone in the oven, a 5-minute preheat is adequate.

12. Just before baking, use a pastry brush to paint the top crust with egg wash (see sidebar), and then sprinkle the crust with poppy seeds.

13. Place the cookie sheet in the oven and bake for about 30 to 35 minutes, until browned and firm. Smaller or larger loaves will require adjustments in resting and baking time.

14. Allow the challah to cool on a rack before slicing and eating.

∽

GETTING A SUPER-SHINE ON CHALLAH: If you follow our eggwash-painting directions exactly, you'll get a lovely loaf and the seeds will stick securely, but it won't be that shiny. If you really want a shiny result, paint the top crust with egg wash twice. First, apply a coat and let it dry. Then, just before baking, paint again and *now* sprinkle on the seeds.

VARIATIONS: SCANDINAVIAN CHRISTMAS BREADS
Our basic lightly enriched dough above can be used in two terrific Scandinavian Christmas favorites: *pulla* (from Finland) and *julekage* (from Norway, Sweden, and Denmark). You can make them with a brioche base (pages 275, 279, and 284) but traditional recipes favor a more lightly enriched and sweetened dough. The secret's in the spices.

PULLA
Simply add 1 teaspoon ground cardamom and ½ teaspoon ground anise seeds to the dry ingredients in the *challah* recipe. Braid the loaf as for challah and paint it with egg wash, but sprinkle it with raw sugar instead of poppy seeds before resting and baking at 350°F as above.

JULEKAGE
Base your *julekage* on the same spiced enriched dough variation that you used for *pulla*, but add ¾ cup dried fruits such as raisins, currants, cranberries, apricots, cherries, candied citron, candied lemon peel, or candied orange peel to the liquid ingredients. Shape the loaf as a flattened round. After resting, bake at 350°F as above. When slightly cooled but still warm, paint it with the icing below, then sprinkle it with toasted slivered or sliced almonds.

Icing for *Julekage*

1½ teaspoons milk
¼ cup confectioners' sugar
¼ teaspoon pure almond extract

Mix together in a small bowl.

Apples and Honey Whole Grain Challah

Apples and honey are the traditional culinary welcome to Jewish New Year, and though they don't usually make their way into the turban-shaped holiday challah, their combination is absolutely irresistible any time of the year. Use Braeburn or another firm variety so that the apples maintain their shape.

Makes enough dough for at least five 1-pound loaves. The recipe is easily doubled or halved.

5 cups whole wheat flour
3 cups unbleached all-purpose flour
¼ cup wheat germ
1½ tablespoons granulated yeast, or 2 packets
1 tablespoon kosher salt (increase or decrease to taste, page 17)
¼ cup vital wheat gluten
3 cups lukewarm water
½ cup neutral-flavored oil, unsalted butter, melted, or zero trans fat, zero hydro-
      genated oil margarine, melted
½ cup honey
3 large eggs
4 large baking apples (Braeburn or other firm variety), peeled and cored, then cut
      into ½-inch dice
Egg wash (1 egg beaten with 1 tablespoon water) for brushing on the loaf
Sesame seeds for sprinkling on top

1. **Mixing and storing the dough:** Whisk together the flours, wheat germ, yeast, salt, and vital wheat gluten in a 5-quart bowl, or a lidded (not airtight) food container.

2. Combine the liquid ingredients and the apples and mix with the dry ingredients without kneading, using a spoon, a 14-cup food processor (with dough attachment), or a heavy-duty stand mixer (with paddle). You might

need to use wet hands to get the last bit of flour to incorporate if you're not using a machine.

3. Cover (not airtight), and allow the dough to rest at room temperature until it rises and collapses (or flattens on top), approximately 2 hours.

4. The dough can be used immediately after its initial rise, though it is easier to handle when cold. Refrigerate it in a lidded (not airtight) container and use over the next 5 days. Or store the dough for up to 2 weeks in the freezer in 1-pound portions. When using frozen dough, thaw it in the refrigerator for 24 hours before use, then allow the usual rest/rise time.

5. **On baking day,** dust the surface of the refrigerated dough with flour and cut off a 1-pound (grapefruit-size) piece. Dust with more flour and quickly shape it into a ball by stretching the surface of the dough around to the bottom on all four sides, rotating the ball a quarter-turn as you go.

6. Gently roll and stretch the dough, dusting with flour so that your hands don't stick to it, until you have a cylinder. Thin out one end so you end up with a tapered rope. You might need to let the dough relax for 5 minutes so that it won't resist your efforts.

7. **Winding the turban:** Keeping the thick end stationary, wind the thinner end around it and, finally, tuck it underneath to seal.

8. Place the turban on a greased cookie sheet, or one prepared with parchment paper or a silicone mat, and allow it to rest, loosely covered with plastic wrap, for 90 minutes (40 minutes if you're using fresh, unrefrigerated dough).

9. **Thirty minutes before baking time, preheat the oven to 350°F,** with a rack placed in the center of the oven. If you're not using a stone in the oven, a 5-minute preheat is adequate.

10. Just before baking, use a pastry brush to paint the top crust with egg wash, and then sprinkle the crust with sesame seeds.

11. Place the cookie sheet in the oven and bake for about 35 minutes, until browned and firm. Smaller or larger loaves will require adjustments in resting and baking time.

12. Allow the challah to cool on a rack before slicing and eating.

Il Bollo (Italian Yom Kippur Challah with Anise and Olive Oil)

"My friend Ralph is my source for all recipes Italian or Italian-American. Years ago, he told me about a challah perfected by medieval Jews in northern Italy. The loaf was enriched with olive oil rather than butter or the traditional goose fat of Eastern Europe. Much healthier!

"Il bollo (which literally means nothing more than 'the ball') is justly famous for its flavor, spiked with olive oil, anise, vanilla, and lemon. It was traditionally eaten to break the fast of Yom Kippur, but it's great anytime. We left this loaf mostly white, but you can increase the whole grain and liquids if you like, and make a version based on the Braided Challah with Whole Wheat and Wheat Germ dough (page 258)."—Jeff

Makes enough dough for at least four 1-pound loaves. The recipe is easily doubled or halved.

1½ cups whole wheat flour
7 cups unbleached all-purpose flour
1½ tablespoons yeast, or 2 packets
1 tablespoon kosher salt (increase or decrease to taste, page 17)
2 tablespoons anise seeds, plus additional for sprinkling
2 tablespoons vital wheat gluten
2 cups lukewarm water
¾ cup honey
½ cup olive oil
2 teaspoons pure vanilla extract
4 large eggs
½ teaspoon grated lemon zest
Egg wash (1 egg beaten with 1 tablespoon of water) for brushing on the loaf

1. **Mixing and storing the dough:** Whisk together the flours, yeast, salt, anise seeds, and vital wheat gluten in a 5-quart bowl, or a lidded (not airtight) food container.

2. Add the liquid ingredients and lemon zest and mix without kneading, using a spoon, a 14-cup food processor (with dough attachment), or a heavy-duty stand mixer (with paddle). You might need to use wet hands to get the last bit of flour to incorporate if you're not using a machine.

3. Cover (not airtight), and allow the dough to rest at room temperature until it rises and collapses (or flattens on top), approximately 2 hours.

4. The dough can be used immediately after its initial rise, though it is easier to handle when cold. Refrigerate it in a lidded (not airtight) container and use over the next 5 days. Or store the dough for up to 2 weeks in the freezer in 1-pound portions. When using frozen dough, thaw it in the refrigerator for 24 hours before use, then allow the usual rest/rise time.

5. **On baking day,** prepare a cookie sheet with olive oil, parchment paper, or a silicone mat. Dust the surface of the refrigerated dough with flour and cut off a 1-pound (grapefruit-size) piece. Dust the piece with more flour and quickly shape it into a ball by stretching the surface of the dough around to the bottom on all four sides, rotating the ball a quarter-turn as you go.

6. Allow the loaf to rest, loosely covered with plastic wrap, on the prepared cookie sheet for 90 minutes (or 40 minutes if you're using fresh, unrefrigerated dough).

7. **Thirty minutes before baking time, preheat the oven to 350°F,** with a rack placed in the center of the oven. If you're not using a stone in the oven, a 5-minute preheat is adequate.

8. Just before baking, use a pastry brush to paint the loaf with egg wash, and then sprinkle the crust lightly with additional anise seeds. Slash the loaf with a ¼-inch-deep slash into the top, using a serrated bread knife.

9. Place the cookie sheet on the stone or on a rack in the center of oven and bake for about 35 minutes, until browned and firm. Smaller or larger loaves will require adjustments in resting and baking time.

10. Allow the *bollo* to cool on a rack before slicing and eating.

Honey Graham Bread

"My kids call this 'daddy' bread because my husband's name is Graham, and graham flour is the key ingredient in this tasty loaf. I was inspired by one of our family's favorite snacks, the ubiquitous cracker of the same name. I love the wheat flavor combined with honey and cinnamon. Toast it with butter and you have a lovely snack or breakfast."—Zoë

Makes enough dough for at least two 2-pound loaves. The recipe is easily doubled or halved. Use any leftover dough to make muffins (see page 199).

4 cups graham flour
3¼ cups unbleached all-purpose flour
1 tablespoon ground cinnamon
1½ tablespoons granulated yeast, or 2 packets
1 tablespoon kosher salt (increase or decrease to taste, page 17)
¼ cup vital wheat gluten
3½ cups lukewarm water
¾ cup honey
⅓ cup neutral-flavored oil, or 6 tablespoons melted unsalted butter, or melted zero trans fat, zero hydrogenated oil margarine

1. **Mixing and storing the dough:** Whisk together the flours, cinnamon, yeast, salt, and vital wheat gluten in a 5-quart bowl, or a lidded (not airtight) food container.

2. Combine the liquid ingredients and mix them with the dry ingredients without kneading, using a spoon, a 14-cup food processor (with dough attachment), or a heavy-duty stand mixer (with paddle). You might need to use wet hands to get the last bit of flour to incorporate if you're not using a machine.

3. Cover (not airtight), and allow the dough to rest at room temperature until it rises and collapses (or flattens on top), approximately 2 hours.

4. The dough can be used immediately after its initial rise, though it is easier to handle when cold. Refrigerate in a lidded (not airtight) container and use over the next 7 days.

5. **On baking day,** lightly grease an 8½×4½-inch nonstick loaf pan. Dust the surface of the refrigerated dough with flour and cut off a 2-pound (cantaloupe-size) piece. Dust the piece with more flour and quickly shape it into a ball by stretching the surface of the dough around to the bottom on all four sides, rotating the ball a quarter-turn as you go.

6. Elongate the ball into an oval and place it into the loaf pan; your goal is to fill the pan about three-quarters full. Cover loosely with plastic wrap. Allow to rest for 1 hour 45 minutes (60 minutes if you're using fresh, unrefrigerated dough).

7. **Thirty minutes before baking time, preheat the oven to 350°F,** with a baking stone placed on the middle rack. The baking stone is not essential for loaf pan breads; if you omit it, the preheat can be as short as 5 minutes.

8. Place the loaf on a rack near the center of the oven and bake for 45 to 50 minutes. Smaller or larger loaf pans will require adjustments in baking time.

9. Remove the bread from the pan (see page 50) and allow it to cool completely on a rack before slicing and eating.

Milk and Honey Raisin Bread

Milk and honey both tenderize wheat breads, so for people who are looking for a soft whole grain bread, this is the one. The raisins are a perfect fit for the sweet, tender crumb. An added bonus is that these flavors are universally loved by children.

Makes enough dough for at least two 2-pound loaves. The recipe is easily doubled or halved. Use leftover dough to make muffins (see page 199).

4¾ cups whole wheat flour
4½ cups unbleached all-purpose flour
1½ tablespoons granulated yeast, or 2 packets
1 tablespoon kosher salt (increase or decrease to taste, page 17)
¼ cup vital wheat gluten

2 cups milk
2 cups lukewarm water
⅓ cup honey or agave syrup
2 large eggs
¾ cup raisins
Egg wash (1 egg beaten with 1 tablespoon water) for brushing the top
Raw sugar for sprinkling on top

∽

MILK IS ONE OF THE BEST WAYS TO GET CAL-CIUM AND VITAMIN D INTO YOUR DIET: There's some evidence that children in particular may not be meeting their recommended daily allowance for calcium. Since milk makes a nice liquid base for bread, this loaf is a great way to get more calcium and vitamin D into your kids' diets. Most adults will also benefit.

Milk is also rich in the mineral zinc.

1. **Mixing and storing the dough:** Whisk together the flours, yeast, salt, and vital wheat gluten.

2. Combine the remaining ingredients and mix them with the dry ingredients without kneading, using a spoon, a food processor (with dough attachment), or a heavy-duty stand mixer

(with paddle). You might need to use wet hands to get the last bit of flour to incorporate if you're not using a machine.

3. Cover (not airtight), and allow the dough to rest at room temperature until it rises and collapses (or flattens on top), approximately 2 hours.

4. The dough can be used immediately after its initial rise, though it is easier to handle when cold. Refrigerate it in a lidded (not airtight) container and use over the next 10 days.

5. **On baking day,** grease an 8 1/2 × 4 1/2-inch nonstick loaf pan. Dust the surface of the refrigerated dough with flour and cut off a 2-pound (cantaloupe-size) piece. Dust the piece with more flour and quickly shape it into a ball by stretching the surface of the dough around to the bottom on all four sides, rotating the ball a quarter-turn as you go.

6. Elongate the ball into an oval and place it in the loaf pan; your goal is to fill the pan about three-quarters full. Allow the loaf to rest, loosely covered with plastic wrap, for 90 minutes (or 40 minutes if you're using fresh, unrefrigerated dough).

7. **Thirty minutes before baking time, preheat the oven to 375°F,** with a rack placed in the center of the oven. A stone is not needed for loaf-pan breads; if you omit it, the preheat time can be as short as 5 minutes.

8. Just before baking, use a pastry brush to paint the top crust with egg wash, and then sprinkle with raw sugar.

9. Bake for about 45 minutes, until richly browned and firm. Smaller or larger loaves will require adjustments in resting and baking time.

10. Remove the bread from the pan (see page 50) and allow to cool on a rack before slicing and eating.

Bran Muffin Bread

This unusual yeasted bread has the flavors of American-style bran muffins, with lots of bran and spice. It's a lot lighter than traditional muffins, which, if truth be told, are very high in fat (especially commercial ones). If you make these as buns (shape as for Whole Wheat Mixed Berry Bread or Muffins on page 197 and bake for about 15 to 20 percent less time), you'll have something a little closer to bran muffins, and you'll be avoiding many, many grams of fat.

Makes enough dough for at least four 1-pound loaves. The recipe is easily doubled or halved.

1½ cups wheat bran
1 cup whole wheat flour
4¼ cups unbleached all-purpose flour
1½ tablespoons granulated yeast, or 2 packets
1 tablespoon kosher salt (increase or decrease to taste, page 17)
1 teaspoon ground cinnamon
¼ teaspoon ground nutmeg
¼ cup vital wheat gluten
2½ cups lukewarm water
½ cup maple syrup
1 tablespoon molasses
½ cup neutral-flavored oil
½ teaspoon pure vanilla extract
2 large eggs
¾ cup raisins

1. **Mixing and storing the dough:** Whisk together the wheat bran, flours, yeast, salt, cinnamon, nutmeg, and vital wheat gluten in a 5-quart bowl, or a lidded (not airtight) food container.

2. Combine the liquid ingredients, and raisins and mix them with the dry ingredients without kneading, using a spoon, a 14-cup food processor (with dough attachment), or a heavy-duty stand mixer (with paddle). You might need to use wet hands to get the last bit of flour to incorporate if you're not using a machine.

3. Cover (not airtight), and allow the dough to rest at room temperature until it rises and collapses (or flattens on top), approximately 2 hours.

4. The dough can be used immediately after its initial rise, though it is easier to handle when cold. Refrigerate it in a lidded (not airtight) container and use over the next 5 days. The dough can be frozen in single-loaf portions and defrosted overnight in the refrigerator.

5. **On baking day,** dust the surface of the refrigerated dough with flour and cut off a 1-pound (grapefruit size) piece. Dust the piece with more flour and quickly shape it into a ball by stretching the surface of the dough around to the bottom on all four sides, rotating the ball a quarter-turn as you go.

6. Elongate the ball into a narrow oval. Allow the loaf to rest, loosely covered with plastic wrap, on a pizza peel prepared with cornmeal or lined with parchment paper for 90 minutes (40 minutes if you're using fresh, unrefrigerated dough). Alternatively, you can rest the loaf on a silicone mat or a greased cookie sheet without using a pizza peel.

7. **Thirty minutes before baking time, preheat the oven to 350°F,** with a baking stone placed on the middle rack. Place an empty metal broiler tray on any other rack that won't interfere with the rising bread.

8. Just before baking, use a pastry brush to paint the top crust with water. Slash the loaf diagonally with deep parallel cuts, using a serrated bread knife.

9. Slide the loaf directly onto the hot stone (or place the silicone mat or cookie sheet on the stone if you used one). Pour 1 cup of hot tap water into the broiler tray, and quickly close the oven door (see pages 27 and 28 for steam alternatives). Bake for about 40 minutes, until richly browned and firm. If you used parchment paper, a silicone mat, or a cookie sheet under the loaf, carefully remove it and bake the loaf directly on the stone or an oven rack two-thirds of the way through baking. Smaller or larger loaves will require adjustments in resting and baking time.

10. Allow the bread to cool on a rack before slicing and eating. Try it with the honey butter on page 197.

Whole Wheat Brioche

"Considering my pastry chef roots it would make sense that I find sweets an important part of the diet. It would have been my preference to put the sweets chapter at the beginning of the book, but perhaps I am alone in thinking that we should eat dessert first. Even though this is a book about eating healthier breads, we didn't want to eliminate the sweets, we just wanted them to fit into our healthier diets. We've used natural sweeteners and made use of nutritious whole grains. The recipes we have based on this lovely dough are both delicious and satisfying."—Zoë

Makes enough dough for at least two 2-pound loaves. The recipe is easily doubled or halved. Use leftover dough for muffins (page 199) or pinwheels (page 299).

4 cups white whole wheat flour

3 cups unbleached all-purpose flour

1½ tablespoons granulated yeast, or 2 packets (decrease to taste, page 15)

1 tablespoon kosher salt (increase or decrease to taste, page 17)

¼ cup vital wheat gluten

2¼ cups lukewarm water

¾ cup (1½ sticks) unsalted butter, melted and cooled slightly, or zero trans fat, zero hydrogenated oil margarine), melted and cooled slightly, or neutral-flavored oil

¾ cup honey

5 large eggs

Egg wash (1 egg beaten with 1 tablespoon water) for brushing on the top crust

1. **Mixing and storing the dough:** Whisk together the flour, yeast, salt, and vital wheat gluten in a 5-quart bowl, or a lidded (not airtight) food container.

2. Combine the liquid ingredients and mix them with the dry ingredients without kneading, using a spoon, a 14-cup food processor (with dough attachment), or a heavy-duty stand mixer (with paddle).

3. The dough will be loose, but it will firm up when chilled. *Don't try to use it without chilling* for at least 2 hours. You may notice lumps in the dough, but they will disappear in your finished products.

4. Cover (not airtight), and allow the dough to rest at room temperature until it rises and collapses (or flattens on top), approximately 2 hours.

5. Refrigerate it in a lidded (not airtight) container and use over the next 5 days, or store the dough in the freezer for up to 2 weeks in an airtight container. Freeze it in 2-pound portions. When using frozen dough, thaw it in the refrigerator for 24 hours before use, then allow the usual rest/rise time.

6. **On baking day,** grease a brioche pan, or an 8½ × 4½-inch nonstick loaf pan. Dust the surface of the refrigerated dough with flour and cut off a 2-pound (cantaloupe-size) piece of dough. Dust the piece with more flour and quickly shape it into a ball. Place the ball in the prepared pan and allow to rest, loosely covered with plastic wrap, for 1 hour 45 minutes.

7. **Thirty minutes before baking time, preheat the oven to 350°F,** with a rack placed in the center of the oven. If you're not using a stone in the oven, a 5-minute preheat is adequate. Steam is not needed.

8. Just before baking, use a pastry brush to brush the loaf's top crust with egg wash.

9. Bake the loaf near the center of the oven for approximately 40 to 45 minutes. Brioche will not form a hard, crackling crust. The loaf is done when it is medium brown and firm. Smaller or larger loaves will require adjustments in resting and baking time.

10. Remove the brioche from the pan (see page 50) and allow it to cool on a rack before slicing or eating.

Apple Strudel Bread

This bread is perfect for breakfast or a Sunday brunch. Inspired by the classic Austrian pastry, the loaf is made from brioche dough that is rolled thin and layered with tons of apples, raisins, and nuts. A sprinkle of cinnamon and raw sugar is the crowning touch. This makes a large loaf, but trust us—there will be none left over.

Makes one 2-pound loaf

Use any of these refrigerated pre-mixed doughs: Braided Challah with Whole Wheat and Wheat Germ (page 258), Whole Wheat Brioche (page 275), 100% Whole Grain Butterfat- and Yolk-Free Brioche (page 282), Pumpkin Pie Brioche (page 284), Soft Whole Wheat Sandwich Bread (page 92), or any other enriched dough

1½ pounds (small cantaloupe-size portion) of any pre-mixed dough listed above, defrosted overnight in the refrigerator if frozen

2 medium apples, skin on, thinly sliced, then finely chopped

½ cup raisins

¾ cup finely chopped walnuts (optional)

¼ cup raw sugar

½ teaspoon ground cinnamon

Egg wash (1 egg beaten with 1 tablespoon water) for brushing on the top crust

Cinnamon-sugar (1 tablespoon raw sugar mixed with ¼ teaspoon ground cinnamon) for sprinkling on top

1. **On baking day,** combine the chopped apples, raisins, optional walnuts, raw sugar, and cinnamon in a bowl. Toss well and set aside.

2. Grease an 8½ × 4½-inch nonstick loaf pan. Dust the surface of the refrigerated dough with flour and cut off a 1½-pound (small cantaloupe-size) piece. Dust with more flour and quickly shape it into a ball by stretching the surface of the dough around to the bottom on all four sides, rotating the ball a quarter-turn as you go.

3. With a rolling pin, roll out the dough until it is a 1/8-inch-thick rectangle. As you roll out the dough, use enough flour to prevent the dough from sticking to the work surface, but not so much as to make it dry.

4. Spread the apple mixture over the rolled-out dough. Roll the dough into a log, starting at the short end. Place the log in the loaf pan and allow the loaf to rest, loosely covered with plastic wrap, for 90 minutes (40 minutes if you're using fresh unrefrigerated dough).

5. **Thirty minutes before baking time, preheat the oven to 350°F,** with a rack placed in the center of the oven. If you're not using a stone in the oven, a 5-minute preheat is adequate.

6. Just before baking, use a pastry brush to paint the top crust with egg wash, and then sprinkle with the cinnamon-sugar.

7. Slide the loaf into the oven. Bake for about 50 to 60 minutes, until deeply browned and firm. Smaller or larger loaves will require adjustments in resting and baking time.

8. Remove the bread from the pan (see page 50) and allow it to cool before slicing or eating.

100% Whole Wheat Christmas Stollen

Our first book, *Artisan Bread in Five Minutes a Day*, was published in November, just in time for holiday baking. Within days we were inundated with requests for *stollen*, a German Christmas specialty rich with butter and eggs, spiced with cardamom, studded with dried and candied fruit, and spiked with just a touch of brandy. Here in Minnesota there is a large German-American population and this festive bread is part of that tradition.

Here is a gorgeous version made with whole grains and marzipan running through the middle. If you find the brandy a bit too festive, then you can replace it with either orange juice or even black tea (see photo, color insert).

Makes enough dough for at least three 1½-pound loaves. The recipe is easily doubled or halved. Use any leftover dough to make muffins (see page 199).

6 cups white whole wheat flour

1½ tablespoons granulated yeast, or 2 packets

1 tablespoon kosher salt (increase or decrease to taste, page 17)

½ teaspoon ground cardamom

¼ cup vital wheat gluten

2 cups lukewarm water

½ cup neutral-flavored oil, unsalted butter, melted, or zero trans fat, zero hydrogenated oil margarine, melted

½ cup honey

4 large eggs

¼ cup brandy (orange juice or lukewarm black tea can be substituted)

1½ cups finely chopped dried or candied fruit (raisins, currants, dried pineapple, dried apricots, dried cherries, candied citron, candied lemon peel, or candied orange peel)

½ cup almond paste, or marzipan, or 1 cup slivered almonds for the center of the loaf

Egg wash (1 egg beaten with 1 tablespoon water) for brushing on the top crust

Confectioners' sugar for the top of the loaf

1. **Mixing and storing the dough:** Whisk together the flour, yeast, salt, cardamom, and vital wheat gluten in a 5-quart bowl, or a lidded (not airtight) food container.

2. Combine the liquid ingredients and dried and or candied fruit and mix with the dry ingredients without kneading, using a spoon, a 14-cup food processor (with dough attachment), or a heavy-duty stand mixer (with paddle). You might need to use wet hands to get the last bit of flour to incorporate if you're not using a machine.

3. The dough will be loose, but it will firm up when chilled. *Don't try to use it without chilling* for at least 2 hours.

4. Cover (not airtight), and allow the dough to rest, loosely covered with plastic wrap, at room temperature until it rises and collapses (or flattens on top), approximately 2 hours.

5. Refrigerate it in a lidded (not airtight) container and use over the next 5 days. Beyond that, the dough stores well in the freezer for up to 2 weeks in an airtight container. Freeze it in 1½-pound portions. When using frozen dough, thaw it in the refrigerator for 24 hours before use, then allow the usual rest/rise time.

6. **On baking day,** dust the surface of the refrigerated dough with flour and cut off a 1½-pound (small cantaloupe-size) piece of dough. Dust the piece with more flour and quickly shape it into a ball.

7. With a rolling pin, roll out the dough to a ¼-inch-thick oval. As you roll out the dough, use enough flour to prevent the dough from sticking to the work surface, but not so much as to make it dry.

8. Place the marzipan or slivered almonds across the short end of the dough about one-third of the way from the end. Lift and fold the remaining two-

thirds of the dough to form an S-shape over the almond filling. The end of the dough will lie near the middle of the top of the loaf. Allow to rest, loosely covered with plastic wrap, on a cookie sheet prepared with parchment paper or a silicone mat, for 90 minutes.

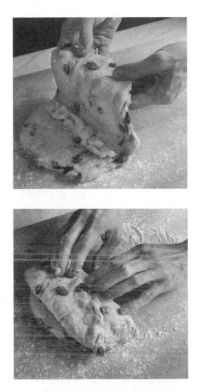

9. **Thirty minutes before baking time, preheat the oven to 350°F,** with a rack placed in the center of the oven. If you're not using a stone in the oven, a 5-minute preheat is adequate.

10. Just before baking, use a pastry brush to paint the top crust with egg wash.

11. Place the cookie sheet in the oven and bake for approximately 35 to 40 minutes, until medium brown and firm.

12. Allow the *stollen* to cool, then sprinkle it generously with confectioners' sugar.

100% Whole Grain Butterfat- and Yolk-Free Brioche

"I developed this brioche for my mom and my dear friend Barb, both of whom were un-expectedly told their cholesterol is high and had to go on drastic diets. Both enjoy great food, but changed their diets dramatically to improve their health. I used a butter sub-stitute that my mother's doctor recommended and eliminated the yolks. This bread is not fat- or calorie-free, but if eaten in moderation it works in their new diets. This dough can be used to make pinwheels, strudel, or any other enriched dough recipe."—Zoë

Makes enough dough for at least two 2-pound loaves. The recipe is easily doubled or halved.

7 cups white whole wheat flour
1½ tablespoons granulated yeast, or 2 packets
1 tablespoon kosher salt (increase or decrease to taste, page 17)
¼ cup vital wheat gluten
2 cups lukewarm water
½ cup honey
8 large egg whites
1 cup zero trans fat, zero hydrogenated oil butter substitute, melted, or neutral-flavored oil
Egg white wash (1 egg white beaten with 1 teaspoon water) for brushing on the top crust

1. **Mixing and storing the dough:** Whisk together the flour, yeast, salt, and vital wheat gluten in a 5-quart bowl, or a lidded (not airtight) food container.

2. Combine the liquid ingredients and mix with the dry ingredients without kneading, using a spoon, a 14-cup food processor (with dough attach-ment), or a heavy-duty stand mixer (with paddle). You might need to use wet hands to get the last bit of flour to incorporate if you're not using a machine.

3. The dough will be loose, but it will firm up when chilled. *Don't try to use it without chilling* for at least 2 hours. You may notice lumps in the dough, but they will disappear in your finished products.

4. Cover (not airtight), and allow the dough to rest at room temperature until it rises and collapses (or flattens on top), approximately 2 hours.

5. Refrigerate it in a lidded (not airtight) container and use over the next 5 days. Beyond that, the dough stores well in the freezer for up to 2 weeks in an airtight container. Freeze in 2-pound portions. When using frozen dough, thaw it in the refrigerator for 24 hours before use, then allow the usual resting time.

6. **On baking day**, grease a brioche pan or an 8 ½ × 4 ½-inch nonstick loaf pan. Dust the surface of the refrigerated dough with flour and cut off a 2-pound (cantaloupe-size) piece of dough. Dust the piece with more flour and quickly shape it into a ball. Place the ball in the prepared pan and allow to rest, loosely covered with plastic wrap, for 1 hour 45 minutes.

7. **Thirty minutes before baking time, preheat the oven to 350°F,** with a rack placed in the center of the oven. If you're not using a stone in the oven, a 5-minute preheat is adequate.

8. Just before baking, use a pastry brush to paint the top crust with egg wash.

9. Bake near the center of the oven for approximately 45 to 50 minutes. Brioche will not form a hard, crackling crust. The loaf is done when it is medium brown and firm. Smaller or larger loaves will require adjustments in resting and baking time.

10. Remove the brioche from the pan (see page 50) and allow it to cool on a rack before slicing and eating.

Pumpkin Pie Brioche

"In the autumn I bake pies using freshly roasted sugar pumpkins. My kids love the flavors and I love that pumpkin is full of vitamins. It struck me that the same amazing flavors could be used in a sweet and spiced brioche. *The pumpkin makes wonderfully moist dough and the bread is so fragrant and tender. It is great with butter and cinnamon-sugar or the cream cheese icing on page 294."*—Zoë

Makes enough dough for at least two 2-pound loaves. The recipe is easily doubled or halved. Use any leftover dough to make muffins (page 199), crescent rolls (page 294), or pinwheels (page 299).

3 cups white whole wheat flour
4½ cups unbleached all-purpose flour
1½ tablespoons granulated yeast, or 2 packets
1 tablespoon kosher salt (increase or decrease to taste, page 17)
2 tablespoons vital wheat gluten
1 teaspoon ground cinnamon
½ teaspoon ground ginger
½ teaspoon ground nutmeg
¼ teaspoon ground allspice
1¼ cups lukewarm water
4 large eggs
½ cup honey
¾ cup neutral-flavored oil, or unsalted butter, melted, or zero trans fat, zero hydrogenated oil margarine, melted
One large pie (or "sugar") pumpkin to yield 1¾ cups pumpkin puree, or use one 15-ounce can pumpkin puree
Egg wash (1 egg beaten with 1 tablespoon water) for brushing on the top crust
Raw sugar for sprinkling on top

1. **If making your own fresh pumpkin puree:** Preheat the oven to 350°F. Split the pumpkin in half, starting at the stem, and place it cut side down on a

lightly greased cookie sheet or one lined with a silicone mat. Bake for about 45 minutes. The pumpkin should be very soft all the way through when poked with a knife. Cool slightly before scooping out the seeds.

2. Scoop out the roasted flesh of the pumpkin and puree it in the food processor. Set aside 1¾ cups for the dough and use any leftover in your favorite pumpkin pie recipe.

3. **Mixing and storing the dough:** Whisk together the flours, yeast, salt, vital wheat gluten, and spices in a 5-quart bowl, or a lidded (not airtight) food container.

4. Combine the liquid ingredients with the pumpkin puree and mix them with the dry ingredients without kneading, using a spoon, a 14-cup food processor (with dough attachment), or a heavy-duty stand mixer (with paddle). You might need to use wet hands to get the last bit of flour to incorporate if you're not using a machine.

5. The dough will be loose, but it will firm up when chilled. *Don't try to use it without chilling* for at least 2 hours. You may notice lumps in the dough, but they will disappear in your finished products.

6. Cover (not airtight), and allow the dough to rest at room temperature until it rises and collapses (or flattens on top), approximately 2 hours.

7. Refrigerate the dough in a lidded (not airtight) container and use over the next 5 days. Beyond that, the dough stores well in the freezer for up to 2 weeks in an airtight container. Freeze it in 2-pound portions. When using frozen dough, thaw it in the refrigerator for 24 hours before use, then allow the usual rest/rise times.

8. **On baking day**, grease a brioche pan or an 8½×4½-inch nonstick loaf pan. Dust the surface of the refrigerated dough with flour and cut off a 2-pound (cantaloupe-size) piece of dough. Dust the piece with more flour and

quickly shape it into a ball. Place the ball in the prepared pan and allow to rest, loosely covered with plastic wrap, for 1 hour 45 minutes.

9. **Thirty minutes before baking time, preheat the oven to 350°F,** with a rack placed in the center of the oven. If you're not using a stone in the oven, a 5-minute preheat is adequate.

10. Just before baking, use a pastry brush to paint the loaf's top with egg wash, and then sprinkle with raw sugar.

11. Bake near the center of the oven for approximately 45 to 50 minutes. Brioche will not form a hard, crackling crust. The loaf is done when it is medium brown and firm. Smaller or larger loaves will require adjustments in resting and baking time.

12. Remove the brioche from the pan (see page 50) and allow it to cool on a rack before slicing or eating.

Indian Spiced Whole Grain Doughnuts

"We are lucky in Minneapolis to have several fabulous farmers' markets. My favorite is the market down by the Mississippi River between the old flour mills and the brand-new Guthrie Theater. It has a superb variety of locally produced foods, including cardamom-scented whole wheat doughnuts. I was so taken with these little fried treats that I decided to re-create them for you. You will love them with tea, coffee, or a big glass of cold milk (see photo, color insert)"—Zoë

Makes twelve 3-inch doughnuts

Use any of these refrigerated pre-mixed doughs: Braided Challah with Whole Wheat and Wheat Germ (page 258), Whole Wheat Brioche (page 275), or Pumpkin Pie Brioche (page 284)

1½ pounds (small cantaloupe-size portion) of any pre-mixed dough listed above

½ cup sugar

½ teaspoon ground ginger

1 teaspoon ground cinnamon

½ teaspoon ground cardamom

¼ teaspoon ground cloves

FRIED DOUGHNUTS DON'T BECOME SATURATED WITH OIL, SO LONG AS YOU FRY THEM RIGHT: So right now you're probably asking, "what are doughnuts doing in a health-conscious book?" But doughnuts don't have to be overly greasy—it's got to do with food's vapor pressure versus the oil's absorptive pressure, or to put it more plainly:

If you fry at high temperature (but not so high that it burns), the water inside the doughnut starts turning to steam immediately, and pushes out through pores in the developing doughnut crust. That outward movement prevents inward movement of oil. If you keep the temperature precisely where Zoë recommends, the finished weight of the doughnut will be remarkably close to where you started—it didn't absorb that much oil after all. After weighing a bunch of doughnuts before and after frying, and accounting for up to a 10 percent water loss in finished baked goods, our best

(continued)

(continued)

estimate is that each doughnut only absorbs between 15 and 45 calories' worth of oil. Use a healthy oil—not lard or hydrogenated shortening—and this will be a reasonable splurge.—Jeff

Neutral-flavored oil for frying (use a high-smoking-point oil like canola, peanut, or vegetable blend), enough to fill a medium saucepan 4 inches from the top

Equipment
3-inch and 1-inch biscuit cutters
Deep saucepan for frying
Candy thermometer
Slotted spoon
Paper towels

1. **Make the spiced sugar mixture:** Combine the sugar and all the spices in a medium bowl and set aside.

2. Dust the surface of the refrigerated dough with flour and cut off a 1½-pound (small cantaloupe-size) piece. Dust the piece with more flour and quickly shape it into a ball by stretching the surface of the dough around to the bottom on all four sides, rotating the ball a quarter-turn as you go.

3. Roll the dough into a ¼-inch-thick rectangle on a lightly floured surface.

4. Heat the frying oil to 360°F to 370°F, as determined by a candy thermometer.

5. While the oil is heating, use a 3-inch biscuit or round cookie cutter to cut the dough into about 12 circles. Use a 1-inch round biscuit or round cookie cutter to remove the centers of the circles to create the doughnut shape. Reserve the centers to fry as well. Return any scraps to the bucket of dough.

6. Drop the doughnuts in the hot oil 2 or 3 at a time so that they have plenty of room to rise to the surface. Be careful not to overcrowd them or they will not rise nicely.

7. After 1 minute, gently flip the doughnuts over with a slotted spoon and fry for another minute or so until golden brown on both sides.

8. Remove the doughnuts from the oil and place them on paper towels to drain the extra oil. While still warm, dredge them in the bowl of spiced sugar.

9. Repeat with the remaining dough until all the doughnuts are fried. Serve slightly warm.

Pear Tarte Tatin with Whole Wheat Brioche

This is a French tart usually made with a pastry dough, but we discovered that it is excellent made with our whole wheat brioche. It comes out like a wonderful caramelized upside-down pancake. It can be served on its own as breakfast or with ice cream for dessert. The whole spices left in the pan as it is cooking and baking impart terrific flavor and look gorgeous. Cooking the pears takes more than 5 minutes, but we promise it is worth the wait (see photo, color insert).

Makes 1 tarte Tatin

Use any of these refrigerated pre-mixed doughs: Braided Challah with Whole Wheat and Wheat Germ (page 258), Whole Wheat Brioche (page 275), or Pumpkin Pie Brioche (page 284)

½ pound (orange-size portion) of any pre-mixed dough listed above

3 tablespoons unsalted butter, or zero trans fat, zero hydrogenated oil margarine

⅓ cup brown sugar

¼ cup honey

1 teaspoon lemon juice

1 cinnamon stick

Two 1-inch round slices fresh ginger

2 whole cardamom pods (optional)

1 star anise (optional)

5 large firm pears, peeled, stemmed, cored, and quartered

1. In a 10-inch cast-iron skillet, melt the butter or margarine over medium heat, and then sprinkle the sugar, honey, and lemon juice over it. Drop the cinnamon stick, ginger, and optional cardamom pods and star anise in the middle. Arrange the pears in a circular pattern, cut side up, in the sugar.

2. Cook slowly over low heat until the pears start to absorb the caramel and the juices are bubbling around them, about 30 to 40 minutes, depending on the size, ripeness, and firmness of the pears. Spoon the sugar over the pears as they cook. Move the pears around slightly so that they are cooked

evenly. If you are using a softer pear, it will go much faster.

3. Once the pears are coloring nicely and the caramel is bubbling, turn off the stove and let them cool while you prepare the dough.

4. **Preheat the oven to 350°F,** with a rack placed in the center of the oven. The baking stone is not essential; if you omit it, the preheat can be as short as 5 minutes.

5. While the pears are cooling, dust the surface of the refrigerated dough with flour and cut off a ½-pound (orange-size) piece. Dust with more flour and quickly shape it into a ball by stretching the surface of the dough around to the bottom on all four sides, rotating the ball a quarter-turn as you go.

6. With a rolling pin, roll out the dough until it is a ⅛-inch-thick circle that fits the pan and extends about 1 inch beyond to make room for any shrinkage while baking. As you roll out the dough, use enough flour to prevent the dough from sticking to the work surface but not so much as to make it dry.

7. Drape the circle of dough over the pears, and tuck the excess between the pears and the edge of the pan.

8. Bake for 20 to 25 minutes, or until the dough is golden brown. Remove the pan from the oven and allow the tarte to cool in the skillet for about 5 minutes. Then carefully invert it onto a serving platter that is large enough that the hot caramel juices don't spill out. Serve warm or cool.

Honey Caramel Sticky Nut Buns

Just because we want to eat healthier doesn't mean that we want to be austere about it. We need to indulge on occasion and here is a way to do just that without compromising our resolve to eat better. The caramel is made with honey and the dough is made from whole grains. It may not make you healthier to eat these, but it will certainly improve your mental state. Joy is an important part of our wellness and this will bring you large doses of it.

Makes 8 to 12 buns

Use any of these refrigerated pre-mixed doughs: Braided Challah with Whole Wheat and Wheat Germ (page 258), Whole Wheat Brioche (page 275), Pumpkin Pie Brioche (page 284), or Master Recipe (page 53)

1½ pounds (small cantaloupe-size portion) of any pre-mixed dough listed above

The Honey-Caramel Topping and Filling

½ cup honey

½ cup brown sugar

½ teaspoon salt

½ teaspoon ground cinnamon

¼ teaspoon ground nutmeg

½ cup (1 stick) unsalted butter, softened, or zero trans fat, zero hydrogenated oil margarine, softened

½ teaspoon orange zest

¾ cup finely chopped nuts (pecans, walnuts, or macadamias are wonderful)

1 cup raisins

1. Cream together all ingredients except the nuts and raisins. Spread half the mixture evenly over the bottom of an 9-inch cake pan. Set aside. Reserve the other half of the mixture for the filling.

2. Dust the surface of the refrigerated dough with flour and cut off a 1½-pound (small cantaloupe-size) piece. Dust with more flour and and quickly shape it into a ball by stretching the surface of the dough around to the bottom on all four sides, rotating the ball a quarter-turn as you go.

3. With a rolling pin, roll out the dough until it is a ⅛-inch-thick rectangle. As you roll out the dough, use enough flour to prevent the dough from sticking to the work surface, but not so much as to make it dry.

4. Spread the remaining honey-caramel filling evenly over the rolled-out dough. Sprinkle on the nuts and raisins. Roll the dough into a log, starting at the long end of the dough. Pinch the seam closed.

5. With a very sharp knife or kitchen shears, cut into 8 to 12 equal pieces and arrange over the caramel-covered pan, with the "swirled" edge visible to you. Cover loosely with plastic wrap and allow to rest for about 1 hour.

6. **Thirty minutes before baking time, preheat the oven to 350°F,** with a rack placed in the center of the oven. If you're not using a stone in the oven, 5 minutes of preheat time is adequate.

7. Bake for about 30 minutes, until golden brown and well set in center. Run a knife around the edge of the pan to release the buns while they're still hot, then invert onto a serving dish immediately. If you let it set too long the buns will stick to the pan and be difficult to unmold.

8. Serve warm.

Cinnamon Crescent Rolls with Cream Cheese Icing

We've all tasted crescent rolls made from dough that popped out of a tube. Those are modeled on the French *croissant* (which just means crescent), the flaky, buttery creation that begs to be dipped into a big bowl of café au lait. Neither the popped dough nor the French original are terribly healthy, so we've updated the crescent roll with doughs made from whole grains and healthy oils rather than white flour and butter (see photo, color insert).

Makes 16 crescent rolls

Use any of these refrigerated pre-mixed doughs: Braided Challah with Whole Wheat and Wheat Germ, (page 258), Whole Wheat Brioche (page 275), Pumpkin Pie Brioche (page 284), Master Recipe (page 53), or Chocolate Espresso Whole Wheat Bread (page 301)

1½ pounds (small cantaloupe-size portion) of any pre-mixed dough listed above

½ cup brown sugar

2 teaspoons ground cinnamon

1 tablespoon neutral-flavored oil or melted butter

Egg wash (1 egg beaten with 1 tablespoon water) for brushing on the top crusts

Raw sugar for sprinkling on top

The Honey Cream Cheese Icing

4 ounces cream cheese, at room temperature (or Neufchâtel cheese)

2 tablespoons unsalted butter, or zero trans fat, zero hydrogenated oil margarine, at room temperature

3 tablespoons honey

½ teaspoon pure vanilla extract

¼ teaspoon lemon zest (optional)

Pinch of salt

1. Combine the sugar, cinnamon, and oil. Set aside.

2. Prepare 2 cookie sheets with parchment paper or a silicone mat.

3. Dust the surface of the refrigerated dough with flour and cut off a 1½-pound (small cantaloupe-size) piece. Dust with more flour and quickly shape it into a ball by stretching the surface of the dough around to the bottom on all four sides, rotating the ball a quarter-turn as you go.

4. With a rolling pin, roll out the dough until it is a ⅛-inch-thick rectangle. As you roll out the dough, use enough flour to prevent the dough from sticking to the work surface, but not so much as to make it dry.

5. Spread the cinnamon-sugar mixture evenly over the rolled-out dough. With a pizza cutter, cut the dough into 8 smaller rectangles. This is done by making 3 evenly spaced cuts along the length of the dough and then cutting the dough in half along the short end. Now cut the 8 rectangles into 2 triangles each.

6. Gently stretch the triangles nearly 50 percent longer and wider than their original length. Lay each piece of dough down and roll it, starting at the thicker end, until the point is tucked under the bottom. Curve the ends to create the crescent shape. Cover them loosely with plastic wrap and allow to rest about 40 minutes.

7. **Thirty minutes before baking time, preheat the oven to 350°F,** with a rack placed in the center of the oven. If you're not using a stone in the oven, 5 minutes of preheat time is adequate.

8. Use a pastry brush to paint the tops with egg wash, and then sprinkle with the raw sugar. Bake the rolls about 20 to 25 minutes, until golden brown and well

set in the center. Remove the crescents from the oven and let cool on a rack.

9. **Make the Honey Cream Cheese Icing:** Cream all the ingredients together. Drizzle over the tops of the crescents and serve. Any leftover icing can be refrigerated for a week, or frozen for a month. This is also wonderful slathered on our Carrot Bread (page 157) and Pumpkin Pie Brioche (page 284).

VARIATIONS
Before rolling up the crescents you can put a tablespoon of almond paste, preserves, apple filling from the Apple Strudel Bread (page 277) or a 1-ounce piece of chocolate on the triangle of dough.

Pistachio Twist

This is inspired by the flavors of *baklava*, a lovely Middle Eastern pastry filled with crushed pistachios and honey and scented with orange blossom water. We love this rich floral combination with the Whole Wheat Brioche, but you can make it with several other doughs, including the Pumpkin Pie Brioche, for a fall treat.

Makes one 2-pound brioche

Use any of these refrigerated pre-mixed doughs: Braided Challah with Whole Wheat and Wheat Germ (page 258), Whole Wheat Brioche (page 275), Pumpkin Pie Brioche (page 284), or any other enriched dough in chapter 10
1½ pounds (small cantaloupe-size portion) of any pre-mixed dough listed above

The Pistachio Filling

1 cup finely ground pistachios
½ cup brown sugar
2½ teaspoons orange blossom water or rose water (found in Middle Eastern markets)
3 tablespoons honey
3 tablespoons unsalted butter, softened, or zero trans fat, zero hydrogenated oil margarine, softened
Pinch of salt

Egg wash (1 egg beaten with 1 tablespoon water) for brushing on the top crust
Raw sugar for sprinkling on top of the loaf
1 tablespoon finely ground pistachios (or other nuts) for sprinkling on top of the loaf

1. **Make the pistachio filling:** Combine the ingredients in a small bowl. Set aside.

2. Dust the surface of the refrigerated dough and cut off a 1½-pound (small cantaloupe-size) piece of dough. Dust with more flour and quickly shape it

into a ball by stretching the surface of the dough around to the bottom on all four sides, rotating the ball a quarter-turn as you go.

3. With a rolling pin, roll out the dough until it is a ⅛-inch-thick rectangle. As you roll out the dough, use enough flour to prevent the dough from sticking to the work surface, but not so much as to make it dry.

4. Spread the pistachio filling evenly over the rolled-out dough. Roll the dough into a log, starting at the long end. Pinch the seam closed.

5. Gently stretch the log of dough so that it becomes thinner, about 1½ inches in diameter. Fold the log in half and gently twist the log like a twist tie. Lay it on a baking sheet covered with parchment paper or a silicone mat. Cover the log loosely with plastic wrap and allow it to rest for about 1 hour.

6. **Thirty minutes before baking time, preheat the oven to 350°F,** with a rack placed in the center of the oven. If you're not using a stone in the oven, 5 minutes of preheat time is adequate.

7. Brush the twist with egg wash and sprinkle with sugar and the 1 tablespoon of ground pistachios. Place the baking sheet in the oven and bake about 30 minutes, until golden brown and well set in the center.

8. Allow the twist to cool on a rack before slicing and eating.

Fruit-filled Pinwheels

A lovely pastry for a Sunday brunch. This is one of those treats that looks so impressive, but is really very simple to create. We've filled these with a bit of cream cheese and fruit preserves, but we're sure you'll come up with your own creations as well.

Makes 12 pinwheels

Use any of these refrigerated pre-mixed doughs: Braided Challah with Whole Wheat and Wheat Germ (page 258), Whole Wheat Brioche (page 275), Pumpkin Pie Brioche (page 284), or Chocolate Espresso Whole Wheat Bread (page 301)

1½ pounds (small cantaloupe-size portion) of any pre-mixed dough listed above

½ cup cream cheese, at room temperature

1 tablespoon honey

¼ teaspoon grated lemon zest

½ cup fruit preserves

Egg wash (1 egg beaten with 1 tablespoon water) for brushing on top crusts

12 raw almonds

Raw sugar for sprinkling on top

1. Combine the cream cheese, honey, and zest in a small bowl, set aside.

2. Prepare two or three cookie sheets with parchment paper or silicone mats.

3. Dust the surface of the refrigerated dough with flour and cut off a 1½-pound (small cantaloupe-size) piece of dough. Dust with more flour and quickly shape it into a ball by stretching the surface of the dough around to the bottom on all four sides, rotating the ball a quarter-turn as you go.

4. With a rolling pin, roll out the dough into a ⅛-inch-thick, 11×15-inch rectangle. As you roll out the dough, use enough flour to prevent the dough from sticking to the work surface, but not so much as to make it dry.

5. With a pizza cutter, cut the dough into 12 small squares. This is done by making 3 evenly spaced cuts along the length of the dough and then 2 along the short end.

6. Fill the center of each square with 2 teaspoons of the cream cheese filling and then top with 2 teaspoons of the preserves. Cut a slash from the filling to each of the corners of the dough. Brush every other point with egg wash, which will act as a glue. Lift one of the egg-washed points up and to the center, repeat with the rest of the egg-washed points, and press them firmly together over the filling. Cover loosely with plastic wrap and allow to rest about 40 minutes

7. **Thirty minutes before baking time, preheat the oven to 350°F,** with a rack placed in the center of the oven. If you're not using a stone in the oven, 5 minutes of preheat time is adequate.

8. Brush the tops with egg wash, push an almond into the center of each pinwheel, and sprinkle with the raw sugar. Bake about 20 to 25 minutes, until golden brown and well set in the center.

9. Serve warm or cool.

Chocolate Espresso Whole Wheat Bread

"I was so pleased when the nutritional powers that be deemed dark chocolate and espresso 'good for you' (see sidebar). Considering what a large portion of my diet they occupy, I was relieved to know I no longer needed to feel guilty, not that I ever really had. So in an attempt to make you all a bit healthier and a lot happier I've come up with Chocolate Espresso Bread. Not too sweet but packed with flavor."—Zoë

Makes enough dough for at least two 2-pound loaves. The recipe is easily doubled or halved. Use any leftover dough to make cupcakes (page 303).

2 cups whole wheat flour

4 cups unbleached all-purpose flour

1 cup cocoa powder

1½ tablespoons granulated yeast, or 2 packets

1 tablespoon kosher salt (increase or decrease to taste, page 17)

¼ cup vital wheat gluten

1 cup lukewarm brewed espresso or strong coffee

1¼ cups lukewarm water

4 large eggs

½ cup neutral-flavored oil

∾

IT'S TRUE, CHOCOLATE MAY HAVE POWERFUL HEALTH BENEFITS: Moderation is the key, because chocolate is high in sugar and fat. But chocolate contains phytochemicals (beneficial plant chemicals) that may increase HDL (good) cholesterol, lower blood pressure, and decrease the likelihood of blood clots. Milk chocolate has less of these phytochemicals than dark chocolate because some of the cocoa is replaced by milk, and white chocolate doesn't have any at all.

Feeling better yet? Well, your coffee contains antioxidants. According to one study, Americans get their highest dose of antioxidants from coffee. It's not yet clear whether that translates into higher body stores of antioxidants, but it's opened up a whole new area of research, not to mention apparently justifying those mocha lattes (careful: sweetened or creamy coffee drinks are a major source of unnecessary calories).

¾ cup honey

6 ounces bittersweet chocolate, finely chopped

Egg wash (1 egg beaten with 1 tablespoon water) for brushing on top crust

Raw sugar for sprinkling on top

1. **Mixing and storing the dough:** Whisk together the flours, cocoa powder, yeast, salt, and vital wheat gluten in a 5-quart bowl, or a lidded (not airtight) food container.

2. Combine the liquid ingredients and the chopped chocolate and mix with the dry ingredients without kneading, using a spoon, a 14-cup food processor (with dough attachment), or a heavy-duty stand mixer (with paddle). You might need to use wet hands to get the last bit of flour to incorporate if you're not using a machine.

3. The dough will be loose, but it will firm up when chilled. *Don't try to use it without chilling at least 2 hours*

4. Cover (not airtight), and allow the dough to rest at room temperature until it rises and collapses (or flattens on top), approximately 2 hours.

5. Refrigerate it in a lidded (not airtight) container and use over the next 5 days. Beyond that, the dough stores well in the freezer for up to 2 weeks in an airtight container. Freeze it in 2-pound portions. When using frozen dough, thaw it in the refrigerator for 24 hours before use, then allow the usual rest/rise time.

6. **On baking day**, grease an 8½×4½-inch nonstick loaf pan. Dust the surface of the refrigerated dough with flour and cut off a 2-pound (cantaloupe-size) piece. Dust the piece with more flour and quickly shape it into a ball by stretching the surface of the dough around to the bottom on all four sides, rotating the ball a quarter-turn as you go.

7. Elongate the ball into an oval and place it into the loaf pan; your goal is to fill the pan about three-quarters full. Cover loosely with plastic wrap and allow to rest and rise for 1 hour 45 minutes.

8. **Thirty minutes before baking time, preheat the oven to 350°F,** with a rack placed in the center of the oven. If you're not using a stone in the oven, a 5-minute preheat is adequate. Steam is not needed.

9. Just before baking, Use a pastry brush to brush the loaf's top crust with egg wash, and then sprinkle with the raw sugar.

10. Bake near the center of the oven for approximately 45 to 50 minutes, until firm.

11. Remove the bread from the pan (see page 50) and allow it to cool on a rack before slicing and eating.

VARIATION: Cupcakes (see photo, color insert)

1. **On baking day, grease a muffin tin.** Dust the surface of the refrigerated dough with flour and cut off a 1½-pound (small cantaloupe-size) piece. Dust the piece with more flour and quickly shape it into a smooth ball by stretching the surface of the dough around to the bottom on all four sides, rotating the ball a quarter-turn as you go.

2. **To form the cupcakes,** divide the ball into 12 roughly equal portions (each about the size of a golf ball). Shape each one into a smooth ball as you did above. Place the buns in the prepared muffin tins. Allow to rest, loosely covered with plastic wrap, for 40 minutes.

3. **Thirty minutes before baking time, preheat the oven to 350°F,** with a rack placed in the middle of the oven. If you're not using a stone in the oven, a 5-minute preheat is adequate.

4. Just before baking, use a pastry brush to paint the top crust with egg wash, and then sprinkle with the raw sugar. Bake for about 20 minutes, until the cupcakes are richly browned and firm.

5. Remove the cupcakes from the tin and allow to cool on a rack before eating.

Chocolate Tangerine Bars

"Don't tell Zoë, but this recipe was inspired by a pre-wrapped treat that I was served on an airplane. It tasted of delicious chocolate and citrus—the wrapper on the bar said it had tangerine oil in it. Where in the world are you supposed to get tangerine oil? For home use, you get the flavor of tangerine oil by using the zest—it's the colored part of the skin that contains the oil. Usually that's done with a micro zester, but this time, go for the coarse effect of a traditional box grater for a more assertive tangerine flavor. Be sure to avoid getting much of the white pith, which can be bitter. After you get your zest, save the tangerine sections to use as a garnish for the bars—bet you'll never see that at 35,000 feet!"—Jeff

Makes about 9 bars

½ pound (orange-size portion) Chocolate Espresso Whole Wheat Bread dough (page 301)

2 ounces coarsely chopped high-quality bittersweet chocolate, preferably Callebaut or the equivalent (or chocolate chips)

½ cup dried cranberries

Zest from 1 tangerine, removed with a coarse grater

Tangerine sections for garnish

1. Grease an 8-inch square baking pan and set aside.

2. Dust the surface of the refrigerated dough with flour and cut off a ½-pound (orange-size) piece of dough.

3. Work the chocolate, dried cranberries, and zest into the dough with your fingers. Don't use any flour. Roughly press the mixture into a ball with wet hands.

4. Flatten the ball to a thickness of about ¾ inch and press it into the prepared pan. Allow to rest, loosely covered with plastic wrap, for 90 minutes.

5. **Thirty minutes before baking time, preheat the oven to 350°F,** with a rack placed in the center of the oven. If you're not using a stone in the oven, a 5-minute preheat is adequate.

6. Bake for about 20 to 25 minutes, until firm and set.

7. Cool the pan completely on a rack, cut into squares, and serve garnished with the tangerine sections.

APPENDIX

~~

The B Vitamins and Their Function

The B vitamins are crucial to energy metabolism: the chemical reactions that allow the body to use "fuels" like carbohydrates, fats, and proteins to release energy:

- **Thiamine:** Energy metabolism, healthy nervous system/brain function
- **Riboflavin:** Energy metabolism
- **Niacin:** Energy metabolism; prevents pellagra, a serious deficiency disease
- **Biotin:** Energy metabolism
- **Pantothenic acid:** Energy metabolism, prevents fatigue (deficiency causes gastrointestinal distress and nervous system/brain problems)
- **Vitamin B_6:** Crucial for protein metabolism, prevents nervous system/brain disorders
- **Folic acid or folate:** Crucial for DNA and vitamin B_{12} metabolism, prevents spina bifida and other neural tube defects, may prevent heart disease by decreasing blood homocysteine
- **Vitamin B_{12}:** Essential for DNA, RNA, and protein metabolism. Healthy bone, stomach, blood, and nervous system/brain depend on vitamin B_{12}.

Flours: Approximate Protein and Fiber Content per 30-Gram Serving

	PROTEIN (GRAMS)	FIBER (GRAMS)
WHOLE WHEAT FLOURS		
Whole wheat flour (Gold Medal)	4	3
Whole wheat flour (Pillsbury)	4	4
White whole wheat flour (King Arthur)	4	3
RYE FLOURS		
Stone-ground whole grain rye (Hodgson Mill)	3	5
Dark rye flour (Bob's Red Mill)	4	7
Light rye flour (Bob's Red Mill)	2	Less than 1
WHITE FLOURS		
Unbleached all-purpose (Gold Medal or Pillsbury)	3	Less than 1
Unbleached all-purpose (King Arthur)	4	Less than 1
MISCELLANEOUS		
Bulgur (Bob's Red Mill)	4	5
Corn masa (Maseca)	3	2
Flaxseed meal (Bob's Red Mill)	7	9
Oatmeal (Quaker Oats)	4	3
Spelt (Bob's Red Mill)	4	4
Teff flour (Bob's Red Mill)	4	4

Saturated Versus Unsaturated Fat (for Budding Chemists)
Saturated fats have more hydrogen atoms appearing on the carbon chain that makes up a fatty acid molecule. Those kinds of fats make great building blocks for so-called "bad cholesterol."

Fat Content of Common Fat Sources for Baking Based on a 1-Tablespoon (14-Gram) Serving
Look for products low in saturated and trans fat, and high in omega-3, polyunsaturated, and monounsaturated fats.

SOURCE	SATURATED FAT	TRANS FAT	POLYUNSATU-RATED FAT	MONOUNSATU-RATED FAT	TOTAL FAT
Canola oil	1	0	4 (28% omega-3)	8	14
Olive oil	2	0	1 (12% omega-3)	11	14
Butter	7	0.3	0.4	3	11
Margarine, solid stick	2.3	2.4	3.8	2.5	11
Margarine, soft tub*	1	0	6	4	11
Vegetable shortening	3	0	6	3	12
Smart Balance Omega Spread	2.7	0	2.7	3.8	9.5

*Seek out soft tub margarine that has zero trans fats and zero hydrogenated oils.

SOURCES FOR
BREAD-BAKING PRODUCTS

Bluebird Grain Farms: www.bluebirdgrainfarms.com, 509-996-3526
Bob's Red Mill: www.bobsredmill.com, 800-349-2173
Cooks of Crocus Hill: www.cooksofcrocushill.com, 651-292-0949, ×40
Fantes Kitchen Wares Shop, www.fantes.com, 800-443-2683
Hodgson Mill: www.hodgsonmill.com, 800-347-0105
King Arthur Flour: www.kingarthurflour.com/shop/, 800-827-6836
Native Seeds/SEARCH: www.nativeseeds.org, 866-622-5561
Penzeys Spices: www.penzeys.com, 800-741-7787
Tupperware: www.tupperware.com, 800-366-3800

The only nationally distributed vital wheat gluten products that we've been able to find in supermarkets are Bob's Red Mill (**www.bobsredmill.com**) and Hodgson Mill (**www.hodgsonmill.com**). King Arthur Flour vital wheat gluten is available through mail order.

SOURCES CONSULTED

Aggarwal, B.B., and Harikumar, K.B. "Potential Therapeutic Effects of Cucurmin, the Anti-Inflammatory Agent, Against Neurodegenerative, Cardiovascular, Pulmonary, Metabolic, Autoimmune and Neoplastic Diseases." *International Journal of Biochemistry and Cell Biology.* 2009; 41(1): 40–59.

American Diabetes Association. "Standards of Medical Care in Diabetes—2008." *Diabetes Care.* 2008; 31(Suppl 1): S12–S54.

Flax Council of Canada. "Flax, a Healthy Food." Storage recommendations and baking temperatures accessed at http://www.flaxcouncil.ca/english/index.jsp?p=g1&mp=nutrition on December 11, 2008.

"Food Chemists Slice Up Healthier Pizza." *Science Daily.* July 1, 2007.

Harding, A., et al. "Plasma Vitamin C Level, Fruit and Vegetable Consumption, and the Risk of New-Onset Diabetes Mellitus." *Archives of Internal Medicine.* 2008; 168(14): 1493–99.

Harvard School of Public Health. "Vegetables and Fruits: Get Plenty Every Day." Accessed at http://www.hsph.harvard.edu/nutritionsource/what-should-you-eat/vegetables-full-story/index.html on December 25, 2008.

Katcher, H.I. "The Effects of a Whole Grain–Enriched Hypocaloric Diet on Cardiovascular Disease Risk Factors in Men and Women with Metabolic Syndrome." *American Journal of Clinical Nutrition.* 2008 (87)1: 79–90.

Nettleton, J.A., et al. "Incident of Heart Failure Is Associated with Lower Whole-Grain Intake and Greater High-Fat Dairy and Egg Intake in the Atherosclerosis Risk in Communities (ARIC) Study." *Journal of the American Dietetic Association.* 2008; 108: 1881–1887.

Newby, P.K., et al. "Intake of Whole Grains, Refined Grains, and Cereal Fiber Measured with 7-D Diet Records and Associations with Risk Factors for Chronic Disease." *American Journal of Clinical Nutrition.* 2007; 86: 1745–53.

Pennington, J.A., and Douglass, J.S. *Bowes and Church's Food Values of Portions Commonly Used,* 18th edition. Philadelphia: Lippincott Williams & Wilkins, 2005.

Oberdoerffer, P., et al. "SIRT1 Redistribution on Chromatin Promotes Genetic Stability But Alters Gene Expression During Aging." *Cell* 2008; 135: 907–18. Harvard research linking resveratrol, found in grape skins and red wine, to a protective effect for human chromosomes.

Rolfes, S.R.; Whitney, E.N.; and Pinna, K. *Understanding Normal and Clinical Nutrition,* 8th edition. Belmont, CA: Wadsworth, 2009.

Slavin, J. "Whole Grains and Human Health." *Nutrition Research Reviews.* 2004; 17: 99–110.

Smith, J.S., Ameri, F., and Gadzil, P. "Effect of marinades on the formation of heterocyclic amines in grilled beef steaks." *Journal of Food Science.* 2008; 73(6): T100–5.

U.S. Department of of Health and Human Services/U.S. Department of Agriculture. *Dietary Guidelines for Americans, 2005.* Accessed at www.healthierus.gov/dietaryguidelines in December 2005.

Wade, N. "Scientists Find Clues to Aging in a Red Wine Ingredient's Role in Activating a Protein." *The New York Times,* November 27, 2008.

Xiaole L. Chen, Hannah R. Silver, Ling Xiong; Irina Belichenko, and Erica S. Johnson. "Spontaneous Topoisomerase I-Dependent DNA Damage in *a Saccharomyces cerevisiae* SUMO Pathway Mutant. *Genetics.* September 2007; 177(1): 17–30.

INDEX

Visit www.healthybreadinfive.com, where you'll find recipes, photos, videos, and instructional material.